The Gospel according to the Harvard Business School

The Gospel according to the Harvard Business School

PETER COHEN
HARVARD M.B.A.

1973
Doubleday & Company, Inc., Garden City, New York

To protect their privacy,
the names of the people appearing in this book,
and, where necessary,
the names of the places in their lives
have been changed.

Because what is told here
really happened.

ACKNOWLEDGMENTS

Excerpt from "Companies Pull Back From MBA Recruiting," January 15, 1970, issue of *The HarBus News.* Reprinted by permission of *The HarBus News.*

Excerpt from *"Bright & Bumptious*–They Chafe If Promotion Is Slow; Often Irk Colleagues Recruiters," April 1, 1969, issue of *The Wall Street Journal.* Copyright © 1969 Dow Jones & Company, Inc. Portions of Tim Metz' story *"B-School Blues*–Demand for Graduates With MBAs Declines and Salary Rise Slows," March 20, 1970, issue of *The Wall Street Journal.* Copyright © 1970 Dow Jones & Company, Inc. Reprinted by permission of *The Wall Street Journal.*

Excerpt of article taken from June 1970 issue of *True* Magazine. Reprinted by permission of *True* Magazine.

ISBN: 0-385-02724-9
LIBRARY OF CONGRESS CATALOG CARD NUMBER 73-79656

PRINTED IN THE UNITED STATES OF AMERICA
FIRST EDITION

CONTENTS

Rooms With a View

This is a book about people who want to get to the top of the world. People who are determined that in their profession nobody is going to do or be better, and who are prepared to pay any price to live up to their expectations.

This is a book about what happens to such people when they are confronted with the first reality of their undertaking; when they realize, some of them, that they aren't going to make it; when the others get within reach of the money and power they dream of.

Most people want to do great things with their lives. They want to be doctors, lawyers, actors, or scientists, and most of them never make it. At which point they are forced to earn a living, which implies tedious tasks and sheer drudgery. It usually means that they go to work for some company making cars, or thumbtacks, or dog food. And when you meet these people, they always talk most heartily about their game of golf or their vacations, as if that is what they did for a living; they are too embarrassed or too bored to talk about the other part, although it is a major part of their lives. So it seems strange that there should be people who actually get a kick out of being in business; self-confident sonsofbitches who know that all the world's dreams would come to nothing if they didn't supply the cars, the thumbtacks, the dog food to make them come true.

This book is about the latter kind of people. About those on the way to the paneled, real-leather rooms with a view that overlook the world's business empires. It describes two and a half years in the life of a group of people who, in the not too-distant future, expect to be in those rooms. Ninety-four graduate students who some recent fall arrived at the Harvard Business School. Most of them in their twenties, some in the early thirties, a few fresh out of college, but most with at least a couple of years of "real world" work experience—all of them after that ticket to paradise called an M.B.A. (Master in Business Administration).

This is an account of their education to become lords over a new kind of army in a new kind of warfare, getting ready to take over from the military who have perfected their technology to the point where its use is guaranteed to leave nothing worth using it for. But since men will continue to be ambitious; since they will still want to be, they don't know what, except different, they will go on fighting for those things of which there aren't enough to go around—money, love, land, praise, power and perquisites. Aggression and the need to excel are looking for new ways to manifest themselves, and business, with its armies of functionaries, its prominent adversaries, its highly visible battlefields, is the perfect fit.

World War III is going to be fought on the shelves of your neighborhood shopping center, and the Harvard Business School is a sneak preview of it. How its generals are prepared. The weapons and tactics they learn to use. How they fight against each other, against humiliation and delusions of grandeur; how they run each other down, yet somehow, desperately at times, seek to maintain at least the appearance of friendship. How, pushed at each other, each pushes himself, battling to ward off the crushing pressures—altering, stretching, refining his self-image in a restless, futile search to cast it into the perfect shape.

Inasmuch as it describes their education, this book is about a place as well as about people. A big building with two rear sides whose alcoves and checkered windows belie the fact that the classrooms inside have no windows at all. The *real*

Harvard Business School, the bricks and mortar behind the thousands of generals and field marshals the school is rumored to have produced; a symbol of the omnipresence of American business in the world; a seal of seeming superhuman ability, a door opener, a launching pad, a status symbol beyond compare among status-minded top corporate managers.

This is a book about what the place says it will do for you, and what it ends up doing to you. How some people only lose their sleep, but some their self-respect. This, in a way, is what it is like to get a professional education in America. Or just plain an American education. How America's prejudices, how some of its warped values, affect not just the tortured present but, through their impact on the schools, the future for generations to come. How America corrupts those it can least afford to corrupt—its lawyers and doctors, its professional managers.

All this is laid out in these pages as something of a case study, in the Harvard Business School's own case-learning style. The facts, not too orderly, with no more interpretation than absolutely needed to get you started on an interpretation of your own. Everything is as close to reality as the author, a participant, could make it. Consider it. Because if the heroes of this book won't be your competitors, one may very well end up as your boss.

I

The Fight for Survival

SEPTEMBER TO JUNE OF THE FIRST YEAR

1
Here We Are

September 8: It's been a long way. Many nights with the light on. The usual detours, the inevitable dead ends. A mess of meandering footsteps which vanity, with the help of hindsight, stretches back into a straight and purposeful line.

But, finally, here we are. Seven hundred and seventy-six survivors out of more than three thousand applicants. And there, across the bright ribbon of the Charles River, is the Harvard Business School. A great many haughty little windows framed in red brick. On top of them a line of chimneys, stiff and somber, which guard the golden cupola in their midst.

A moment of equilibrium, while the voracious ego smacks its lips from the fat chunk of approval that came with being admitted here. But already, like a swarm of frightened birds, questions rise up and dot the mind's horizon. What kind of people are these? What do they really want here? Is it the promise of more? The temptation of going higher and farther? Is it the satisfaction of being good, very good at something? Or are they no more than cowards, running from risk and uncertainty, trying to hide in some vast human machine in which everybody has a share and nobody has the responsibility? Or, wrong again, are they out to brave that very surge toward bigness? The cruel law of size which says that the bigger an organization gets, the more of everything it must include; and the more of everything it includes, the more average it gets?

You remember the people who started out with you in

grade school; who haven't, some of them, made it through high school; who haven't, most of them, made it through college. How the faces got fewer and fewer, until you are dead sure somebody has to be a real genius to get into the Harvard Business School.

And the more you think about it, the more you become convinced that it really is going to be like the pictures in the catalogue. With everybody running around in suits and ties, probably saying "sir" to each other. That these are going to be unbelievably smart, unbelievably self-confident, unbelievably aggressive people, and that a regular, willing guy like yourself is going to be in very hot water.

But what the hell, you have been through it before. The feeling of apprehension. The strange faces. Not knowing what lies in front of you. Everybody is starting from a common denominator which is uncertainty.

Supplies for Fall Term

Supply Kit #1 (including $7.00 for Slide Rule) – $19.96

Required

3 packages	Report Paper
9	Report Envelopes

(Additional supplies of the above will be needed for the spring term.)

*Suggested**

1	2-Inch Ring Binder
2	1-Inch Ring Binders
6	Acco Binders
1	Subject Index for 2-Inch Binder
1	Columnar Pad for Ring Binder, No. 6013
6	Scratch Pads
1	6-Inch Flexible Rule
1	Slide Rule

* Any of the suggested items which are included in the kit may be returned for credit or refund ten days *after* registration.

September 11: Registration and a first look at the premises.

The first floor of Aldrich Hall, together with its carbon copies, the second and the basement floors, is a moving tribute to so total a lack of imagination as to make the entire building stand out, even among the dull and faceless newer buildings at the Business School as an achievement of monumental non-distinction. On every floor, the same drafty alcoves, the same hallway wrapped around the same classrooms. (Except that on the second floor the Coke machines are at the opposite end.)

Section B's classroom—Aldrich 108—is on the first floor, just off the hallway which, in exact intervals, is decorated with life-size photographs of bald professors, staring out into the slow waters of the Charles. As the second of the two heavy doors swings shut behind you, there opens up a windowless realm of everlasting neon light where only the silent electric clock above the door tells of the changing light outside. Rising up against the bare, faint beige walls, forming a half circle which opens toward the blackboards, are the benches and wooden swivel chairs of Section B. An uninviting, strictly functional arena where, if what we've heard is true, the play goes on in the stands and the lonely spectator, the professor, sits down front, in the middle of the stage.

Tomorrow we'll know. The first day of classes.

September 12: One day but for some reason it feels like ten or a hundred.

The welcoming ceremony began at 8:30 A.M., in Carey Cage, which is an old Harvard gym. Squeezed in, on bench, amid bench after jammed bench of spiffed-up, shivering guys, you endure all kinds of threats in the guise of good advice and a terrible draft that makes your teeth chatter.

Over to Aldrich 108, at 9:30, to meet your ninety-four new friends who, from now till next June, will be known collectively as Section B. These are the people you will be together with, four and a half hours a day, five days a week, always in this same room. Too many new names to remember, even with the name tags everybody is wearing.

Then, in the third and final class, we meet Duncan McKay. He stands with one foot on the teacher's table, tall, even bent as he is, his massive face resting on the pointing stick he has planted on the table. Looking at nobody in particular, he says that he doesn't want us to love him. That he doesn't care if we hate him. That if we are lucky, *some* of us are going to be leaders and that we shouldn't bother to come to his class without a coat and tie.

That said, he takes his foot off the table, announces tomorrow's case, and piles into the classroom door so that its wings scream in their hinges for some time after he has left. The class is too stunned to even breathe.

A tall fellow named Sam Maguire is making an obvious effort to call everybody by their first name. So after the second class, he goes over to a guy named Rush, saying, "Hiya, Paul," and the guy says, "No, it's Tony."

September 19: The case method is to the Harvard Business School what the crooked tower is to Pisa. The Harvard Business School invented the method; the Harvard Business School succeeded with it; the Harvard Business School swears by it, and we have to put up with it, every grinding minute of every grinding day. There are no lectures, no labs, few textbooks even. Only cases, cases, and more cases.

In its outward appearance, a case is a bundle of mimeographed pages—some thirty to forty on the average—written in a heavy-handed, lumbering prose that creaks from an overload of nouns. It describes a real event (although the names may be disguised) that happened in the course of some real business campaign, at times giving a general's grand view, at times a corporal's blurred impressions; it reports on the conditions in the trenches and bunkers of the business front; on the progress of armies of salesmen marching against each other, of supply convoys steaming down channels of distribution. It is a factual listing of men, money, and materials risked; of brilliant victory, of losses beyond imagination.

It often begins with grandiose flourishes: "For J. Hamilton Peacock, chairman of the board of the First Haverhill National Bank, planning was not a luxury . . ." Invariably it ends with a question that is beginning to haunt us in our sleep: "What would *you* do?"

These aren't the "case histories" people get in law or medical school. You know, and here is what the judge said. Or here is what the doctor ordered. Our cases have no ending. They just kind of dump the whole mess into your lap—tables, columns, exhibits, and all—and you can't run away from it because tomorrow ninety-four people—the entire Section—will be waiting for your decision. You may not be the guy the professor calls on "to lay out the case," but then again you may, which makes for a lot of motivation.

Three cases a day; sixty, maybe a hundred, maybe more than a hundred pages a night. You almost read yourself to death, just to find out what the *problem* is. And then, of course, you need a *solution.*

Here you are, a strapping production manager, or financial vice-president, or marketing executive, alone in a jungle of unfamiliar terms and technology, with no lecture notes, no fundamentals, or formulas to go by; with, perhaps, a reading list and a textbook and an equally confused, dry-mouthed roommate. And if you haven't done so already, you do a lot of growing up in a hurry, because you've got a problem. And no time. And little help. And something like your life depending on your finding a solution.

Same day: At noon, there were Baxter, Maguire, Tuck, Howell, and Terner, married men who have developed a habit of eating together in one of the alcoves just outside the classroom. This is one of the many groups that crowd Aldrich during the noon hours. Groups of people called "brown-baggers" (after the brown paperbags in which they bring their sandwiches). Nobody seemed to be able to make much sense of today's cases so we just talked. Max Tuck complains that he just can't get through to Professor Rosen. That whatever he says hits the wall rather than the professor. Max always seems to make a point in class—one an hour. Not bad ones, but slightly technical ones. The kind that are hard to remember.

September 20: At lunch Max said that some test in high school had shown him to have the aptitude to be a mechanic. And, of course, the brown-baggers laughed. But there really *is* something mechanical about Max. Something too predictable in what he says. Something very average about the schools he has gone to, the positions he has held. Max doesn't seem the kind of guy you would expect to find here.

From the way he participates in class you certainly can't say that Max doesn't have determination. But somehow, determination—determination and nothing else is not a very inspiring combination. Perhaps it's still too early to tell. After all, there must be a reason why they let him come here. Well today, as during previous lunch sessions, everybody more or less talked to Max. He was the one who cut people off. He was the one everybody was asking questions. Max, obviously and naturally, was in charge. And that must be why he is here. Although you kind of hate to admit it.

September 21: After the first full week of classes our first test. To save us bother during the week they schedule it for a Saturday! The material to be studied had arrived during the summer. And most people had treated it like material for the fall that arrives during summer. Now a lot of them are regretting it. Some guys have been up all night, tracing gold certificates from Bank X to Bank Y to a never-never land called "treasury" or "the general public."

Preliminary examination on Macroeconomics—a first chance to find out not only what but whom we're up against. Now that it's over it can be said for a fact that the exam lived up to our worst expectations. An hour and a half; it turned out a real bastard and to more than the normal extent, passing should be a matter of sheer luck.

September 23, Monday: A change in weather has come with the suddenness of a thunderstorm, whipping thick gusts of rain into the trees. The leaves that seemed to stay up there forever are finally beginning to fall. Gone are the frisbees, the footballs, the bicycles. Gone the light suits, gone the loud and reckless colors of summer. Subtle shades of brown are hushing the landscape.

It was as if the weather had decided to dramatize the change that has come over Al Terner's life since he entered the Business School; the feeling of anguish that wrenches his insides every time he crosses the bridge over the Charles. Because that bridge, whose three low spans on calm days seem anchored in their own mirror image, leads from baby carriages and casually dressed husbands into the land of suits and black briefcases, into the province of return on investment, into the kingdom of gross margin. To Terner, coming from the warm and soft comfort of the weekend, struggling against the driving rain, it seemed today to end in everlasting Monday.

September 24, lunch hour:

(FRANK CHARVIS *talking*)

"I thought, if nothing else, going to the Business School will give me flexibility. It's going to give me mobility. I can probably live any place in the country I want; do things I might not even be aware of today. Let's face it, it's very difficult, once you're in a company, to cast yourself in something other than the job you have. If you're in advertising as a copywriter, you're known as a copywriter. If you're in sales, you're known as a salesguy.

"Anyway, I was in New York at the time and I called up Jackson & Wade and another consulting firm—Eastern Consultants—to try to talk to somebody to see what they thought about business school and what they thought of the various ones. Luckily enough, Eastern let me talk with several people. They were very, very helpful and, of course, Eastern is very Harvard oriented. They said, you know, 'If we could get all the bodies we feel are qualified, we'd get them all from Harvard.'"

October 2: The name of the game is to make a point. Both, the kind that proves something and the kind that can be added up to give a grade. McKay has announced that he will grade every sound we make in class. Although the others haven't told us so, we know that they are doing more or less the same.

The trouble is that with ninety-four players and the time per game limited to ninety minutes, it's difficult to score. It often isn't so much a matter of knowing the stuff but knowing how to let the professor know that you know it. To overcome these difficulties, we are developing a number of special techniques. Like the "preventive attack" in which you start the class by "laying out the case," showing what, according to you, is the problem and what should be done, which gives you some five to ten uninterrupted minutes.

If, as is normal, you find yourself playing someone else's game, there are a number of "defensive" techniques. Of these, the most effective is the "questioning of premises." While the guy who is laying out the case is building the second and third levels of his argument, you demolish the foundations. If those foundations should prove too well made, try "pseudo participation" or "the single point technique." The latter is useful when you don't know what the case is all about. You relax and let yourself be inspired by what other people are saying. Sooner or later you will be led to some (usually minor) point, some dot on the "i" that the main speakers have overlooked.

Pseudo participation is more demanding. It is the opposite of the single point for it applies where you are well prepared, where you have a point to make, but not the discussion in which to make it. You cannot blatantly change the topic. So the trick is to start your "contribution" with a smoke screen and then with a quick "however" to turn the whole thing around to suit your purpose. As a kind of last resort, you can always fall back on sheer "trifling." You may not score, but at least you show that you are there.

Whatever happens, jump at the argument as if it were a loose ball. Develop a unique pattern of waving your hand. And most of all, be unscrupulous. Try to corner the argument, get it into a little nook all of your own, and hammer away at it there until the angry mob catches up with you.

Yet, lest all of the above give you a false sense of security, it is never easy—even with all this preparation and technique—to join the action. More often than not, you will find yourself sitting there, well prepared and eager, with the public argument dancing in front of your eyes, like a piece of paper torn out of your hand by the wind, almost within reach, yet again and again eluding your grasp.

Ever since his first class, it has become a kind of game to figure out what makes Duncan McKay tick. Max Tuck, for one, swears that McKay is a mad genius. That some of the things which seem rude, impulsive, and sometimes unfair to us are really parts of a well-laid plan, leading to some mythical achievement that we are still too small to comprehend. And there are many in the Section who seem to feel the way Max does.

McKay can flex his ego the way a weight lifter does his biceps, casting a huge, defiant shadow on our ambitions. A challenge far more intense even than the fear he inspires. So we're beginning to fight in his class, as we do in no other. Fight one another hard and relentlessly as if trying to prove to the somber, taciturn man up front that we are every inch as tough as he is.

Duncan McKay is playing a dangerous game because sooner or later somebody is going to look beyond his shadow to his real size.

October 9: After the last class, Professor Francis handed out mimeographed sheets to five or six people in the Section. According to McGrady, who got one, the sheets said that the people who received them flunked the Macroeconomics test. No grades, no individual scores, no comment. It was like getting yourself all worked up for a great race only to find that most of the entrants crossed the finish line together.

October 10: On its way through Cambridge the river Charles is a smelly, unpleasant fellow, rolling its waters back and forth through numerous bends like a Sunday sleeper, unwilling to get out of bed. In fact, because of its many bends, the Charles seems like the only river in the world that you can cross and end up on the same shore.

Following the border between the townships of Brookline and Cambridge, it gently bends around the Business School, cutting it off from the rest of the Harvard campus—if you can call it a campus. Sure, across from the Business School, there is Harvard Yard, guarded by a heavy, wrought-iron fence, dotted with undergraduate dorms and class buildings. But the Yard measures no more than about five walking minutes in breadth and length. All the rest of the university is tucked away in the maze of narrow Cambridge streets, amid businesses and barbershops, boutiques and boardinghouses.

Aside from the Yard, the Business School is the only part of Harvard that you could really call a campus. Built on the riverbank opposite the rest of the school, it sits at the edge of a small plain, worn into the landscape by the Charles. Surrounded by athletic fields, a huge parking lot, and farther to the rear, by storage houses, car dealers, and gas stations. An elegant front for a sprawling commercial area that is crisscrossed by multiple lane highways and throughways.

Still, for all the complicated local geography, back "across the river" isn't a place, it's a state of mind.

From the Business School, as we are beginning to find out, across the river means the hippies, the "kids"—the emotional people, the shouters. Those who discuss problems instead of solving them.

From the Business School, "across the river" is a threat. Something stirring up fears that the crowds from over there—

the daydreamers, the self-righteous idealists, the critics blinded by their own enthusiasm, the fools who mistake a flash of insight for the light of truth—might try to smash the whole intricate apparatus of which we very much want to be a part.

But across the river also is where the girls are, the coffee houses, the subway trains into Boston, and an ice-cream cone with jimmies in one of the greasy spoons around Harvard Square.

And, although they never admit it, across the river for many of us is the slightly bitter taste of a dream only partly come true. Of an undergraduate education spent at a small, obscure place where the work was just as hard but the prestige infinitely smaller. The view of the Harvard Yard. The realization that we, as graduate students—and especially as graduate students of business—are kind of stepsons of this prestigious family.

"Abolish the B School," someone has written on a wall, over in the Yard. That's what across the river seems to mean to them over there: a subsidiary of IBM. A farm club for the CIA. A machine spewing out briefcase-carrying tin soldiers —mercenaries in the battle for higher profits; little schmucks who are willing to sell their left hand for the right to build a new Coca-Cola factory in outer Swaziland.

And so, when somebody says, "across the river," it isn't which but whose side he is on. Though there are two convenient bridges, each side has neither the time nor the interest to cross over for anything other than football, sex, or ice-cream cones.

October 11: When he finally spoke everybody turned around and looked. Just like McKay had said: "The longer you wait to speak up, the more difficult it will be."

The voice was Blotner's who sits in the last row, all the way over to the door. He isn't a big guy, Blotner, of middle height and at twenty-two he looks very much his age. The force of the seesawing argument kneads the soft mold of his face, making the mouth twitch nervously as he rocks his chair, his hands fiddling with a heavy golden class ring. You could hear in his voice the urgent desire to speak up, to claim his place in the Section. But you could also hear the terror of being rebuked, contradicted, or worse—ignored. His gesticulating hands, rather than adding emphasis, told of a vain attempt to grab hold of himself. But already his voice stuttered and stalled, his argument broke before anybody got a chance to jump on it.

"Now Leroi shoots down Goodwin," Allan McGrady said afterward, "and Goodwin shoots down Leroi and, you know, what do we learn? Nothing. You got a few guys that have enough nerve to do something like that, while other people clam up even more, saying: 'Jesus, I don't want to get shot down like that.'

"I don't think I ever saw a blood bath solve a goddamn thing."

October 16: Today, McKay brought a big fish to class. He had wrapped it into a newspaper and the newspaper into two layers of plastic foil.

He carefully pulled it out, down at the table, and laid it on the newspaper for everybody to see. The fish had a reddish head and a yellow, almost golden belly.

"Here's what happens," McKay said, pointing to the dead fish, "to those who open their mouth at the wrong time."

October 18:

MANAGERIAL ECONOMICS, REPORTING, AND CONTROL II
Prepare: Dayton Manufacturing Company EA-C 153

That is what the weekly assignment sheet listed for MERC II (Managerial Economics, Reporting, and Control II), and here is what the case was about: After seven years of trying, the Dayton Manufacturing Company finally gets the order it has been waiting for, from the Rickenback Electric Company. Dayton is to build a flatbed railroad car that Rickenback is going to use for the transport of heavy transformers. So they build and ship it, and the next thing they hear from Rickenback is that the car derailed.

What happened? Well, based on specs by Rickenback, the car was built with non-oscillating trucks. But the track Rickenback is using it on is banked in such a way that a car with non-oscillating trucks is bound to derail. So Rickenback refuses to accept it. And since Dayton is hoping for further business from Rickenback, they are hesitant to insist.

What should Dayton do now? Rebuild the car with oscillating trucks? But then the cost of the car will be higher than what Rickenback is willing to pay. Rebuild but offer below cost to save at least part of the investment? But what if the car even with oscillating trucks still derails? Rebuild and offer it at full cost to other companies that might be interested? But what if it derails on their tracks too? What about the cost of trying to sell it to other companies?

Not rebuild? Scrap? Or offer to others as is?

Suppose that you are on Dayton's board of directors. But that, unlike the real directors, you haven't got a month to make up your mind. That you only had from yesterday evening until nine-forty this morning.

You are getting called on. What would *you* do?

It was Holton's turn, and he lucked out. From the wad of paper he pulled from his briefcase it was obvious that he had put last night's effort into the right case. With barely concealed triumph he read off a decision tree which Jake Kamholz put on the board something like this:

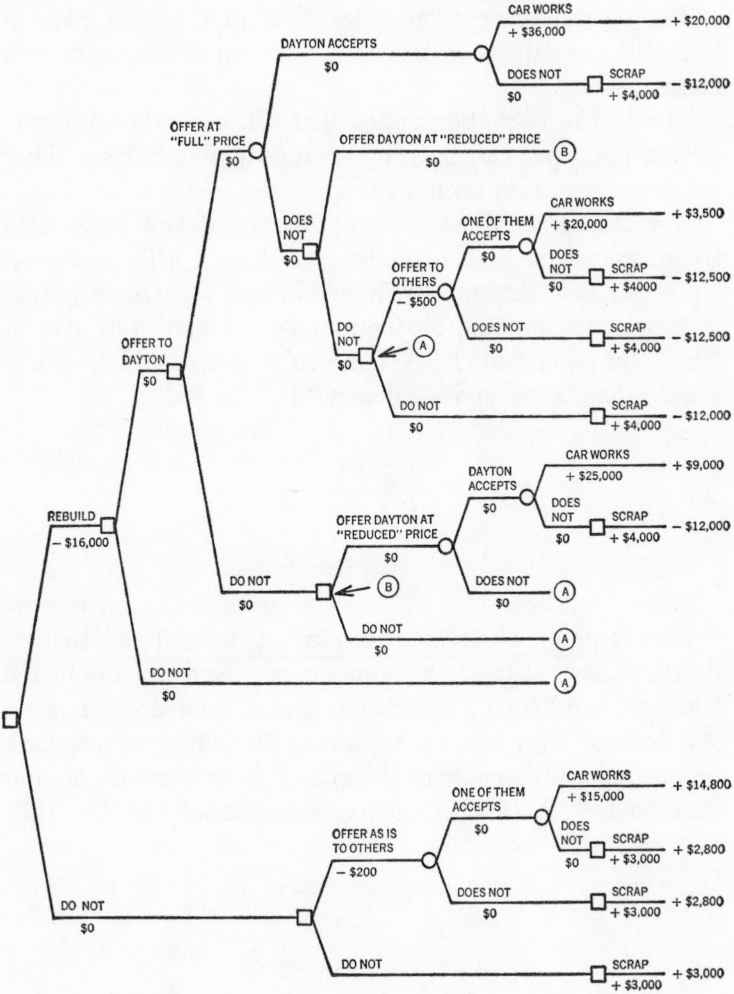

Dayton Manufacturing Co. Decision Problem

A decision tree (Holton's included) is really a way to order complicated decisions on a piece of paper. It is a diagram based on three simple but useful observations:

The first observation holds that even the most complex decision must end in a simple choice: to do or not to do a certain thing.

The second observation notes that all decisions have at least one consequence. And that even no consequence is a consequence.

The third observation states that all, even the most uncertain consequences, have one certainty about them: They either occur or they do not occur.

If you diagram these observations and if you begin with the decision you have to make, you draw a little square—it represents your decision—with two branches emanating from it. Now, remembering observation No. 1, mark one branch "do," the other "don't." What you've got should look like the diagram below and is called a "decision fork":

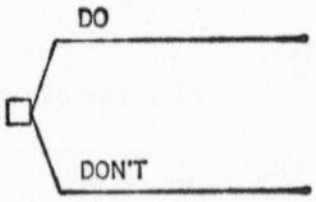

At this point, observation No. 2 will remind you that all decisions have at least one consequence. And since both the "do" and the "don't" branch are part of your decision, each will have at least one consequence. Mark that consequence by putting a little circle at the end of both branches of your decision fork. Your decision tree now should look like this:

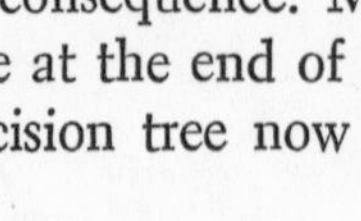

Observation No. 3 tells you that consequences either occur or do not occur. In terms of your diagram, this means that each of your little circles will grow two branches. One branch saying "consequence occurs," the other saying "consequence does not occur." The little circles now have become what are called "event forks." Your decision tree describing one decision with one consequence is complete. It should look as follows:

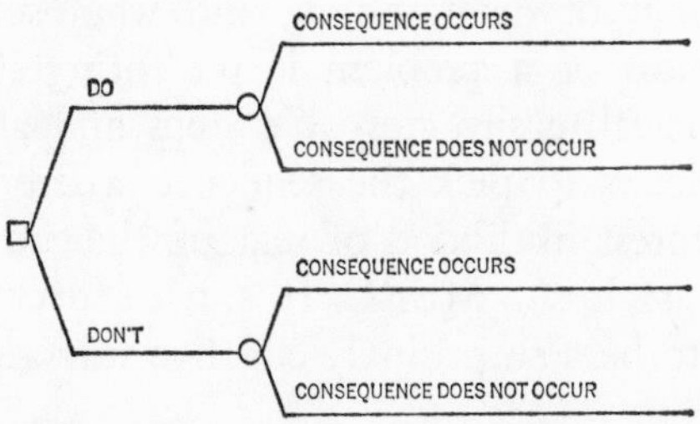

If you go back now to Holton's decision tree, you will see what he is trying to do. The immediate decision facing Dayton—whether to rebuild or not to rebuild the car—is his starting point. If he goes the "do" route, he faces a second decision: whether or not to offer the rebuilt car to Dayton. If he does offer it to Dayton, he has to decide whether or not to offer the car at "full" price. If he opts for "full" price, the consequence will be that Dayton does or does not accept, and if Dayton does accept, the car will either derail again or it will not, and so forth.

To determine the *financial* impact of his alternatives or "options", Holton has put into his tree the dollar amounts corresponding to each decision and consequence. A plus means: Money is coming in. A minus means: Money is going out. All of which enables him to read off at the end of each sequence of decisions and events, the total dollar impact that following that particular route will have.

Of course, those dollar amounts by themselves are quite meaningless, if you don't also know something about *how likely* they are. What is worth more: $20,000 that you have only one chance in a hundred of winning, or $2,800 where your chance of winning is ninety-nine in a hundred? So Holton has figured into his decision tree the likelihood for each of his events to occur (these numbers are left out so as to not clutter the tree too much).

Half an hour of diagramming and what seemed an impenetrable mess of a problem is presenting itself as a sequence of logical, easily graspable steps and all that is left for you to do, is to pick the sequence where the numbers show the greatest likelihood of making the most money (or suffer the least loss). MERC II and its decision trees are turning out to be a surprisingly effective way around a lot of headaches.

October 21, lunch hour:

(JAMES ERWINGER *talking*)

"I didn't know Baxter too well, Lindsay—I really didn't know him too well either—who else? I think McGrady came along with us, this was Saturday, we all took off to the 'Pearly Gate' and got shit-faced.

"Yeah, we all kind of . . . really were looking and searching, trying to get to know each other just by . . . by doing something and . . . all right, here we were at a bar, there is a bunch of girls, there's a bunch of guys . . . the bartender is mixing our drinks . . . we're looking and commenting on the same things together, finding out about each other.

"I mean this is . . . it's part of getting along in life . . . getting to understand the people you're with. But, anyway."

October 22: Professor Richard W. Francis and his book on accounting have instilled such respect in Section B that the way to do things in MERC I is "according to St. Francis."

Richard Francis is the type of man you probably wouldn't notice in a room full of people. If everybody were wearing suits and ties, that is. He is a sort of *Saturday Evening Post* American: self-assured, calm, and helpful in a strangely distant way. You can't say that he doesn't care. But in contrast to McKay, who comes so close that he fills up your entire field of vision, Francis stays aloof and distant, hidden by the task which he has set before us.

To illustrate the concept of "funds flow," Professor Francis today drew on his experience in a high government office. Somebody in his department, he said, had used a scheme called a "people flow" to help determine what was happening in Vietnam.

The scheme had a column, "Sources of People," listing where the soldiers had come from, and a column, "Applications of People," listing where they had gone. And, presumably, when the "Applications" exceeded the "Sources," the department had to ask for more Americans to make up the difference.

It was a very peculiar example because, on one hand, you couldn't avoid a flattering sense of your own importance, from being allowed to share with this man an experience the consequences of which are far more lasting and inalterable than anything most of us are ever likely to do. On the other hand, there was this feeling of bewilderment that the lives of so many men should add up to no more than two simple columns.

October 23, evening: Beale Company was the MERC I case. About what it *really* costs to make a product. You know, as opposed to what it costs to keep up the machines and the building and pay for administration. What costs do you look at to set prices? To figure out your profit? For inventory and taxes?

Our MERC I notes are beginning to look pretty complex with break-even diagrams, absorbed and estimated, fixed and variable costs. The idea is sinking in that accounting is really an information system; the business officer's map, if you want to use a military analogy.

The basic elements of that information system are quite simple. To understand them, try to think of the most basic kind of business situation imaginable: say, a man who wants to start up a factory making red socks.

Now ask yourself what you, as this man, would have to know to be able to run that business.

Well, before you could take orders, you would have to be sure you have the tools and the raw materials to use them on. Without tools you can do nothing, and without wool to process, the tools are useless.

Assume now that you have the sock-making equipment needed and that your machines are turning out socks by the mile. You surely would want to know how many socks your machines are making; how much money you'll take in after selling the socks; how much red wool you could buy for that money; how much of the wool you will feed back into the machines to make more socks, and, of course, how much money will be left over from all transactions for you to keep as profit.

So you will want to know not only whether you *have* the necessary tools, but also *how much business activity your tools have generated.*

And that—a list of your tools as well as the amount of business activity generated by those tools—is what the information system called "accounting" is designed to tell you. In the language of the business officer, the list of tools is called a "balance sheet"; the piece of paper describing how much business activity has been generated by those tools is called an "income statement."

The balance sheet (as shown below) is arranged in the form of a "T." On the left side it lists all the tools or assets a company has; on the right side, under the heading "equities," it lists the people and institutions who, as owners, partners, or stockholders in the company, own those tools.

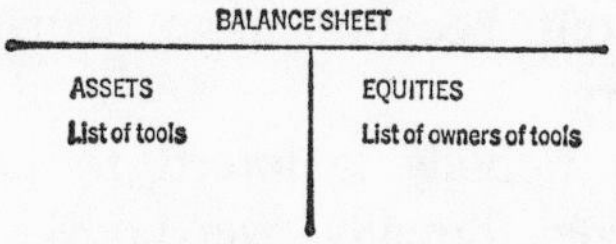

And since all tools are paid for and owned by somebody, the total amount of what the owners claim to own must be the same as the total value of all the tools in the company. Which is why a balance sheet balances.

As for the income statement, it usually is a single column composed of additions and subtractions. What went into the company's tools during the period—the value of the raw material—is subtracted from what came out—the finished product. If the result is zero, you broke even. If you get a positive number, you've made a profit. If you get a negative number, you're fired.

Midnight: An afterthought. To call a business administrator a business "officer" is more than just a military analogy, because that's what the top administrators of businesses are called. Which makes a graduate school of business administration, like this one, an officer candidate school and all of us business officer candidates.

October 24: When you read about it in the school catalogue, this thing called a "study group" sounds like the ideal cure for all possible ills of the Business School. It seems like a human haven made of shared misery and joint effort. A point from which to stem the tide of losing, of trying to cram ten or twelve hours of work into six hours of evening. A way of putting an end to the silly catch-up game that forces you to tackle tomorrow's cases with yesterday's barely mastered techniques. And when you hear McKay saying that people who are in a study group have a greater chance of making it, then the study group becomes more than a convenience, it becomes a necessity.

Thus, although nobody is forced to join and although they aren't organized formally, everybody is eager to be part of one. What started as brief, exploratory chats during the first couple of weeks is turning into an eleventh-hour, often desperate behind-the-scenes struggle. What could have been a group of guys working together, sharing their experience (which seems to be rich and varied in Section B) is turning into just another source of pressure and anxiety. "Now Reddick," you begin to calculate, "he seems to know a lot about accounting . . . with his experience in accounting and my experience in marketing . . ."

But what if, like some of the guys, you don't have any experience in accounting, have never worked in marketing? What if you're left to face those overly long cases alone? Alone to face the larger than life figures of the professors. A thought that sends people scurrying for shelter, willing to risk rejection and insult. For at this stage, even the illusion of belonging is better than the certainty of being on your own. And so the strong, as they get together, become stronger while the weak, afraid of dragging one another down to defeat, stay apart.

Our own fault? A fault of the school? A mirror of the real world? Comparing people to diamonds, some sloganeer in the Section exclaimed that "diamonds are made of pressure." Diamonds, yes. But not the light that gives a diamond its fire.

October 25:

According to a statistic put together by Sam Maguire, forty-five of the ninety-four people in the Section are between ages twenty and twenty-four; thirty-nine of them are between twenty-five and twenty-nine; ten are in their thirties.

Fifty-eight of the men and one of the four girls are married.

Almost 20 per cent of the Section are foreigners: six from Canada, three from England, two each from France, the Philippines, South America, or other European countries.

The seventy-seven Americans are from thirty-two states, most of which are represented by one or two persons. The states with the heaviest representation are California, six, New York, twelve, Massachusetts, eleven, and Pennsylvania, five.

The most heavily emphasized undergraduate discipline is the social sciences (especially economics), followed by engineering and business administration. Twelve were liberal arts majors, six were natural science majors, two hold undergraduate degrees in law, and one has a degree in architecture.

Among their alma maters you find a whole string of famous universities plus places you probably never heard of:

Harvard (seven)
Princeton (three)

Yale (four)
University of California at Berkeley (one)
MIT (two)
Stanford (two)
Business University of Puget Sound
Trinity College, Dublin
University of Chile
Manilla University
United States Air Force Academy
École Centrale, Paris
Vassar
University of Guelph, Canada
Christ Church College, Oxford
Institut d'Études Politiques, Paris
Iowa State
United States Naval Academy
South Dakota School of Mines

Ten members of the Section have more than one degree. One holds a graduate degree in economics, one, a graduate degree in international relations, one, a degree in philosophy, three, degrees in law, and six, degrees in engineering. One even holds two graduate degrees, and thus, with his undergraduate diploma and the M.B.A., will have a grand total of four degrees.

Of course, this being the Business School, everybody has some work experience: twenty-three have more than four years, thirty-one have worked between one and four years, and forty have had less than a year of continuous work experience.

For seventy-three, the employer has been private industry, thirteen have been or still are part of the armed forces, five have worked for the government, and three were owners and operators of their own business.

But the most varied and also the most reassuring information is the following sample of the kinds of jobs held. It shows that there must be a million ways, if not to success at least into the Harvard Business School:

Charter pilot
Assistant bank branch manager
Summer shutdown co-ordinator
Legal researcher
Industrial engineer
Marketing executive
Nuclear research engineer
Economic analyst
Creative director, advertising
Riding master, Playboy Club
Lawyer
Trainee, French Atomic Energy Commission
Investment analyst
Captain, chief of staff for maintenance
Intern, labor and race relations
Farm manager
Insurance adjustor
Tool engineer
Owner of a construction company
Lieutenant, French Army
Teletype operator
Marketing consultant
Draftsman
B52 Co-pilot
Statistical clerk
Battalion officer
Senior accountant
Electronic data processing programmer
Captain security police
Computer salesman
Production foreman

Bank vault attendant
Jet propulsion system analyst
Federal Reserve Board, field staff, examiner
Teaching assistant
Owner and founder of painting company

October 25, afternoon: The Section elected two representatives to the SA (Student Association). Everybody kind of played it down, but we all were aware that, starting today, it would no longer be easy to be friends with everybody. And given the kind of environment we're in, nobody particularly likes to have any more enemies than is absolutely necessary.

For the first time, we will have to tell what we think of one another. Sure, we will only have to name two persons whom we particularly like. But that's also saying something about some of the people whom we do not like at all.

Two second-year men took names, and after we had gone through with it, there were about ten or fifteen names on the board. The names of almost all the people who, in one way or another, have caught the fancy of the Section.

Kaplan, the lawyer, the dominant force in our PBE (Planning in the Business Environment) anti-trust cases. Goodwin, whose intricate and informed way of speaking has made him a point of reference from the first day. Argus, the All-American boy, broad shouldered and slightly chubby, with strands of blond hair dangling into his handsome face. Max Tuck, the incarnation of what people call a "mature individual."

When the candidates had left the room, somebody put in a word for the late nomination of Leroi. A thin, waspish guy whose frequent outbursts in class alternately bother and amuse people. Gilfeder also was nominated late, as "the guy who has made an effort to meet every man in the Section."

Well, the way the vote went, neither Kaplan nor Goodwin made it, nor anybody who really is anybody. Except for

Allan—Allan McGrady—who always has a smile, a minute, a willingness to listen.

But with the second guy, things got difficult. It took three rounds and almost ended with Gilfeder; a tall, pale individual whose face is cast into the expression of grave and stately concern that you see in ads aimed at executives; a crusader for the obvious, a revolutionary for causes that are already won; helpful and concerned where help and concern don't cost anything.

Everybody was shaking McGrady's and Flagg's hands. But everybody knew that the whole thing had ended in a draw. That, except for Allan, we hadn't elected anybody, but had decided to wait and let the real power relationships in the Section work themselves out; we weren't willing or ready yet to show our true feelings.

October 30: Sam Maguire, our social chairman, had said that last night's thing would be an informal get-together of the Section, that there would be beer and, if anybody had a tape recorder, to please bring it to have some music.

Still it wasn't quite clear, at first, what sort of thing this would be, and the married men wondered whether they were meant to bring their wives.

At a quarter to eight, there were already a number of couples strewn about the place with Blotner's tape recorder filling in the pauses. And Allan McGrady, with a smile, was passing out beer.

At about eleven, almost everybody was there, and the party boiled with lively conversation, filling up the impersonal, hotel-lobby type of lounge.

Somewhere, at the fringe of the crowd, Mel Kandel was finishing another beer, and his face, that slightly puffed-up face that projects a state of perpetual hangover, almost hid his eyes as he laughed loud and happy, hanging on to this big-eyed little thing who punctuated his sentences with cheery bits of southern drawl.

Russ Baxter had installed himself at an important intersection between a couple of easy chairs, extracting a heavy toll of conversation, while Duane Gilfeder had gotten hold of Jake Kamholz, our young and very brilliant MERC II professor and—as everybody tried to get in on the deal—scored what points he could until Kamholz fled to a group that had given refuge to his wife.

Mr. O'Neil, our WAC (Written Analysis of Cases) instructor, said that he had been in Switzerland—was it in '57 or '58? And that he had gone over the—was it the Gotthardpass?

And all this time, Allan was smiling and passing out beer.

October 31: The only thing we will probably remember of Paul Stahl is that he looked smaller than he was, that he wore glasses, and that he had the misfortune of being picked on to give a presentation in one of the first of McKay's classes.

It wasn't that he hadn't prepared. It was just that the case was about forty pages long, full of tables, and that nobody could really handle it, specially not Stahl.

Stahl was the kind of guy you never noticed much in the Section. He didn't dress loud. He didn't talk loud. And having just graduated from college, he wasn't prepared for something like McKay. So when McKay made him give a second presentation because he had gotten lost in the first one, he got himself into trouble all over again. He had done a tremendous amount of work—hard to imagine how he ever found the time—and all that did for him was make things worse. He spoke for about fifteen minutes on what you had to do right to succeed in this particular industry and on trends in the market until McKay, who hadn't said a word, interrupted him testily: "Tell me, what is the *problem* here?"

McKay was right. Stahl had thought of practically everything. Except what was really the key question. Red and wiping the sweat from underneath his glasses, Stahl sank without so much as a gurgle. McKay then told him, in front of the whole Section that he had to rate him "Unsat"—unsatisfactory.

The Section, afterward, tried to cheer Stahl up by giving him the "Sacrificial Lamb Award—for the guy who deserves most protection from harassment."

Chatting a bit today, at the beginning of class, McKay mentioned among other things that Stahl has left for the Army.

The Stahl incident shows that case learning is a rough business. Sometimes they deliberately don't give you enough information; sometimes, deliberately, they give you too much. And always there is the deadline of the next morning and the chance that you may be asked to present a decision.

Which is the way it is in the real world. You never know all you ought to know. And what you could know is often hidden in a mess of garbled information and cluttered with useless detail. But not everybody in the Section has been out in the real world. And traditional education with its lectures, its ready-made questions, and prefabricated answers doesn't teach it. Most people in the Section have picked it up quickly. Stahl just happened to be a little slow.

November 1: At first it looked like the most normal HBO (Human Behavior in Organizations) class ever. There was none of the groping, rambling discussion. This time Rosen seemed determined to talk business. It was dull and very unlike the HBO classes that had gone before. At least until

Leroi suggested that instead of fiddling with the case, why not use the "systems approach" to look at ourselves? Why not treat the Section as a "social system"? But Kearney had another idea. Could we not, he asked, look at the professors too?

"Please put up two columns," Kearney requested of Professor Rosen.

"Put 'Rosen' at the top of one, 'McKay' at the top of the other."

"Write 'small' under the name Rosen."

Rosen wrote.

"Write 'insecure.'"

Rosen wrote.

"Write 'marshmallow.'"

Rosen started to write.

"Stop this!" Tom Benson suddenly shouted from the back. For a moment, it was absolutely quiet.

"Mr. Benson . . ." Rosen made some kind of effort. "Mr. Benson, please . . ."

"No," Tom said with an eerily controlled voice, "this doesn't serve anything . . . it's no good . . . let's stop!"

It wasn't just the things that had been said about Rosen. It was that Rosen didn't or couldn't or wouldn't fight back. Kearney was lying afterward when he said that this was a misunderstanding, that he hadn't meant to insult Rosen, that by "marshmallow" he had meant Rosen's habit of absorbing our comments rather than dealing with them.

A strange, almost perverse twist of fate that this should be happening to Rosen. Because here is a man who is trying and risking something. A man who on the first day—we were still speechless from the threats of McKay—had come in without a jacket, in just shirt and tie, drinking a cup of coffee. It was like after a bad dream. This man was real, our size. The first human event in a succession of clockwork ceremonies.

Rosen never tried to use his power on us. Surely because he thought he never would have to. Recently, however, he has begun to remind us that he knows more about HBO than we do, that after all he has a Ph.D. Perhaps because he is sensing that things are beginning to go wrong. That his knowledge isn't working. Rosen somehow never has become a landmark in the shifting web of Section B's relationships: He has changed from a solitary human being to a vague reminder of the power the Harvard Business School holds over us, and finally to an object of discontent and ridicule.

What happened? Why him? The man who is trying to be understanding? Who is permitting students to call him by his first name? Why him?

Perhaps such a man doesn't belong with such a large group of people as Section B.

Or perhaps the world which he sees is not the world in which we live. He never seems to hear our words although he has made a habit of repeating them.

Was it us? Was it him?

Was it just words?

Whatever it was, this class has done something to our relationship with Rosen that nothing, especially not words, can repair.

November 5: Kandel almost fell out of his chair, yawning. Baxter sat there with his eyes closed, and Mark Holton rocked his chair to keep his flickering lights from going out altogether. The lack of sleep, the tension and turmoil of the first weeks finally seem to catch up with Section B.

The even stream of MERC I and MERC II numbers is carrying us out, away from reality into a strangely familiar land where trees grow numbers, where numbers form weird lines that befuddle the mind.

As for Rosen, there seems to be even a physical distance now between him and us, as he moves farther away to the door, to the blackboard. He is quite pale and on the verge, it seems, of having his mind flee from our curious glances, humming about him like a swarm of flies.

There is less reinterpretation by him. There is less exploration. There is less of everything. He tries to be concise and to the point. It is as if we—the Section and he—have exhausted ourselves on one another, and now all that is left is time and an increasing distance.

A kind of underhanded, slightly rebellious humor is all that at the moment is left of Section B. Like this morning, when Mr. Kamholz lowered the electric blackboard to find that somebody had written on the board behind: "God is alive and failing MERC II."

November 9, Saturday: Somebody over in Morgan seems to think that we haven't seen anything yet. That the weeks gone by have been only warm-ups. That it is about time to show us. This morning they did.

It was an exam made of Chinese boxes, with boxes inside boxes inside boxes inside boxes. Even if you could read the thing, chances are you still couldn't understand it. And even if you could understand it, you still couldn't handle the complexities of it.

Four hours this time.

It was a matter of drawing a very complicated decision tree, and the way people were talking afterward, many of those trees never grew higher than rhubarb.

Blotner said all he had was leaves.

In one of the exam rooms a guy got up after about an hour and, with a snap that could be heard all the way down the hall, broke his slide rule into a handful of pieces.

December 7: There were more people drunk than usual. There were more loose ends of loose conversation. More girls. More perfume, more hairdos, more giggling than usual.

There were more people running around, looking for somebody. More people saying, "hello," more floors to get lost on.

They say that it is usually quite unusual, the Harvard Business School Christmas formal.

2

Petra Cement

(Or the Agony of a WAC)

WEEK OF DECEMBER 2

Monday: Of all the instruments of fear and terror at the disposal of the Business School, none can match a WAC's effectiveness in reducing a healthy first-year body to a mess of gastric disorders, fluttering eyelids, and recurring nightmares that make the poor bastard jump up in the middle of the night, screaming for Mother.

A set of instructions told us at the beginning of the year:

> The substance of the WAC course is the process of analysis. It is useful to think of the evolution of a WAC report, the product of that process, as having three related but separate stages. The first stage or phase is the actual analysis of the assigned case, leading to the development of a plan of action. The second phase is the selection and organization of ideas that have been developed in the analysis in preparation for the third stage, which is the presentation of the analysis in written form.

In written form (typewritten) and on special green paper on which it is almost impossible to erase. Due: Every other Saturday, in a brown, clearly labeled envelope, at the West End of Baker Library by 6 P.M.

We picked up a twenty-page case at Baker 20 today, of which the cover sheet contained the following information:

Written Assignment #5
December 14, 19–

HARVARD UNIVERSITY
GRADUATE SCHOOL OF BUSINESS
ADMINISTRATION
George F. Baker Foundation

WRITTEN ANALYSIS OF CASES
Written Assignment #5
The Petra Cement Company EA-G 265

Assignment: What should Petra Cement do? Why?
Word Limit: 1500 words, excluding exhibits if any
Due: West End of Baker Library by 6:00 P.M., on Saturday, December 14, 19–

Wednesday: As far as you understand it, a committee of executives recommends that Petra's new cement plant should be built at Kuta. Unless Petra's bid for the nearby river dam fails. Then the plant should be built at Pelam. Petra's economic department, on the other hand recommends Verna as the plant site best suited—bid or no bid. As for the Kuta site—there are rumors that Petra's major competitor, the Davon Cement Corporation, is going to build a plant at Belton. And Belton is only twelve miles from Kuta.

Six pages of exhibits and two appendixes provide the numbers.

Thursday: The first discussions are springing up. Quietly, in small groups of friends. Insights into a WAC are too valuable to be wasted on just anybody.

The consensus seems to be that Petra must do everything to win the bid for the river dam. Because whoever wins it will have to build so much cement production capacity that he will dominate the entire region. It's an all-or-nothing proposition. Compared to winning the bid, the problem of site selection seems of secondary importance. But what if they *do* win the bid?

Friday: The discussions are becoming more frequent, louder, more intense. People are hoping to get a lead they can follow up over the weekend. Especially those who can't type and have to hand their drafts to the typists early.

Discussion is permitted but, at the same time, everybody is supposed to write the WAC on their own. So even among friends, the discussion always stays kind of cautious, general, almost superficial.

Maguire and Erwinger think that Pelam is out of the question because of a bad geological structure there. Maguire is going to try with a decision tree. He works extremely fast and probably will be done by the end of the weekend. But he is an exception.

Saturday and Sunday: You've been able to take the case apart all right but you can't, for all you try, put it back together. It's like sitting in the front row of a CinemaScope movie. Everything melts into one big blur.

You have spent Saturday and almost all of Sunday, but no progress, except a wad of yellow note paper filled with beginnings of beginnings and worthless diagrams.

Everything is related to everything else in this bloody case. By picking up one tiny piece you pick up the whole mess. A real merry-go-round. There is nothing so demoralizing as to try hard and get nowhere. The incredibly tight rules of a WAC strangle your thoughts. No leaps of faith allowed; no grandiose assumptions permitted. You've got to slug it out, covering all your bases.

THE WEEK FOLLOWING

Monday: In order to be done in time, you are forced to spend at least an hour a day on the WAC—in addition to the three daily cases. You are thinking Petra Cement as you brush your teeth. You think Petra Cement as you sip your coffee, as you walk to school. You think Petra Cement while you are supposed to listen to class discussion. You eat Petra Cement, you sleep Petra Cement, you've got Petra Cement oozing out of your ears.

Tuesday: WAC classes, like so many other aspects of our life as a Section, are caught in the conflicting demands of competition and co-operation. And while, earlier in the year, co-operation had seemed to win out, the growing familiarity with our surroundings is loosening the bond of fear, is tipping the scales in favor of competition. The anonymous mass that used to offer shelter from the school's pressures is breaking up into a federation of groups, an alliance of cliques—each with its distinct traits, each with its own ambitions.

Especially in WAC class—a regular class held about a week before each WAC is due—people no longer make a real effort. WAC classes have turned into a ritual in which everybody pays lip service to a goal that nobody is really interested in attaining. As a result, WAC classes move along slowly, haltingly, frequently retracing their steps, irresolutely searching for a promising direction.

Still, a good number of people do speak up. Some because called on by Mr. O'Neil, but most of them voluntarily. Their motives too diverse to allow for a clear explanation. For some it's the habit of impressing others. For others it's a securing of flanks by trying to assure themselves of the good will of Mr. O'Neil. (Although no grade is given in WAC for class participation.) For still others it's a genuine interest in the case or a true or naive generosity. Because of such people, even the slowest, most difficult WAC class is not without its meaning, its helpful bits and pieces of information.

Today's class on Petra Cement was no exception.

Wednesday: The way things are going, or rather the way they aren't going, you'll have to make some real wild assumptions. But that's taking your chances. Because No. 13 may not like it.

No. 13 is your WAC reader; the girl who has been assigned to read and grade your WACs. All you've seen and all you probably will ever see of her is the comments she makes in the margins. She writes neatly and straight up. The shapes of her letters are soft and round, and there is an elegant down swing to her "gs." Like somebody tall and cautious with a lovely, symmetrical face.

As it is, you're not exactly getting love letters from her. The first comments were devastating. But once you began to force your thoughts through the rigor of the WAC-type analysis—dressing each one of them up in a three-piece suit with tie—things began to look up. Up to about a P+ (Pass Plus). And that's the level on which No. 13 and you have continued to carry on your mute conversation. She, meticulous but fair. You, gnashing your teeth and trying harder.

Friday, morning: Time is running out. You can't afford to miss today's classes but you can't really afford to go, either. So you won't go. The WAC doesn't let you.

Midnight: It's no longer funny. You're getting clutched. You *must* begin to write if you want to have it done by tomorrow evening. Verna, Kuta, Pelam . . . if, if, if . . . a haze of ifs.

You truly want this Harvard degree, but it is getting a little costly.

Saturday, three in the morning: The stream of cars outside has slowed to a trickle. The late, late show must be over. There isn't a sound—except for your typewriter. You hope it won't wake up anybody.

Everything is kind of light and automatic now. The anger is giving way to detachment. A numbing indifference is setting in. Still, you have no beginning, but decide to go ahead and write anyway. You can't do better than your best and with a little bit of luck you'll come out in the right place.

Eight in the morning: Finally to bed a little after three. After you'd gone just far enough to make sure that you would have something to hand in.

Some people go straight through the whole night. But after a day and half a night of intense concentration you just couldn't go any further. These four and a half hours of sleep have somewhat refreshed. And now, on to finishing the rough draft.

Noon: You're getting there. But the finished draft is still three pages too long.

Five o'clock: Night is falling. You're done. Done and done for. It reads coherently, amazing considering the circumstances.

You proofread and staple it together. You slip it into the

carefully labeled, heavy brown envelope. Outside it's cold —even through the coat—and the banks of the Charles lie totally deserted.

At the West End of Baker Library it's the big circus. People are popping out of the twilight, queueing up at the slot in the basement window. You hear the hissing sound as the envelopes go down the chute and the fat "plop" as they fall into the WAC box.

Five-thirty: There is a long line of headlights and idling motors. With people jumping out, dropping off their envelopes, jumping back in.

People start arriving at a trot. Five more minutes.

Six: Rien ne va plus! The university watchman, down in the cellar, has closed the box. There is the sound of diminishing footsteps, and soon the street is restored to its desolate quiet, typical of late-winter evenings. Some people will undoubtedly be coming, but their papers will end up on top of the closed WAC box, at a full grade less.

Ten after six: It isn't easy to get your bearings in the dense smoke, the din of elated voices, the swirling crowd. What used to be the lounge of Gallatin Hall has been converted into a pub, has been divided into some six alcoves with a large round table in each, all the alcoves opening toward the center of the room where there is a bar. The alcoves make the large room quite cozy and especially after a WAC, the place is jam-packed.

McGrady's massive, balding head, set on an equally massive six-foot frame, like a bell tower, signals the location of Section B. Their table is loaded with brimful pitchers of beer and they are in the sorry sort of state to which only a WAC can reduce people. Torn and soiled slacks, the sort most suitable to spend a night in at the typewriter; shirts as crumpled as yesterday's newspaper; the faces marked by a day's growth of beard.

"Worst paper I ever wrote," Holton claims with a silly grin, to which O'Mara adds that "an outfit with that kind of an operation . . ." but somehow gets sidetracked. Somebody lets off a sharp burp and the only thing that gets finished in this conversation is the beer. McGrady feels an urge to play a game of darts but nobody can really warm up to the idea. Baxter, meanwhile, hangs slumped over in his chair and somebody, for about the sixth time, says he has to go, he really has to go home now . . .

And in a couple of weeks, usually at the end of an eleven-ten class, our two SA reps will walk in, each with an armful of brown envelopes, and the Section, like a flock of geese, will go: "WAC, WAC, WAC." The brown envelopes will fly through the air, landing amid a flurry of excited hands.

Petra Cement! You will look frantically for the little white slip, and you don't care what Petra Cement should or could have done, what your mistakes were, or the flaws in your argument, or whatever No. 13 has got you down for; all you want to know is that she put at least a *P* (for Pass) on the slip; that you have made it past yet another one, and that—thank God—five WACs down. Only six to go.

3

For What? For Whom?

December 17: The waiting line outside Baker 20 went all the way down the hall and people were cracking jokes to ease the tension. Inside, the lady behind the counter wanted to know your student number. Walking over to a pushcart loaded with file boxes—each box subdivided by tall pieces of cardboard, each piece of cardboard marked with large numbers—she would pull out a white envelope, hand it over, one after another as the line inched by the counter.

What you got was a regular white, business envelope. "After 5 days return to Harvard University Graduate School of Business Administration, Soldiers Field, Boston, Mass. 02163," it said in the upper left corner. And in the window just below: "Student Number 02340" and the beginning of something that said: "Harvard Business S . . ." printed by a computer. You didn't have to open it because it wasn't sealed. The flap was inside, holding back a printout, the size of a large postcard:

Terner, Allan P.

Human Behavior in Org	LP+
Merc II	P
Planning + Bus Env	P+

And that's all the thing said.

Some guys' faces were red with excitement and some carried their envelopes away to a corner like hungry dogs. Others stuffed them away quickly, nervously, as something too personal to share.

Outside, the inevitable questions: "What did you get? How did you do?" And on the floor, a scattering of empty white envelopes.

December 19: According to figures that McKay read off at the end of his class, Section B came up with the following grades in the courses MERC II and PBE:

	PBE	MERC II
D– (Distinction Minus)	0	1
HP+ (High Pass Plus)	1	1
HP (High Pass)	4	2
HP– (High Pass Minus)	9	8
P+ (Pass Plus)	16	15
P (Pass)	25	13
P– (Pass Minus)	23	22
LP+ (Low Pass Plus)	12	13
LP (Low Pass)	2	15
LP– (Low Pass Minus)	1	2
U (Unsatisfactory)	0	1

December 20: It just may be that they forgot them—after Thanksgiving, after the exams and all. The fact is that some guys no longer bring the white placards with their names on them. These are white cards about six inches high and ten inches long, that fit into slits provided on the desk tops. So maybe they just forgot them. But why so many? Why Goodwin? Why O'Mara? Why Reddick? Why five or six others?

But then, why bring them? Who doesn't know Schwartz, the tall, spindly guy on the left by the door? Who doesn't know that whenever there is question of anybody "having some experience in it," all faces turn toward Parsons? After the fourteen weeks we now have spent together, who doesn't know?

So why the cards? Could it be, is it perhaps that those cards no longer reflect the true state of things? That some should be bigger, some smaller than others? That some should no longer be there at all? Perhaps we are no longer names. The real stuff is showing. In a way a word is said, a hand is moved, a presence is felt. We who make such a fuss about being rational, who dread nothing so much as becoming involved, of losing control, of getting too close. We are no longer free. We are no longer objective. Dislike and affection color our views of one another and make our decisions, despite the rigorous logic of our professional education, something less than rational.

Tomorrow the Christmas recess begins. Inconclusively the first act ends in rain. A heavy downpour is washing away the groans and yawns, the small moments of triumph, the instants of defeat. The watery curtain yields a welcome moment of relief.

What has it all been? What does it mean?

Boot camp? Another obstacle to make sure that there won't be too many eaters to share the pie? A unique opportunity? A colossal mistake?

It's hard to tell. Perhaps because there was so much. Perhaps because we haven't had the time yet to tidy our cluttered minds.

What can you say? Except that a lot of once-strange terms now look a lot more familiar. That we are beginning to feel at home in a world that four months ago was still so provocatively and dismayingly foreign.

There is something convincing and practical about the things they teach us here. About their way of breaking the big ones down to pieces you can manage. It's obvious that it works.

The question is: for what? for whom?

4

The Battle Begins in Earnest

January 6: A week ago—remember?—you told yourself: in a week. Three days ago you warned yourself: just three more days. Well, the week has gone. The three days are over. It's a new year now. It's Monday and again it's school.

It was as though a projector which had unexplainably stopped was suddenly switched on again. And the movie that had stood still—weirdly still with all its actors frozen in bizarre positions—continues.

In fact, after five minutes, you began to wonder whether there had been a break at all. Whether the sun, the snow, the long cozy evenings had been just another daydream. And you looked around at the faces, the ninety-three faces, as if to find proof of the good days just gone by. But these faces were as deserted as a beach in winter.

A number of seats were still empty, and even McKay had not returned from his trip to Europe. Nobody really had much to say about the First Plainsville National Bank. Not that it was a bad case. It might have been interesting any time except perhaps today, on the first day. When our ears were tuned inward, listening to the fading echoes of music, laughter, and happy gibberish.

January 8: Mary's pencil, following her restless thoughts, had wandered off, away from the large round letters it had strung together, tracing memories that had suddenly danced up from oblivion and, bursting like bubbles, had spilled a strange and scintillating array of images. Mary's short brown hair is parted on the right—a boy's cut, almost—yet with strands of it falling onto a small, frail face. The features are drawn in clear, thin lines as though time, discarding sketches of her youth, had settled too quickly on a definite draft. The short line of her mouth, an accountant's double line, balances the sparse but delicate assets of her face with a puzzling finality.

We know little of Mary, other than what it says in one of the listings on Section S: "Emerson, Mrs. Mary, 41, Riceville, Tennessee. Business administration (undergraduate major), University of Tennessee. Systems analyst and computer programmer. Brad (husband's name). Two children."

In fact, by openly, half jokingly referring to her age, she constantly emphasizes the distance between her and the Section, as though to snuff out any emotional contacts. You cannot help but admire her courage, her willingness to suffer through the trials of the first year. Yet, with all of us scheming for a glorious future, Mary at times seems like a relic of her own past.

January 10: The MERC II assignment was a thirty-one-page note on simulation, which sums up a lot of what we've been doing lately. The idea is that since you are in business to make money, you want to stay away from decisions whose likely consequence will be that you lose money. You want to know about possible negative consequences before they hit you.

The trouble is that there are many decisions for which there seems no meaningful ways to predict consequences—either positive or negative. Take the Weston case: If the flatbed car is rebuilt, will it or will it not derail again? No way to predict that, is there? Well, there is. The idea is that if you don't know about the future of an event, you may know something about its past. And that if you have no past to go by, you can make one up by simulating the event. By, for example, driving a car similar to the rebuilt Dayton car over Rickenback's tracks. If, by doing so, you should find that your experimental car derailed ninety-nine times out of a hundred, then you could say that there is a 99 per cent chance that the improved Dayton flatbed will derail too.

The past (whether genuine or simulated) cannot tell you what will happen in the case of the one *particular* event you're trying to predict because the flatbed you are looking at may just be the one out of a hundred that happens not to derail. But by giving you patterns and averages, the past can give you at least *a feel* for what might happen; it can tell you what the *likely* consequences will be. Which is a lot better than leaving things to chance.

And the past is only one of several tools you can use to bring greater certainty into your decision. You can, for example, try to understand your own attitude toward risk. Through an ingenious set of questions you can convert the fact that you are a daredevil (or its opposite) into numbers and work those numbers into your decision problem, which will lead you to a still more objective evaluation of the risks involved.

All of which is why we are struggling so intensively with decision analysis and why MERC II—you can't help but choke at the thought of it—is in the first-year curriculum.

We had a wild discussion on ethics in PBE yesterday, on just what the business of business is. Tony Rush had gone way out on a limb, saying that business and private life are two entirely different things, with different standards and objectives. Others had agreed that this is the way it is in the real world, whether we like it or not.

Mark Holton got up in anger and said that the way everybody was talking, he wouldn't hire two thirds of us.

Today, at the beginning of PBE, Mark got up again and apologized. Said that he still thinks he was right, that there is no excuse for being one thing in private and another in business. But that he didn't mean to insult us.

That's how sensitive we are to one another's feelings. How deeply each of us has come to depend on the others, even though we may hate one another's guts.

January 13: Black is what John Reddick is. And Leo Traver. And Dale Hughes. Or that's what you think black is. If you haven't heard Leo Traver talk.

When Leo held up his hand today we were talking about some white company hiring blacks. It was a PBE race-relations case in which different black groups were competing with one another for influence. The question was what the white manager should do.

Leo knew what the man should do: Split the black front. Make the radicals turn against the moderates.

Whom are you talking for, Leo?

You dress like a well-to-do white man—in fact, there is nothing so obviously white as that shirt covering your black skin. You lean back in your chair with the same relaxed gestures white men make. You select your words with the same care. But aren't these your people? You are black, aren't you?

Why are you talking this way, Leo? Or are we misunderstanding you? Is it bitter humor? Are you trying to tell us that you know too well what the white man is up to? That you will not be fooled?

Or could it be that opportunity—and most of all this tremendous "opportunity" named Harvard Business School—has fogged up your lenses? Is it that our elaborate arguments have given you a false sense of security?

Or is it that you no longer want to have anything to do with the whole thing? That your life is your own business?

What have other blacks done for you that you should fight for them?

White people don't go out on a limb for other white people.

Why should you care?

It's hard work at the Business School. You've got to give it all you have. For others?

What do they care—about your flunking out of school, out of your job, out of life?

There are many good reasons, Leo. Not just good reasons but real, very real reasons.

We may not like them but we understand.

January 14, morning: Holden doesn't arrive at conclusions slowly and deliberately. He jumps at them with the abandon of a man who has nothing to lose.

In fact, his conclusions are far more than conclusions. They are almost embarrassing insights into a personality. A deliberate, desperate self-exposure that you cannot answer with technical niceties. Holden doesn't want a discussion. He wants a fight. He speaks in ultimatums that force you to take a stand on Stanley Holden.

To top that, he isn't an enemy to be taken lightly. For, although nobody seems to be particularly close to him, almost everybody respects him. In our discussions of MERC II, he has shown himself an undoubted master in matters of statistics. Yet, the less we talk of statistics and the more we know of Stan, the further he seems to drift from the main body of the Section, orbiting around it, aloof and inaccessible as the moon. His face is hard and somber to look at, the mouth folded inward in intense concentration. The dark-gray suits, which he wears without fail or variation, and the strands of thick brown hair glued across the forehead heighten the faint sense of terror his appearance inspires.

It seems that all the success in his life—high honors in college and the prospect of going to the Business School—hasn't been able to relax Stanley Holden. Somewhere in all this struggling, he seems to have gotten off on the wrong track. Seems to have thought that love and affection can be bought with effort. Seems to have come to believe that peace with oneself depends on victory over others.

So there he goes, fighting with all the will he can muster to prop up the teetering image of himself. Like the big hand of a clock forever running after his smaller but more weighty companion that he continually passes but cannot beat. A victim of the enemy he himself has created. A man who, because he cannot, knows that he must.

Evening:

(MEL KANDEL *talking*)

"We never stop talking about cases. We never stop.
We are always talking about business or the Business
School, and I love it. Every minute of it. I have
planned on devoting a year to doing nothing but that.
And I'm doing nothing but that. I'm dead serious.
I *love* talking about business. It's like a hobby. Even
if I were teaching music I would read, you know,
the *Wall Street Journal* and *Business Week*
as a hobby."

(MARK HOLTON *talking*)

"You're so tied up between Baker Library, Aldrich,
and the dorm that unless you have a car, unless you have
a lot of contacts in the city, you really don't tend to
go out that much. And when you do, the only time

you really have available is Saturday night, you know,
and that is five or six hours maybe . . .

"I constantly feel I have to begin the cases
immediately upon return from the classroom. Well,
I just know the work is there and it has to be lengthy:
Each case a couple of hours' long anyway, if you want
to do a decent job. And if you put it off until after
dinner, you know, you watch the news, you sit around
and talk awhile, and by that time, you know, you're
lost unless you want to stay up all night."

January 17: Living day after day in this windowless room is having a strange effect on people. They move around, changing their seat from one day to the next, sometimes from one class to the other. "To get a look at it from the other side," as they say, or simply to hide at the periphery of the professor's field of vision. So it's kind of hard to tell who is and who isn't there on a given day. And although they have put the holy fear into us about missing classes ("You can't have a discussion with nobody there"), we have discovered that they won't give you trouble if you're kind of careful about it and don't do it too often.

This constant moving and shifting, this slightly irregular attendance provides an ideal backdrop for people with out-of-the-ordinary habits.

All the looking in the world, for example, couldn't change the fact that Chico Perez wasn't here today. He has left—somebody said at lunch—for a prolonged weekend in the Virgin Islands, and nobody really was very much surprised at that. Chico has entered our scene, flashing his white teeth with the self-confident, relaxed smile of a singer about to give a performance to a room full of middle-aged ladies. He seems to approach the Business School with the sporty eagerness of an amateur golfer—out for a good, clean challenge. With everybody mired down by the weight of their worries, Chico soars along overhead—given to the occasional concern of a man who does not like his faultless record (including a Harvard undergraduate degree) spoiled—but otherwise cool and collected, always game for a fine joke.

Because of his father, back in Montevideo, Chico commands the reputation of a man who has got it made. And with shoes in the latest Paris style, an English Rover, painted racing green (picked up over there last summer), Chico does his natural best to look the part.

So people in Section B almost expect and discreetly overlook the fact that Chico's seat is empty a little more frequently. That the broad flashy tie is missing every so often, gone the hands playfully flipping a heavy golden pencil whose dull surface produces a muffled flash as it tumbles through the air.

In contrast to Chico's obvious presence—when he is here at all—it's very difficult to tell whether or not Hank Schwartz is around. Schwartz never talks. The only time he ever said anything was when McKay made him. Still—he is there. If he is there. His thin body runs up through his pants and jacket like a line of stitches, up to the respectable altitude of about six feet. Up there, a swell of straight black hair breaks over his forehead; the face—a bony face with hollow cheeks—is dominated by dark brows which hide two hesitant eyes.

Hank Schwartz was the first man in the Section to get a grade of "distinction." Understandably, there is little in first-year life that creates as lasting an impression as that. Silently, invisibly almost, Hank lives both in the everyday world and in our imagination; admired by all but not really known by anybody.

It's a peculiar thing about our wasteland of a classroom. With nothing but us to give it life, it's quite easy, in spite of all the moving around, to tell who is and who isn't there on a given day.

Here, a sampling of the jargon that identifies us as members of Section B and, more generally, as students at the Harvard Business School: *A ballpark number.* Still in fair territory; never far enough for a home run but a sure way to get on base. *Thou* or *K.* Stands for $1,000. Gets away from all this dull talk about money. Makes you sound as though you had been around this sort of thing all your life. *To eyeball.* To size up in one quick glance. To substitute insight for investigation. *Hobo problems.* Stems from HBO, which are the initials of the first-year course in Human Behavior in Organizations. Means having some kind of hang-up with somebody. *To massage data.* The ability to reach the right conclusions from the wrong data. *The real world.* As opposed to what's going on in Aldrich 108. *The quits. Having the quits.* Being unable to convince yourself that you came here voluntarily. The shakes. Over the hill and off the orbit. The shrieks.

January 21: His room is on the second floor of Morgan, down the hall and to the left. It's in the wing with the odd-numbered rooms, and on the glass-paneled door, on eye level, there is the small sticker with his and his secretary's name.

You knock, you turn the brass doorknob, and later you don't really remember much of the room. You think there was a carpet. It sure felt like a carpet. In that kind of room, with that kind of man, there had to be a carpet. One thing you are quite sure of is the size of the room. It felt bigger, more empty than it is. Perhaps because of the order, because of the books neatly stacked behind the desk. And the desk, funny, perhaps there were things on it but you remember it wide and empty. You remember the man getting up, the "hello." You can still sense the ring of curiosity in that greeting. You can almost hear the clicking of the extraordinary brain, pulling your name like a file card, out of its vast and complex stores. You can see the recognition flick across the face. You remember the hand stretched out to meet yours, your saying: "How do you do, sir," and the echo of the reply: "What can I do for you?" and a brief relaxing smile.

Here you sit—across from Professor Francis. "Your" professor, yet as you sit there, it's a thousand miles across that desk to the man with that slow, even voice. The graying hair on the sides of the angular head is closely, cleanly cut and parted. There is nothing really on which to fasten your glance except the tiny red rosette in his left lapel. A decoration, undoubtedly, that was conferred on him for his work in government office.

There is nothing that is obvious or varying about him except his eyes. The eyes attentively fasten, first on you, then on your student card, which he has drawn out of a steel closet. You can see his round, even handwriting and you see his eyes coming back to you. There you sit, a student doing lousy in MERC I, explaining what you are going to do about it. And all the time you feel his eyes urging you, pushing you on, gentle but determined.

You come out, knowing that you will get a fair chance. That it's up to you. That there is no talking yourself into or out of something with this man. That he will look at your blue book with the same detached interest that he accords your person.

Yet, somehow, this visit hasn't done it for you. Here is a man whose impact on your career may make itself felt forever after and you don't just want to sit there, awaiting his verdict. You want to tell him that you are working hard. That you are making every conceivable effort, and that slowly but surely your performance in class will reflect that.

But now the door has closed. Perhaps there is no other way for a man of his influence to organize his affairs. Surely, his tasks are too urgent, his burden already too heavy to allow room for the individual hopes and problems of a lowly M.B.A.

Yet, as you stand out there, as you think of the things he said. Of the things that could and perhaps should have been said. Standing out there—those urgent tasks and all that heavy burden seem quite irrelevant to you.

January 22: Even in class, Ralph Parke has the stance of a football player. A blind eagerness to charge, a kind of I've-got-to-hit-you-before-you-hit-me attitude. A view of the world as a source of infinite and varied aggression that must be met head on, with all the force at one's disposal.

In spite of his relatively small size, Parke has been a mainstay of the Section's athletic teams, converting even a harmless game like softball into a tense, crunching encounter of bodies. There seems to be neither pause nor deliberation in his life. Instead, there is an unbroken sequence of all-out charges, designed to do away with any trace of opposition. Likewise in class, he seldom bothers to raise his hand but shouts right over people, ripping apart the delicate web of the discussion, leaving his own argument to dangle meaninglessly in mid-air.

At twenty-two, Parke just graduated from a place called Lanigan University with a degree in civil engineering. He comes from way out there on a farm, where he went to school, met his wife and where their two children were born. But there is nothing of the modesty that you might expect to flow from so obscure a background. Rather, Parke displays the hollow self-confidence of a man who has never been seriously challenged.

What is this fellow but an oversized gadget, the sad result of an educational process that mistakes efficiency for the end toward which it should have been a means. A piece of equipment produced on that assembly line leading from Sunday school to high school, from high school to college, from college to graduate school, from graduate school to the corporation.

January 23: In violent contrast to our generally subdued and quite formal way of dressing, Parke showed up today in a pair of worn, stained jeans and a smudgy Hawaiian shirt that looked as if he had cleaned his car with it. An attire that was neither funny nor imaginative nor hip nor anything but an eyesore.

Parke seemed to be telling us that because he had proved himself exceedingly adept in handling cases, that because he could *do* more, he *was* more, and by being more, he had the right to violate the feelings of his less gifted Section mates. Few people bothered to comment and those who did seemed to be doing it in the gentle, ironic sort of manner that people like Parke have been educated not to understand.

January 24: The answer to the Butcher Polish case was so obvious, it had to be wrong. Green Stripe, a high-quality, liquid, self-polishing wax is Butcher Polish's best seller. And although Butcher is a small, family-owned company, Green Stripe is holding its own against nationally advertised brands of much larger companies. Butcher's problem seems to be that Green Stripe isn't sold in enough places and that the places, where it is sold—hardware, grocery, and variety stores—don't have enough customers to build up the sales volume of which Green Stripe is capable.

The answer had to be: supermarkets! That they should go for the big-volume outlets.

"You must be aware," Professor Poole interrupted, "that supermarket shelves are crowded as they are?"

"Yes, sir, I am." Leroi was very sure. "That's why I recommend the heavy advertising. Make the product known! Create a lot of new customers."

"What about the money? The advertising money?" Poole, who had waited patiently for Leroi to get all the way out, was beginning to apply saw to limb.

"I believe," Leroi said with somewhat less conviction, "that they should cut their high retailer's margin. The dealers are making more money off Butcher's products than off anyone else's."

"Fine," Professor Poole said, "but you have thought, haven't you, what this will do to the retailers? Mr. Baxter, you want to address this point?"

"I would like to say this," Baxter said eagerly, "that so far what has sold Green Stripe wasn't advertising at all—page three of the case—they are doing almost no advertising. What they are doing is giving the advertising money to the retailers in the form of a high margin. *That*'s what's selling the product. That's why the dealers are pushing it."

"And if you cut that margin . . ." Poole was encouraging Baxter to go on.

"If you cut that margin, you cut yourself off from all your present dealers. You no longer have any channels of distribution."

That's where the catch was! By changing your outlets, you weren't just changing your outlets, you were changing your whole marketing strategy. After you saw the case laid out as we did, you really had to admit, Butcher does have a strategy and a coherent one at that. Now it may not be the most dynamic, and, what's worse, there may be no way of changing it short of selling out to a big conglomerate, but it *is* a strategy: You let the corner grocer sell the product by paying him a high margin. By letting the corner grocer sell, you don't really need a lot of advertising. Which gives you the money to pay for the grocer's margin. You let the grocer *push* the goods out the door. As opposed to what Butcher's competitors are doing: going to the big-volume supermarkets where you don't have anybody pushing the goods. Where, consequently, you can save yourself the high grocer's margin. Which you then have to use for advertising, to sell by *pulling* the goods out the door.

Two major marketing strategies; one, the opposite of the other; each effective under very different circumstances: *push* or *pull.*

That's first-year marketing for you. "Marketing" which really means no more than what it actually says: getting the goods from the door of the factory to the people waiting for it in the market. Yet, a job which has come a long way since the days when you packed your widgets into a couple of wicker baskets, loaded them onto a cart, pushed the cart to the market in the town square; and advertised the widgets by shouting louder than your competitor.

January 27: In the center section of Aldrich 108 there usually sits a solitary figure, separated by an empty seat or two from everybody else. A short figure, halfway hidden by the black briefcase which he props up in front of himself like a sandbag. So only the head shows, a crop of medium-length, curly hair that points whichever way the wind blows; a roly-poly face with a tiny mouth and red eyelids which vainly try to bare a pair of tired eyes.

The head gently sways to some inaudible rhythm, sinks ever lower until suddenly jerked up, it slowly settles on another downward trip.

But every so often, the jerking of the head becomes a full awakening and the arm shoots up and you hear the professor's voice: "Mr. Fontaine?" And Luc gamely takes off with the words—the words slowly, haltingly assembled in a heavy French accent, seeming to go this way and that. "What it's tell you," Luc says to explain his explanations, "what it's tell you . . ." It is as if the thread of his argument becomes entangled, not just in the difficulties of presenting it in another language, but in the mind itself. He wraps it around his shoulders, wraps himself entirely up and away, disappearing into a sort of cocoon, together with his message.

Luc doesn't understand his troubles. He, always among the first in his class, not getting through! "They are not consistent," he says, vaguely referring to the school or the professors or the courses or something. You don't really understand either, except that he is bothered. Not sad or discouraged or anything, but a bit confused.

The discussion busily moves on, leaving Luc in its wake and he, having said his thing, settles back, folds his arms over the genteel bump of his belly which forces his jacket to stay forever unbuttoned, and soon the head is swaying again, gently swaying and ever so often, a mysterious giggle ripples over his relaxed face.

January 28: LaRue Textiles is a large mill, dominating the little town of Tugaloo, Alabama. Their problem, like the problems of the companies in the preceding PBE cases, is how to survive the conflicting claims of black and white pressure groups; the second trying to block any and all exits from the status quo; the first yanking, at times violently, at the social and employment patterns built on a long and unfortunate tradition of segregation.

The Equal Employment Opportunity provisions of the Civil Rights Act of 1964: LaRue Textiles gingerly but determinedly goes along. And right away you have white backlash, intimidation by the Ku Klux Klan. A speech by a black congressman in Tugaloo is called off "for security reasons" by the town's mayor. CORE is reacting. Demands, ultimatums almost, are presented to Tugaloo and LaRue Textiles.

What would *you* do?

The consensus seems to be: Abide by the law but go slow. *Don't rock the boat!*

John Reddick, who hadn't said a word, held up his hand. "I'm disturbed," he said, and in the little pause following you could almost hear his insides burn. "I'm very disturbed.

"See, you've been telling the black man for years: Just wait and it will get better. Well, we've listened. And we've waited.

"We have waited too goddamn long.

"Look what happened to the Jews," Reddick said. "You in here, you may not be like that. But a lot of people in this country are. We aren't going to take any chances. We aren't going to let this happen again. You want to know how urgent it is? You *really* want to know? You want to know how much it takes to stop a lot of traffic in this country? A few bombs in a few places—that's all it takes."

After an instant of disbelief that Reddick had really said what he said, a big argument started. Kaplan accused Reddick of making the same sick generalizations that he, Reddick, had said white people were making. That Reddick is seeing whites not as people but as a category.

And the more people talked—and from here on Reddick kept quiet for the most part—the more the whole thing moved away, got hung up in abstractions. With the naive belief in the power of argument, one guy after another tried to sum it all up cleanly and logically. But their big words melted like snowflakes on the seething surface of Reddick's barely controlled emotions.

Evening of the same day:

(SID O'MARA *on those PBE cases*)

"You know, just what responsibility does business
have to society? Over and above providing a way in

which resources can be allocated efficiently? We talk about the social responsibility of the businessman—well, I'm not sure I like the idea. I'm not exactly sure that I want a company president to make up his mind what acts are socially responsible and which ones are not.

"All the money which businesses spend on matters of social concern are expenses; which means that tax revenue to the United States Government is decreased. Now I've always thought that it is the primary concern of business to do certain things more efficiently than government, and that it is the primary concern of government to do certain things more efficiently than business. And I don't know whether it's a good idea for either to get involved in the business of the other.

"After all, the private company still is one of the last vestiges of dictatorship we have in this country. By God, as long as a company is making money, and a chairman or president wants to wheel and deal and get *his* will across, he can do it. And that—that is a dictatorship. And I'm not sure I like dictators allocating money for me as opposed to the government, which I have supposedly elected."

January 29: We weren't more than two minutes into PBE when two guys came running into the classroom, their heads covered by hoods with slits for the eyes. They ran up to the blackboard where they drew a Confederate flag and wrote: "The South shall rise again," raising the board with the flag on it.

As it turned out, the simulated clan members were Kandel and Karr. Their demonstration, they said, was to "give us a feel for the southern extremist point of view" (which, one must say, they do not share). But we are obviously running out of things to say in these race-relation cases.

January 30: "It's a real panic experience," Jake Kamholz says, "you're scared out of your mind the first class . . . you think: Here are ninety-four brilliant guys . . . there is bound to be a guy who knows more than you do . . .

"It isn't like other schools where the professor just gives his lecture . . . where you're in control of the environment . . . here it's you guys . . .

"Sure, you're only supposed to be a moderator . . . keep the discussion going . . . but that isn't really enough . . . you want to be better than your students . . . something you're really good at . . .

"This year, in your class, they had one man who knew the stuff cold . . . this kind of guy can lay you wide open . . .

"I think it's a great advantage to have gone through the School yourself . . . you have a feeling for what's going on . . . like around the second set of exams, when we really put you guys through the mill . . . you watch for the little things . . . like the things the Section puts up on the sideboards . . . but sometimes you come into a class, everybody seems all excited . . . you don't really know why . . .

"Sure, you check on the kind of guys you're getting in the Section . . . you know, there are going to be the HBO-type guys who shudder in their boots when they see numbers . . . but I guess—don't you think? —learning never comes easy . . . it's a pain . . . if it's real learning it's pain . . .

"You watch for the guy who says a lot of stuff that isn't really relevant . . . that's the guy you jump on . . . and you know the big wheels in the Section . . . you can't ignore them . . . ignoring them sometimes turns the whole Section off . . .

"You challenge some of the bright guys and sometimes the whole Section comes on real strong . . .

"And because you work so closely with the students, it's important to get to know them . . . personally . . . But some faculty go overboard . . . they try to be a father or something to their students . . . I don't think that's the answer . . . this isn't undergraduate education, this is graduate school . . .

"You've got to have something going for you when you teach here . . . some guys are very funny . . . some guys try to be their title . . . of course a real 'technician' can always try to pull off an escalation of 'technology' . . . like talking calculus . . . putting an integral sign in front of the stuff . . .

"But this kind of system really rewards teaching . . . some people here haven't published more than two books—their doctoral thesis and some pamphlet —when their name first comes up for promotion . . . it isn't just research and publishing and to hell with teaching . . . it looks like you're not such an important part of a class by just guiding . . . but you're working with the students a lot more closely . . .

"I guess it's like everything in life . . . you've got to know when you're scared . . . and you can't let that bother you . . ."

January 31: It's a strangely mixed and mixed-up group of people that meets twice a week now in one of the neighboring classrooms. A bizarre assortment of foreign accents and about five or six black guys—nearly half the blacks in the first-year class. Three or four girls are also coming and about twenty others—thin and fat ones, flashy and dull ones. A group of some forty altogether. All the people who are in academic trouble.

There is a rumor that this is a record year, with the highest number of people in trouble, and the school has finally, for the first time, decided to step in and help. As a result, Professor Byron, a kind man in his late forties or early fifties, and Stan Mills, an equally patient doctoral student, are teaching something evasively named "Special Sessions."

It's kind of paradoxical to be at the Harvard Business School and to be in academic trouble.

So, at first, many never spoke lest their confusion and ignorance reveal themselves, and some are still too embarrassed to bring the placard with their name on it.

However hard we may have tried to conceal this from ourselves and from admiring friends, we can no longer deny that we are not all geniuses. Even at the Business School, there are a good many quite ordinary people. But they are ordinary people making an extraordinary effort, which is kind of extraordinary in itself.

February 1: In a life, four hours are close to nothing. An afternoon at the stadium. An "if," a "maybe," a shadow passing across the wall. Except when the four hours are spent in one of the rooms of Aldrich, or over in Baker Library, in a Business School exam.

"Examination rooms will be open at 8:30 A.M.," an underlined sentence says on the weekly assignment sheet, "Saturday, February 1, 9:00–1:00; room assignments are as follows: 16050 Debrooke P., 13954 Finkbiner W. R., Aldrich 107 . . ."

On every second desk there is a blue book with some plain, white scratch paper inserted, and down at the table, a proctor—a guy our age—guards the sealed package with the examination assignments.

With a well-rehearsed calm, people are laying out their pens and pencils, their slide rules and thermos bottles. Only a quick, sudden grimace and the frenzied drumming of fingers tell of the tension that's gripping their minds.

The minutes bend and stretch, dissolve into a sequence of dreamlike flowing motions, broken up at irregular intervals by long yawns. At 9:00 exact, the proctor rips open the package, hands out the assignment: a case, twenty-two pages in length, eleven of which are numbers and tables.

". . . whether or not Mr. Stuard should lower the price from $79.95 to $49.95 and at the same time expand distribution into several thousand new retail outlets . . ."

10:00. An hour just to read through the case. The exam is "open book." People are fiddling with their notes and outlines.

10:30. Where are the fixed costs for the break-even calculation?

10:45. No luck. No fixed costs. And because of no fixed costs, no calculation. And without the calculation no advice to Mr. Stuard. The words are beginning to dance in front of your eyes.

The little red hand on the clock is moving, but you are going nowhere.

You are thinking now. Thinking how little it takes to spoil an exam, a career, a lifetime. Four hours. Or not even that. A tiny, lousy little number, a split second of insight.

"Funny," you are thinking, "here I've put in all this work—Saturdays, Sundays, all this time—and now everything could go down the drain—just like that.

"And when you go home, they will know that you weren't good enough to make it. They may never say it. They may not even actually think it. But you will always hear it—hear it in everything they say."

10:50. "Come *on*," you are saying to yourself, "come on now. You've still got time—two hours and ten minutes. You've still got a chance. It isn't over yet. Come on, goddamnit!"

11:30. Noise. Right next to you. A ripping, tearing sound. From the guy one seat over. The short, chubby guy. He's all red, and there are big tears of sweat on his forehead.

There! He's eating his coffee cup. Tearing it apart with his teeth—completely oblivious. Then, suddenly coming to, he flings the rest of the cup on the floor, glaring vacantly over the forty-odd backs bent over their exam papers.

1:00. The proctor checks off the names as people hand in their blue books. Outside, there isn't a single cloud and the sun, reflecting in the snow, makes things look brighter than ever.

February 6: Jake Kamholz is a mountain of a man. A six-foot cliff towering above Section B. Its peak, a massive head, capped by blond hair with cool blue eyes blinking down on us. The chest dropping onto the prominent bulge of the stomach. And all of this anchored on a pair of huge flopping feet which half seem to propel him, half seem to be dragged along.

Yet, having created so substantial a man, nature—as if to fake the onlooker—has fitted the massive body with a most nimble soul. "I don't see how I could take MERC II without Kamholz," someone recently said, expressing a feeling that's pretty unanimous in Section B.

There is a contagious cheerfulness in whatever Kamholz says and does. As though the view from up there had banned the trifling and bickering that seem to obstruct the view of men of lesser stature. His prominence is not merely physical, appointed by nature, but one to which—through his knowledge and character—he has elevated himself.

A mere four years ago Jake Kamholz was sitting where we sit now, sweating through M.B.A. cases. But the climb was rapid: a position as one of Defense Secretary McNamara's "whiz kids"—a guy of twenty-four dealing with colonels and generals. Now this—the call back to the Business School.

We are his first Section, sat through his first class when even he was nervous. But not for long. It took him but a class or two to find that he could handle us, and now, if anything, the flow of quips and images is even richer. Kamholz is but a year or two older than a good many of his students. So it isn't his age, just as it isn't his position that sets him apart from us. It's the point of view, the self-confidence of a man to whom success has given a sense of his own value and ability.

At the end of MERC II and Jake Kamholz's last class today, the Section gave him an engraved cigarette lighter and a standing ovation.

February 7:

"Mr. Terner?"

The professor's question hits you like a brilliant light, with a sharp pain that cuts you loose, plunging you into a silence of faint, garbled sounds like recording tape run backward, sending you tumbling through this crazy, windowless room, head over heels, head over heels.

Your body, a dumb broken machine now, moves mechanically to no purpose, with no sense. Too much of a job, too much of a challenge, too sudden.

"Mr. Terner?"

The silence is shattered like a glass whose splinters pierce your flesh down to the bones. You've been waiting for it since the first day; every day, at the beginning of every class, you've been waiting for it. Always sitting frozen, so as not to create a stir in the professor's eye. Sooner or later. In your case later —but today it came.

"Ahem! . . . Mr. Terner?"

It isn't guilt. It's being laid out like that, in front of everybody. Jesus Christ, you sonofabitch.

"I . . . I'm not prepared, sir."

Well said. A thread of will is still holding you together. You've taken a bad bounce. You've hit the wrong number.

Like roulette. The large, gently sloping bowl. The polished metal spindle turning at its center. The hand that turns the spindle also flicks the little ball. On purpose, it moves the two in opposite directions. One hand controls it all and yet, the outcome is uncertain.

February 8:

(Ben Davidson *talking*)

"I really had no idea what I was getting into.

"I came out here, for a weekend, to find out how big the closets were in the dormitory and to ask if there was anything that I should perhaps prepare before I came. I mean, I was amazed that I was going to Harvard Business School. I mean, personally, I didn't go to an Ivy League college. So for me it is like a new ball game.

"I just don't feel I am as smart as the rest of the boys . . . and I certainly am not as eloquent, nor will I ever be as eloquent . . . I don't think I have the quantitative ability. I'm not sure I got past MERC II. I . . . I have these visions of flunking out.

"It's a tense situation, but my attitude is that I'm going to do it. And, of course, you know, after the fact we will probably see that it was really not quite that bad by any means. But, nevertheless, when you're going through it, it . . . it seems terrible. It seems *terrible*. And I go to, you know, go to bed at night, at two o'clock in the morning and look up at the ceiling and say, you know: "What am I doing here? What am I doing at this place?"

5

The Man in the Middle

JOHN REDDICK'S *side of the story*

"My title is administrative assistant to the president. Not that that tells you a lot. I mean, titles don't impress me.

"I'm at Beckridge Bank and Trust Company in Beckridge, which was started two years ago, and what I do is, I assist in different areas of the bank, in straightening out their problems. The bank is having a lot of operational problems and the president and senior management wanted me to go in and try to straighten them out.

"The president of this bank is only thirty-six. He's a high school graduate who went into real estate and was able to maneuver into the presidency. So he doesn't have a lot of background, in terms of education. And he . . . he's somewhat afraid of people who are educated. But, you know, that's quite natural because he fears that they might challenge his job.

"But I think I've kind of smoothed that over, to the point of, you know, 'I don't really want your job. All I want is to make some changes.' Which, I think, for the moment is pretty genuine.

"But I think that, in a way, I'd rather . . . there's so much else that I could be doing than being president of a bank. I want to start a whole new company that would in essence be a . . . a mini-conglomerate, acquiring businesses, starting businesses in many, many fields.

Initially probably service fields: consulting, financial services, housing, construction. And, if possible, branching out into manufacturing. But I'm still working on a . . . on a plan as to how I might attack this whole thing.

"I want to write. I would like to teach. Write books on economic development. And on power.

"You know, McKay gave a second-year course on power. Which I really enjoyed. I learned a lot from it. Got a lot of new insights into things. And I'd like to share those with . . . a lot of other people. It's like—if you've ever read Machiavelli, *The Prince*—how to become a prince. The course enabled me to think along lines like this. How *would* you gain power?

"It's like a game of chess. It's strategy, in a very logical sequence. And once you learn to think in that sequence, you can . . . you'll be able to gain power.

"And that's why . . . that's why I feel that, OK, I could be president of that bank in three years. I could sit down and scheme on how to do it. You know, taking into consideration all the factors: who's on the board of directors, faults of the president, faults of the system. How you could play upon these things.

"But I'm looking more toward the . . . toward the outside. How to get people to . . . become aware . . . of their own potential. That's why I say teaching, eventually. I would use the concepts I learned to enable others to go out and, more effectively, more quickly, gain economic and political power. If that's the course things are going to take. And they might take some other course . . . like revolution.

"You have to be a strategist. And that's what I'm working toward: being a master strategist.

"It's like MERC II. You consider the alternatives. You can go left or you can go right. If you go left, there is going to be an event happening; if you go right, there is going to be an event happening. Even though people might be irrational, you know, they're only going to act in certain ways. If a person gets emotional, there are only certain things that he's going to do unless he's really crazy.

"It's how I perceive the world. It's how I go about effectuating changes in the world. I'm not saying the world is completely rational, because it isn't. It's very irrational at times. But, sooner or later, things are going to fall into a pattern. Because you can predict to a great degree people's behavior, their attitudes. And once you study people, you learn to manipulate them. You know, in a very smooth manner. Without a lot of fuss. Without a lot of bother. Almost like sneaking up on them. They don't know it's coming. And then it's there. What can they do about it?

"Initially I felt I couldn't cope with the Harvard Business School. I came . . . I spent the first week and I saw what was going on in class. And I said, 'Well . . . this is . . . this is pretty rough here.' I never doubted my intelligence. But I just felt so far behind in terms of what I knew about what went on in business and about the effect, the immense effect that business has on everybody's life. It really shocked me.

"I remember that first weekend. We had had a week of class and Dale Hughes and I went back to Stimson College. I was going to see this professor who recommended that I go to Harvard and ask him: Why the hell did he tell me to go there? Why was he going to put me through all that hassle?

"Because to me the place, really, you know . . . it was different from anything I'd ever experienced . . . even though I felt that I had, you know—I was twenty-two —I'd been around a little bit. But I hadn't experienced this other world to the degree that I did when I got to the B School. And it was really frightening at first. It was just . . . it was like going to the moon. Here you are on earth and all of a sudden you are on the moon. Without a space suit on or anything. Naked.

"So I had to put up a front, initially. I had had economics. I was really good at it. And here we had all these graphs and charts in one case. So I went to a doctoral student. Said, 'Here . . . explain all these things to me. Which ones are important?'

"So he explained it to me. I said, 'Fine, thank you.' And then I went to class. And I ran down all that I knew about these graphs. I took what this doctoral student had said and then I added my own twist to it. And I was able to do a better job with the graphs than anybody else in the class. At least anybody that volunteered.

"Which more or less put me in good stead. Because it gave people a certain image. And I was able to play upon that image, to get me over, while I was getting used to the school.

"But once I knew what people were trying to do . . . I'd sit in class and I'd daydream and I'd make notes on people. People would speak and I'd write their names down. I said, 'Now what do I think about that guy? What's he really trying to do? What's he like?'

"And after that I figured, well, these people aren't that smart. Because even though I came in with a disadvantage, I was able to get higher grades in some courses than they were, and probably with less work.

"It was just a matter of knowing how the system worked. What they wanted. Rather than being frightened by it, you used it to your own advantage.

"And that was, I guess, the catching up I had to do. I had never really been concerned with a business. It was strange to be talking about, you know, millions of dollars. When all you might have talked about before was hundreds or maybe thousands. And here you're tossing around millions. And it, you know, it's . . . it's a new sensation. Something I really had to get used to.

"I couldn't be phony about it. I never had anything to do with . . . millions of dollars. See, I'm from Beckridge. And . . . if you've lived in a ghetto, it's a real fight for survival every day. And you have to know how to deal. How to talk, to get yourself out of situations. You know, lots of times you might take your life into your hands, just going out of the house. When somebody says, 'Gimme a dime, kid,' what are you gonna do? You've got to be able to talk your way out of things . . . to scheme, basically. To be creative with whatever you say or do.

"The street is not sophisticated. It's very basic. It's the type of thing, you know . . . it's you or I. One of us has got to win. And then you get into a situation where things are very subtle. And you don't just come out and say, 'I don't like you.' You know, you do it in very subtle ways. You downgrade people very nicely. And you go from being very blunt to being very nice. If you're not used to it, it puts you at a real disadvantage because you might get very, very emotional. And blow up. And then the other person has you over the barrel. So you have to be cool to maintain yourself.

"I never . . . I never wanted for anything really. I went to a good high school, the Beckridge Latin School, which offered more or less the classical curriculum. I went on to Stimson College at Springfield and I didn't really like it . . . but I was . . . I survived because I was well prepared. In my freshman year, you know, I really hated the place. Nothing but white people. I wasn't used to that. They didn't particularly like me. And I didn't particularly like them. But I was able to get away with it because I had such a good high school education. Everything that I had in my freshman year in college I had already had before. So it was just a matter of going to class, of going to the exams, and the rest of the time I'd sleep. Which would upset my white roommate because he couldn't understand how I could sleep all the time. And still, you know, I'd make the Dean's List and he wouldn't.

"My father worked at Sorensen Manufacturing Company, which is a manufacturer of electric circuit breakers outside of Beckridge. He's retired now. He just retired last year. He was the clerk in the shipping department. He had gone to college two years (my mother graduated from college), but his father died, so he had to drop out to support his family. We are from the South—I was born in Tennessee—we could have been all right in Tennessee but my mother and my father didn't like the overt discrimination. So we moved up here, where we could capitalize on the covert discrimination. But that was in 1950, and you couldn't really come in and expect to get a good job. If it was difficult for the people already here to find work, it was even more difficult for a newcomer, even a man with many skills such as my father. But they struggled and we were . . . we were able to make something out of it.

"I was a little cocky at times in class . . . which was good . . . I thought it was good. It gave people something special. They weren't used to seeing that. And, as a matter of fact, I wasn't really that used to doing it. But once I found out I could, I enjoyed it, and I came out . . . not really fearing anybody.

"OK—maybe fearing people less. You always are going to have some fear about people, about a situation. But I came out with enough confidence . . . I could really control myself in any situation. Or, better than that, I could control the situation. Which was, you know . . . it was a very startling thing. You'd always thought of yourself as the underdog. You can't control anything. And here you find out: *you can!* And that, in a way, it's a very beautiful thing.

"I think a really perfect example of what I just talked about was the PBE class. McKay came in there like a bull and frightened everybody. And he'd lay down his ground rules. You know, you were supposed to wear a coat and tie every day, and you were supposed to do this; you were not supposed to do that. And at first I went along with the program. But then, one day, I just didn't feel like wearing a tie. He jumped on me and I was upset because I really prepared the case that day. So I wanted to talk about the case, not about my tie. And he jumped on that, and I made the comment that he couldn't really tell me what I was supposed to wear to class. And that if I wanted to come wrapped in Saran Wrap, I'd come in Saran Wrap.

"But then we started to get into it, and Dick Angus made the point that he wasn't sure who would win but that he would put his money on me. And after that I, you know, I really wasn't afraid of McKay any more. We talked about it afterward, he and I, about what he could have done to me, but I knew then that I had him, and that I too could control the situation, just as he controlled everybody when he first came into that room.

"It's . . . it's difficult to describe the Harvard Business School experience. You really have to live it, if you come from my situation, to see how . . . how much it affects your life. You know, I lived in Beckridge, on Samuels Avenue from about, well, just after second year started until early spring. But I had to—I had to move. I moved to Bayside because I really . . . almost couldn't cope with the two worlds I had to face.

"Every day I'd go to the Business School. We're talking about all this money. Everybody is dressed up nicely. And

I'd go back to Beckridge and see all this poverty. And at a point it really got difficult for me to reconcile . . . the difference in life styles. Even though, you know, you have to do this all your life, being black. In my high school graduating class of three hundred there were seven black students. See, you . . . you get used to it. But not at the Business School. Because at the Business School it was so much more, you know, compete, compete, compete, you've got to win, you've got to succeed. And you hit that on the one hand and you go back to the ghetto and it is completely different. Everybody is . . . it is like—like you are on dope or something, like you're in a nod. You don't really want to compete. Then, one afternoon, a black girl gets raped; it was a May afternoon, early May or late April. She just gets lifted off the street and some guy, some black guy, rapes and kills her.

"I was at home because that was the period we were writing our research reports. And I was driving through this park . . . and a few minutes before I got through there, somebody had found her body. So I . . . I had been thinking about all these negative things anyway and then I see this. And I said, 'Wow, how much of this can I take?' I just couldn't . . . just too many differences. You know, and everybody . . . you try to move toward equilibrium. So I moved out to neutral ground. Where I was still close to the ghetto. Because that's where my friends were. But I could still go to the other side if I had to. And I had to. Because I was going to school.

"It just—the whole experience is completely different from anything I've ever seen and experienced. Just getting over that whole attitude you had about yourself —the negative attitude. You see, at Stimson College, you had mostly poor whites. Some middle-class whites. Who in a lot of ways, they were just there to get the piece of paper. Everybody would go out and drink beer, have a good time and goof off. It wasn't on a plane of being cutthroat. But once you got to the Business School, you had a different stratum of society. You had a lot of people who *could* talk intelligently about a lot of problems. Who all tried to act confident.

"At a point in the first spring, like the world just kind of fell in on me. I was almost helpless. I really couldn't think. Couldn't eat. Couldn't sleep. But when I finally worked that out I had a base I could work from. Something that I knew was strong. I wasn't . . . I wasn't phony any more. I realized the immense capacity of the mind; the strength it has to move you, to move that physical part of you. If you don't realize this you're lost, because the way you think about yourself and about the world really determines what you can do. But now I *do* realize it and I'm able—I can go between either world. I can get down into the street and curse and swear like anybody else. And I can go with the very nice set—you know, exclusive clubs. And fit in there too.

"It's a game. And all a game is, is strategy. In some situations you might get a little emotional. But after you learn how the whole thing is set up that emotion kind of fades. In a way that's bad because it . . . it seems you almost lose part of your humanity. You become stiffer. You become more calculating. And it's tough just to relax, just to let yourself go and don't worry about people attacking you. You know, I could see a definite change in myself. In terms of being sensitive . . . in terms of being what I call 'good.' And I'm still going through those changes—as to just which way I'm going to play this thing. I know that there are going to come occasions where you can't be . . . humane. Where you just can't lose control of the situation. So you have to be hard. But as the old biblical saying goes: For everything there is a time. And you have to know *when* to be cutthroat.

And when to be humane. What I'm saying is, that the emphasis of the Business School was such that you were cutthroat 102 per cent of the time. The people be damned.

"It's fine to give logic and order to things. Because if you have a business and the other guy is competing against you, you can't worry too much about his feelings. But the manner in which you deal with your own people doesn't always have to be as hard and as cold. There has to be a way of setting up an organization, of getting it to function effectively and still be . . . humane about it.

"At Beckridge Bank and Trust, to a great extent, the people there, it's like a big family. Where people *do* talk to each other. People go out with each other, you know, laugh and joke. It's . . . a very friendly atmosphere. And you'll find a lot of occasions when people will come into that bank, not to make a deposit, not to cash a check, but just to find somebody to talk to. And that's something that has to be reconciled, you know. People complain that the service in the bank is slow. The tellers are slow. And there may be a lot of reasons for this: The tellers might not have all the knowledge they need. A lot of the customers might not have the knowledge *they* need about banking—a lot of them, before Beckridge Bank and Trust opened, have never been in a bank.

"But the main reason is that the tellers take time to know people, where they live and what they do, their kids—it does slow down things. But that's a trade-off you have to make.

"Either we slow it down—still making progress now, but humane—or we're going to be very hard about the whole thing. This is a business; you come in and do it this way and that's it. Which way is it going to be?

"I'm saying that I think you *do* have a choice. I'm

saying that the dollar isn't worth that much. You have to find the mix that makes you efficient, lets you do your job and do it well. And yet keeps everybody contented and sane.

"Look at a . . . look at a singing group, OK? I used to be in a singing group. And it got to the point where—even though it was a business proposition—you could have fun doing it. Because if somebody goofed you could anticipate it and fill in, so that nobody in the audience really knew that somebody had goofed. We knew each other and if somebody was doing something wrong you didn't come down on him with an ax. You said, 'You can do that right.' You offered support in a friendly fashion.

"It seems like you might tend to slip more because you're not afraid; you might say, well if I slip, somebody is going to be there to pick me up. But if you're working as a group and you feel good about it, you're not going to let the others down. You're going to do the best you possibly can.

"Entertainment is the perfect example of what people, working together, can do. So why can't that same thing carry over into business?"

6

An Ideal Friend

PARSONS' *story*

"When I think back through my life, I found people that have been kind of like my fraternity brothers—they didn't help very much. You know, they didn't do anything. I found people who actually took advantage of me and I guess everybody goes through this process . . . as they get more mature and more worldly or however you want to put it.

"And then there . . . then there are people who really help you. Like this guy Bill Raskin. He didn't have to. But if he hadn't been there, I never would have . . . Maybe I never would have gotten into Harvard Business School.

"I had a fairly good scholastic record. Not great. But fairly good. I had, I imagine, a very outstanding extracurricular record. And then, one evening, Mr. Raskin called. He used to drop by every once in a while to see how things were going. Well, that night he called and he said: 'Peter, I've put in a good word for you with Dean Moynihan.' So at the end of that summer, my wife and Catherine, our little girl, we left the West Coast and I came to Harvard.

"When I was going through Stanford, I didn't have much time to go to parties and stuff and I was going to try and do something about it this time. I don't look upon myself as a supermature person. I kind of had this feeling, I had a lot of growing up to do. See, there has never been a situation, a problem that I haven't understood. Or at least I thought I haven't understood. And there have been very few people in my life that I thought understood things better than I did. So . . . I have a problem communicating with people . . . conveying to them my understanding.

"You know, throughout my life I've found safety in developing my intellectual capabilities. And striving to understand things. I . . . I've always felt that if you understand something . . . well, if you understand it, it can't hurt you.

"When I was in high school, I tried to understand why my father was the way he was; why my brothers were the way they were; why my mother was the way she was. You know, my mother would pick us up every Thursday afternoon and there was a constant thing about how bad my father was, what a nasty man he was. My father . . . it's just sad, he is a very, very good man. He has worked for the government for forty years and he has put the three of us through school on a government salary. I think he understands his own shortcomings and only once can I remember, did he ever say anything against my mother. He never really said anything at all. He never socialized, never went to parties. You know, he never really had any friends.

"I don't know if you know much about Quakerism. But religion, any religion, is basically a good thing because it can make people feel good. But when you *really* believe in God, when you wake up in the morning, looking for a sign of what you should do that day—that's ridiculous. That's just crazy. And that's what Quakerism is, if you take it literally.

"One of the basic theses of Quakerism is self-sacrifice. You're not a reverent person if you take enjoyment of something. So, you know, Quakers are . . . are anti-cosmetics, anti-kissing, anti-drinking, anti-smoking, anti just about everything. And that can be a good idea, because if a guy doesn't drink and he doesn't smoke and he doesn't fool around, he can become a very wealthy man. But you can take this kind of thing to an extreme. You know, a guy may not drink, he may not smoke, and he may not fool around—OK, but he may say: 'Geez, I enjoy making money.' Then making money must be bad. And this is, you know . . . I think this is the kind of thing that affected my father.

"Quakerism is a way of thinking that just doesn't fit into the world. When you believe it, then it's like the guy—he is crazy because he doesn't know he is crazy. Because if he knew he were crazy he would fix it and then he wouldn't be crazy. If you get brought up wrong you get put in a situation where you don't know that you can't work with the world; you don't know there is something the matter with you.

"I have thought a lot about this, obviously, because I realize I've got a lot of it too. I didn't . . . didn't date that much when I was in high school and when I was in college. And, you know, it's basically one of the reasons why I find it very difficult to enjoy myself. I mean it's . . . it's kind of hereditary. You know, it's been a long line of Quakers and this self-sacrifice thing just doesn't work in this day and age. There are too damned many people around, too damned many problems. And if you are sitting there, beating yourself over the head, people will say: 'Fine,' you know, 'so what?' And they feel sorry for you, perhaps a little pity. That's all.

"You can say: Self-sacrifice is a very nice thing to do.

But you don't make the world go round by just saying: 'Here I am, destroy me.' You can self-sacrifice, but you have to do it in a rational manner. There are some things that are just not worth sacrificing for.

"But I guess, I kind of follow along after my father in many respects. I try to, you know, especially to my friends, I try to give them more than I ever receive from them. The interesting thing is, most of what other people have to give doesn't mean anything to me. I don't have the . . . the social needs. Or maybe I do have social needs but I don't have the capability of accepting them. I find it very difficult to do something without a reason. Whereas, I think, a lot of people . . . a lot of people do things just for the hell of it.

"Until very recently, it was difficult for me to understand that other people might be considerably, I mean, *considerably* different from me. I never thought that there might be people in the world who just don't give a damn about anything. I mean they just literally don't give a damn. But now I understand that there are people who like to be bossed. There are people who—they don't think for themselves. It's hard for me to imagine that there should be anybody who would not want to think. But in some people there is simply no thought process. I mean it's just . . . it's not there. This is what I mean by not giving a damn. To those kind of people, if you show too much consideration, they find it difficult to relate to you. Because you are asking them to think. Which is something that, for them, is impossible.

"So when I've got a job to do I get in there and I work like hell and I'm pretty sure, the way I want to do it is the right way. Or at least, it's a more efficient way than the way of other people who aren't working as hard and who haven't thought about it as much as I have.

"Human relationships, throughout my life, have been basically disappointing. I don't find it difficult to make friends. I might even be what you'd call an 'ideal friend.' Because I'm always willing to help somebody. On the other hand . . . I don't personally commit myself to anybody. See, I don't understand this personal commitment to other people. I'll always do a good job on my side. But I don't really receive much . . . I don't really get that much out of what you call friendship.

"I don't think there was anybody in the Section I was particularly close to. You know, if I had good discussions with them, they were kind of wasted on me. Because I'd sit there and analyze it. Sure, I relate to the guy, but it doesn't involve me personally. There are people, I guess they call them 'friends of location.' When you move away from the neighborhood, that's it. They are forgotten. I guess, I'm talking about . . . I'm just, you know, I'm trying to draw a parallel."

7

The Stuff Heroes Are Made Of

February 27: For Bill Meehan, success has come early and in unusual measure. At thirty-five he is associate professor of finance—one of the youngest ever to hold such high rank. At thirty-five he has been consulted by government ministers, by much older executives of large American companies. After barely two months, he has become one of the favorite professors of Section B.

It is a tribute to Meehan's extraordinary character that he has been able to stay in the bright light of success without becoming blind to his own swaying shadow. His demeanor, his way of dressing are so unassuming that you might easily mistake him for one of his students. Clad in short-sleeve shirt, tie, and slightly baggy pants, he restlessly paces the distance between the table and the nearest desk, often ending up sitting on either one, arms slung around the pulled-up knees. This constant moving, the handful of straight brown hair that threatens forever to sweep over his face, and the glasses make him appear even younger than he really is.

In human, as in strictly material, terms, generosity, it seems, is the privilege of the rich. Of those in whom good fortune has welded extraordinary ability and a strong will into an unshakeable self-confidence. And although Meehan sometimes likes to talk tough—as if to live up to his (true) reputation as a sometime professional football player—he never tries to scare us into action. Rather by cheering us up when we're down, by making an effort to find what's good, what's promising in our work, he encourages us to do our damnedest.

Finding himself in one of his tougher moods, Meehan said the other day that there is no quick and easy way to make money in finance. That there are the intricacies of the law to consider, the hazards of chance, the complex interrelationship of the economy. And there are pressures. Tremendous pressures. "Finance," Meehan added, "is no place for poets."

If you listened closely, it sounded much like the man talking to himself. There was a tremor in his voice; a tremor reflecting intense excitement. The echo of a struggle between a rebellious imagination and the well-trained reflexes of reality. Perhaps that's what makes Meehan the sort of man he is: the ability to walk the thin line. Gifted with both sensitivity and exceptional powers of reason, he manages to balance between the two like a tightrope walker—flattered by both, conquered by neither.

February 28: How much should the three grandsons of Jeremiah Burke pay their cousin Mrs. Wilson for her one thousand shares of common stock in the Burke Candy Co.?

Max Tuck argues that since all of Burke's stock is family owned and not traded, there is no market price to go by and "capitalization of expected income" is the right approach. Jeremiah's grandsons, he says, are holding the stock mainly for the income they are expecting on their shares. And so, to arrive at a fair value for a share, one should figure out what a fair income per share should be. The Burke Candy Co.'s future, he says, looks pretty uncertain to him. So he would need about a 20 per cent return. Now if, for the next several years, he could expect around $10 a year returned per share, and if, as he says, he needs a 20 per cent return, then the value of a share should be $50 ($10 = 20 per cent; 100 per cent = $50).

Should it? Professor Meehan asks Max whether it makes

sense to capitalize an expected income that quite likely may not be there? Isn't there a more reliable way to figure the value of Mrs. Wilson's one thousand shares?

Kearney sees an alternative in the "asset approach." The company should be worth what all its tools are worth—machines, buildings, cash, everything it works with to make candy. The way he figures it, he adds up the total value of the tools; subtracts from that the amount owed to banks and lenders and arrives at the value of the tools actually owned by the company. That, he says, is what the company and its shares are worth.

Yes, a number of people said, but how did he determine the value of those tools? Is it right to merely take them at the value at which they are listed in the company's books? Or should you look at what you could sell them for? Or even what it would cost to replace them? And, anyhow, a company isn't just tools; isn't Kearney going to pay anything for reputation and know-how?

We never really resolved the question except to say that if you aren't going to sell the business, why look at the value of its tools? Future earnings, in spite of their uncertainty, seem to make a lot more sense.

Meehan ended the class with a preview of our next topic: long-term financing and capital structure. If you need money, what kind should you get? Money that is lent for a limited time at a fixed interest? Or partner money that stays in the business but wants a share of your profits?

There is good and bad, cheap and expensive, risky and safe, healthy and sick money—finance is teaching us which is which.

March 1: While he was at St. Andrew's University, Georgia, today's *Wall Street Journal* said that Joey Karr operated a fleet of five battered hearses, each of which cost $25. For a dollar a day, he sold local merchants advertising space on the sides of the hearses and then rented them to classmates who needed a car and kind of liked the idea of driving a hearse. The idea netted him five K (thousand), the *Journal* said, and helped him become what he is now: A first-year nothing at the Harvard Business School.

"I've gone to at least three different colleges," JOEY KARR says, "and in every case I organized things so that I could always do a lot and yet didn't have a demanding course load; and even if it might have been demanding, in some way I was able to work with people so that I never had to do all the work.

"I'm sort of an organizer.

"One of the more successful promotions I did was where we had a hearse that performed as a dragster. We added headers to give it the effect of a big engine and we hired an announcer who would travel with us. And we would receive—this group would—15 per cent of the gate.

"We had a police escort lead the hearse out on the strip and the announcer would say: 'Ladies and gentlemen, we have this funeral procession on the strip. Would you kindly stand up and take your hat off?' And out of the hearse comes this kind of a professor who demands the right to race the hearse.

"The speaker would read off the script saying: 'What? You want to race that hearse? It doesn't even *look* like a dragster.'

"So the professor opens another door and out comes this monster. He had stilted shoes—platform shoes—and he was tall enough to paint a racing stripe, using white shoe polish, across the hood and the windshield all the way back down.

" 'All right,' the announcer would say, 'so you've got a racing stripe. But the engine still sounds like a hearse.'

"So the monster gets underneath and opens up some pipes. The professor revs it up and it caroms like a dragster.

" 'All right,' the announcer would say, 'bring up the fastest car. We're gonna give you a chance. Ladies and gentlemen, please sit down.'

"So the starting lights go down and the announcer says: 'Ready.' And all of a sudden, the professor jumps out and the announcer says: 'What the hell is wrong now?' and the professor says: 'We got too much dead weight.' Now in the back of the hearse is this casket. I'm lying down in it with a sheet over the top of me and nothing on but some polka-dot underwear. I've been lying in his hot hearse for like thirty minutes.

" 'Well, look,' the announcer says, 'would the driver of the other car please help the men?'

"He'd come and they'd get the casket out and get back into the cars. Well, now I flip the lid and start coming out like I'm floating. It says in the script that the driver of the other car, when he sees this body, puts his car in reverse and the hearse starts chugging toward the finish line. But then the other driver screeches up and starts chasing me and I rip off my sheet and there I am in my polka-dot underwear. We'd win the trophy every time.

"And the way we would bill this thing; I would advertise it saying: 'At Harmon's race track, on Sunday —live: The Overtaker driven by the Undertaker.' "

Joseph—or Joey as he is called affectionately—Karr is the natural underdog the way another guy is a natural athlete. Rather short, with quick, excited eyes and a balding head, he could be anywhere from eighteen to thirty. It is as if his lack of height, his accommodating friendliness triggers some sort of mothering complex in people. They keep throwing their arms around his shoulder, slapping him on the back so that the dust flies; gestures which normally signify close friendship but which, here, were a verdict of total, utter harmlessness. Until the *Wall Street Journal* article of today. Now people suddenly act as if Joey were eight feet tall.

"I worked my way through college with projects and ideas," Joey says. "I always had some project where I owned my own company and spent more time doing that than going to class. I always had these very novel ideas."

Joey hasn't changed his habits just for the Harvard Business School. In fact, he has been missing so many classes recently that people are beginning to talk about it. The rumor is that he and Rush are working on some fantastic computer model to beat the bond market, and that Joey is in New York, trying to sell it.

"In my senior year in college," Joey says, "I grew some twenty acres of sunflower seed. Well, I had this idea—they do it in Russia—sunflower oil is competitive with soybean oil. In terms of growing it down South, it brings more revenue per acre than soybeans. So I was going to grow sunflowers commercially for their oil, to compete against soybeans.

"But when I found I couldn't grow it successfully in terms of mass acreage—I had lined up like a thousand acres—I said, well why not grow it on less acreage and market the seeds as a snack food?

"I come from a Southern Baptist home," Joey says, "where my parents do not drink or smoke. And I went away to college trying to find my limit, and the only way to find your limit, is by trying for something bigger every time. I tried a small school. I tried a larger school. I tried the biggest school. By then I realized, I was most probably a bigger person. I felt my skills and knowledge were bigger than staying in Georgia. And most probably bigger than staying in the South. So I left and here I am."

Early last fall, as Joey opened his window at midnight to catch a final breath of air—window after window, floor after floor, the rooms were lit as far as he could see. Filling his lungs with all the air they would hold, he shouted: "Rate-busters!" And, having challenged the world, he went to bed.

March 3:

(ERWINGER *talking*)

"My roommate met Muffy right at a party surrounded by—it was a couple of B-School guys who ran it. And it's tough living with someone, no matter who it is —this says nothing against Bill—but anyone will tell you this: In a dorm, at our age, we like privacy. We like . . . well, if you want to have a girl in for the weekend . . . well, you just can't do it.

"It . . . it depends on what type character, but I'm not gonna sleep with a girl with my roommate next to me, watching TV. . . . We had this problem. He, when he used to have Muffy in, he figured I was over to Ann's, but the last month, Ann moved back home so I had to sleep in at the dorm. And I'd come walking in around one or two in the morning and they'd be in there and I, you know, I just didn't say anything. I . . . I didn't like it, you know, because I wouldn't have done it to him. Of course, you know, I don't want to, I mean I don't think that's funny."

March 4: The OP (Organizational Problems) assignment called for the Section to split into three groups. So Mike Daks got together Benson, Kurowski, Karr, Terner, Blotner, Baxter, and a couple of others. The task: to design a "non-directive" type organization in connection with the upcoming computer game.

Today, in the main dining hall of Kresge, we had the first meeting. To be honest, with everything else we have to do, we needed this non-directive business about as much as we needed a fist in the eye. But the longer we sat, the more Mike's enthusiasm caught on, and soon we found ourselves laughing and talking all at once, with hands scribbling explanations into the surrounding air.

Mike Daks, a carpetlayer's son, displays the drive and eagerness that must come from seeing a reassuringly close horizon explode and reveal the highest peaks of wealth and opportunity. Still his zest is tempered by a relaxed, easy kindness, a matter-of-fact honesty. A strangely unpolished but, perhaps for that, an all the more believable character. This is perhaps why some of us in his group—veterans of life compared to his twenty-two years—are willing to submit to his leadership, to let ourselves be carried along by this jumping, swirling stream.

March 5: Daks's group, today, had to present their organization.

After briefly stating the group's purpose, Mike asked Russ Baxter to begin. "Me—begin? Oh, no!" Baxter said. "Not me—ask him," pointing to Steve Blotner. "What do you mean?"

Blotner protested. "I thought Keith was . . ." which almost popped Kurowski out of his seat. "Come on now!" Keith yelled at Baxter and Blotner, "what's the matter with you guys? Let's not be funny. You were supposed to begin and you know it." Which gave Gross an idea: "Terner—let him take it." But, of course, like everybody else, Terner knew better: "What about Karr?" By which time the entire group was standing (practically on their desks) with arms flailing, shouting at one another at the top of their lungs. It was the most beautifully orchestrated chaos and the Section was strictly dumbfounded. Until Mike finally shut it down with a flourish of his arms.

"Welcome to the wonderful world of non-directive leadership," Mike said. And judging from the round of laughter and applause, the Section felt right at home.

March 6: His name is Len, Len Lambeau, and he comes from a maze of strange tales, doubtful credits, and vague ambitions, drifting out of an obscure past that includes language studies, a year or two at a Belgian university, and—as he says—a stint as pilot with the Belgian Air Force. A past of beginnings but no clear end, no definite direction.

He sits in the front row, like a piece of driftwood haphazardly washed ashore. Silent. Making little effort to explore the human landscape, on which fate has landed him. He hasn't, it seems, struck up any solid friendships; rather, wrapped in silence, he keeps on drifting, his hair tousled, perenially unkempt, his eyes narrow and sleepy, curiously uninvolved, his pencil dropping a disorderly muddle of notes into a bundle of ruffled yellow papers.

And yet he cares. Cares desperately, for this is his biggest and perhaps his last chance to become the master of his destiny. But the years of drifting, having worn and softened his will power, seem to make it difficult for him. He is not doing well. He is, in fact, doing lousy. And perhaps the worse he does, the more his already weak will to fight is sapped, the more he falls back, resigns himself to drifting out of our view on to some undetermined fate.

Today, we got the grades of our second series of exams. Lambeau didn't say much, but looked, perhaps, a trifle more sleepy, a trifle paler, as though the current had really gotten hold of him now, sweeping him away faster and faster.

March 8: Baker Library is a grandiose, six-pillared temple of learning dating back to the turn of the century when education was largely financed by elderly gentlemen who, in the true fashion of the American self-made man, had not come in much contact with education at all, or else had undergone it as a sort of dignified ritual that lay somewhere between breakfast and the daily game of tennis.

Dwarfed by the three-story-high pillars, a large door opens into the main hallway, which is a combination of drained swimming pool and bus terminal, two floors high, all decked out in beige marble. Tubelike hallways lead off to either side, and flanking the one to the right, there is a chest-high pedestal with a bronze on top of it—a polished head with a built-in stare, seeming to examine the incessant parade of briefcase carriers who troop by.

Even further to the right, there is a wide stairwell disappearing into the wall, turning in front of another bronze, leading up to the main desk and the main reading room. The main desk is thirty feet long with two floors of bookracks behind and groups of chatting customers before it. Behind the customers, two large fans spread the stale smell of tons of aged paper.

The doors leading from the desk to the main reading room are soundproofed with thick leather padding. The universe inside is of strictly intimidating proportions: a room almost the length of a football field and as wide as a doubles court in tennis. Even if many people are in it, there is an oppressive emptiness that bears down on the little odds and ends of humanity strewn about the long, ten-men tables. Along one of the walls, about one floor above the ground, there is a narrow balcony-type walkway, the sort from which you expect armed guards to peer down upon you. Further up, finally, in the zenith of this plaster heaven, there are rows of heavy steel-rimmed chandeliers that make you never want to look up, and you hope that they don't have earthquakes in this region.

In a world that has made a fetish of change, this place spells permanence. In a time that puts unbounded faith in man's ability to overcome the obstacles to his survival, this place, in its vast amount of stone and marble, spells out man's frailty and insignificance.

It's only fifty years since Baker Library was built. Lauded and still respected by some as an expression of inalterable truths, it has become a weird monument to another generation's illusions.

March 10: Tom Benson has the ability to be conciliatory enough to relax people, yet determined enough not to become their prey. He radiates a quiet self-confidence that is at once reassuring and that saves him the frantic efforts, typical of so many, who try to shore up crumbling egos by courting the approval and flattery of others.

Yet it isn't just self-confidence that permits Tom to be patient and generous with the people around him. There is also an almost religious optimism that lifts him above the doubts and fears of his more timid contemporaries: an optimism that with good effort and a little bit of luck things are bound to turn out well.

Perhaps it is that nordic, Norwegian ancestry of his. That natural sense of solidarity that you would expect of people who live in inhospitable lands, in vast, isolated expanses. Perhaps, too, it is his childhood in a small town in Nebraska. It's almost naive sometimes but it's never phony.

Yet for all that self-confidence, Tom is very sensitive. Almost six feet tall, thin, often white as a sheet of paper, he doesn't take well to pressures such as we experience here. It is a fair bet that Tom won't be a millionaire by the time he is ninety. Tom isn't made for the big corporations. His plans and daydreams revolve around that large town out West where he has bought an old and roomy house. Where he has left a lively circle of friends, to which he and his family will go back after graduation.

It's the fewer but more resounding human contacts that are Tom's bag. An environment in which the knowledge he has accumulated is exciting news. Where his influence changes people rather than figures on a balance sheet.

Tom isn't made for the make-believe of the cities, the carefully memorized first names, the gluey smiles. Instead, he talks of the problems of the Indians, what could be done to get a bit of zap into the local business out West.

Seeing how some men struggle all of their lives to win the trust and respect of but a few of their peers, it strikes one as unjust that men like Tom should have it so easy. That some should be so obviously gifted in evoking sympathy and affection. But that's the real world for you. Everybody is forced to go out there and struggle but only a few are told how.

March 11: Somehow, Professor Claffin doesn't get along with the electric switches that raise and lower the three blackboards. After at first vainly fiddling with them, he has turned to pushing and straining to get the boards up and down. While this sort of thing was funny at the beginning, it is becoming more and more ridiculous and embarrassing as time goes on.

Why doesn't he figure out how to use the switches?

The other day, Tom Benson had a possible answer: "He doesn't dare to use the switches," said Tom, "because he is afraid he can't figure them out. He is afraid of being afraid, so he won't take any chances.

"The man," Tom said, "has got an ego to defend."

March 12, morning: All the things, the ingredients that on some other guy would add up to something very ordinary, in the case of Wallston add up to a human landmark that you can't overlook.

His black hair, although well groomed and parted, adorns the massive fortress of his face like a coat of arms, heralding a violent will to independence and an all too easy use of force. His sideburns, dim forests, lead down to a bridge of thin lips arching over a scowling, drooping mouth. His glasses, sitting at the tip of his nose, change the impression to that of a sinister bird, perched on one of the back rows, waiting for a mistake, some inaccuracy or weakness, which will cause him to plunge down and finish off the hapless victim.

Wallston is given to the kind of harsh judgments that are the mark of one whose punishing drive toward self-perfection has made intolerant of failure and defect, except for his own self-righteous arrogance. He is a graduate of West Point; an economist loaded with all the right numbers. A man who early in the morning can be seen in one of Aldrich's alcoves, discussing the day's cases with his buddy, Tom Lamb.

Now Lamb is a kind of footsoldier in this crusade for fortune. Directed by accident, commanded by circumstances, willing to submit to the excessive demands of school rather than face the unknown horrors of life outside.

Tom does not think it fair. All his life, he says, he has known but one thing: work and pressure. He has a face to prove it—an almost liquid mass, a faithful, though involuntary mirror of fear and anxiety.

Urged on by a vague desire to control the powers whose punches have knocked him hither and yon, Tom has struggled through an engineering curriculum at Frederick Drake University and, without enthusiasm, went into the insurance industry. He has been climbing the corporate ladder for the last four years. And though he complains and seems to suffer from an inability to get a firm grip on himself, he seems to have settled into a tolerable routine. But his obvious defenselessness invites all sorts of aggression and violence.

Lamb hasn't spoken much until recently. Now, he's coming along, riding a small wave of self-confidence, started, perhaps, by decent grades. These must have convinced him that there is a lot more fight in him than he is getting credit for. The confidence might also come from, who knows, having as strong an ally as Dan Wallston.

Later that morning: The Blitz Company is having so many problems that one production class wasn't enough to sort them all out. The difficulty at first had seemed minor: Recent shipments have been an average of nine days' late and Alfred Jodal, president, is worried about the loyalty of Blitz' customers.

Should he change the company's method of production scheduling? There really isn't any. That is, the president, the sales manager, and a newly hired supervisor are doing one kind of scheduling; the design engineer and the shop foreman are doing another.

The reason the shop foreman does his own scheduling is that he usually has to wait a couple of days before the raw material for an order arrives. And the raw material doesn't arrive because the treasurer who buys it doesn't keep enough of it in stock.

So before the president does anything about the *method* of scheduling, he should make someone clearly *responsible* for it. And, of course, he should talk to the treasurer about the firm's raw-material procurement. Which brings up the question of how large Blitz' stocks should be; because anything above what's needed not only ties up cash but even costs storage charges.

The way the Blitz Company works, no method can solve its scheduling problem. Its production bottlenecks shift around like so many clouds because Blitz almost never makes the same product two days in a row. Small orders, large orders; orders requiring few, and others requiring many operations; rush and regular orders, and nearly every order based on a different kind of basic design. The problem is as much what to offer as how to make it.

But the most formidable obstacle to a smoother operation is the layout of the plant itself, the design of the various work stations. The place was set up to minimize installation costs and to protect the various departments from one another's dust and odors. Little attention was paid to the flow of work. So people keep walking back and forth. Some of their tools, which may have been cheap to buy, are turning out to be very expensive in terms of added labor. What would it cost to change the layout? How much would the president have to figure for more efficient tools?

Here is one of those cases where, rather than being chairman or president, you're content to be a first-year student at the Harvard Business School.

Evening:

(ROBERT CHASEY III *talking*)

"I don't recall ever having met a genius around here, but I did meet a number of people who impressed me as exceedingly sharp. I think they have common sense and I think they have intelligence as measured by IQ tests. That kind of intelligence. I mean, there are some people, it seems to me, that . . . it's difficult to talk with. They won't accept your ideas and things like that, but they are still intelligent. What I'm saying is: Their brains really aren't pre-eminent. I think other qualities are. Qualities of . . . well, ambition, an analytical bent . . . materialistic bent, perhaps . . . organized. Those qualities plus the fact that they're bright.

"I would say that . . . most people here, in one way or another are . . . are somewhat insecure. I don't mean, you know, in a sense where a person is afraid of the world. I mean in the sense that many people here are looking for something, hunting for something. They're not satisfied, they're not fulfilled. They're insecure in either what they have been doing or how they feel at this moment of time. They are looking at the school as a way of . . . of satisfying some need, some desire . . . In that sense I mean, people are insecure. In talking, we called it something like a second identity crisis that . . . people experience at the Harvard Business School."

March 13: Laratti's placard is like Laratti's shoes or Laratti's shirt. It's part of what we see of him every day. A very familiar part. It's no longer white and anonymous or perfectly straight. It is as though every hour its owner has spent behind it has left some kind of mark. Bored, impatient fingers have imprinted their irreverent message. Pencil points and crayons have traced incoherently the history of Section B. The blows of heavy book covers, of backs, and elbows in the crowded hallways have frayed its edges; and the serene front that used to face the class is wrinkled.

Laratti's placard, all our placards, in fact, are no longer the glaring signals of attack of last September. Rather, with their blotches and notches, they have turned into weary flags of truce.

Time, Laratti has written on his side of the placard, *slips by like a field mouse not shaking the grass.*

March 14: They passed it along in Production—the discussion had stalled and we were all glad to have some diversion. It was an article from the *Wall Street Journal,* a long write-up on the "bright and bumptious" Harvard Business grads. It told tales of fabulous salaries and boundless ambition and there was, to prove it, an impressive list of Harvards who are commanding some of the world's biggest corporations.

One management consultant compared his Harvard man to a combination of vacuum cleaner and computer, sucking up vast quantities of disorderly data and ordering them faster than an IBM. "The bidding for Harvard guys is worse than for college quarterbacks," one recruiter said. "It isn't uncommon for a Harvard man to get a dozen good job offers."

"Finally got myself a job," said one of the two
second-year students as they walked across the windy
footbridge. "You'd be amazed, it doesn't pay that
well . . . some really big deals aren't all that much,
when you come down to it, even with the money . . .
it isn't the money. . . ."

"Know what you mean," the other guy said and both their coattails were flailing the wind. "No, I haven't gotten a job yet . . . it's difficult . . . a good job. . . .

"Some guys really learn a lot about themselves," the second guy continued after a little while.

"Yeah."

"Some guys start feeling good. But a whole lot'a guys find out they aren't everything."

"I suppose," the first guy added, "you find out what you can really do, what you are worth or something . . ." He chuckled.

"You know," the second guy fell in, "you discover that in the end . . . what you really need is enough gas to get you there in the morning. . . ."

"And back in the evening." The first guy laughed.

"And back—right," the second guy said.

8

A First-Generation American

RUSCETTA's *story*

Light seeped through the screen of the kitchen door, lighting up the few steps that led down into the garden and a low retaining wall on which he rested his feet. A shadow stained the near side of his face, a massive but not harsh face. In the imperfect darkness you could see the profiles of tall trees.

Art's place is only about three quarters of an hour away from the crowds and the strangling midsummer heat of Manhattan. There are lawns of short, soft grass and brilliantly white houses and large mansions with intricate roofs, with many trees, like umbrellas, to keep away much of the humid urban air. A little wind, leaping in from the water, moves the leaves and only about a block away, in the gap caused by the main road, you can see a narrow, shiny ribbon—Long Island Sound.

Art moves in a little bit from the edge of the light. He talks slowly, reflectively, with long pauses. Sometimes the noise of airplanes getting ready to touch down at La Guardia interrupts him and sometimes, in counterpoint to his searchingly, tentative sentences, there is the laughter of women from the living room. The voices of Mamma; of Cynthia, his wife; and of Aunt Gianna.

"I guess I came because, at the time, I didn't know what else to do. I didn't like what I was doing. In fact,

I hated what I was doing. As I look back on it now, I am still very confused as to why. I had received a first-level promotion but the accounting and auditing I was doing was a lot of detail work, a lot of very tedious work. I think it was a function of growing up, too. Of being very restless, having a difficult time accepting the responsibility of working and being married. I'd get up in the morning and I'd have to convince myself to go to work. And several times I decided: 'To hell with it.' I wasn't going to, and I'd take the day off. I knew that I couldn't go on doing that much longer. It was time to leave.

"The question was: Where do you go?

"I guess, without really meaning to, I thought of myself as a businessman and the natural place to go, since I was a businessman, was a business school. Plus the fact, you know, Harvard was a good place to spend two years when you didn't know what you wanted to do. It could always be viewed as a 'constructive experience.' There'd be no question about your wasting time by going two years to the Harvard Business School. And I guess that was a factor in it, too.

"But maybe it was really that, being a first-generation American, I was more or less controlled by material desires which had been instilled in me for many years. I'd never really taken the time or had the need to think for myself, what I wanted, where I was going. It was more a reflex action than anything else.

"I guess it's really quite a common thing. My mother and father were born in Sicily, in the same town. My mother was the second oldest of my grandmother's children. And her oldest sister married my father's cousin. The neighborhood I grew up in was at the time—it was a Jewish neighborhood then. Russian Jews. There was a little grocery store in the house in which we lived and as long as I can remember, that store was always owned by a pair of Jewish brothers. One of the brothers was in bad health, so they sold out to another pair and one of them—of the second pair —had a heart attack, so they sold the store to two brothers who were also Jewish. But not too long ago, the last pair sold out to a young Puerto Rican. There were also some Germans and a vestige of what once was a German neighborhood. Small Irish population. Substantial Italian population. So it was very much of a mixed bag.

"Our house had a fancy name, Ainvillier D'Arms, but there was nothing fancy about it. It was three floors and narrow, very narrow. The houses there are all built together and ours was the second to the last, just off the street corner. The area was always quite a bit crowded because there were government projects and apartment buildings, none or very few single family houses. Always a lot of kids, which was a good aspect of it. In the building where I lived, it was practically all families and you were almost never alone, which I very much appreciated then and sort of still do now.

"I lived in that neighborhood till I was eleven or twelve years old, and then my parents, who had been separated since I was very, very young, resumed living together. I guess, primarily, because of me. And we moved out of the area to a suburb, to nicer surroundings. We stayed there until I was eighteen and it was probably the worst period of my life. We had a very stormy, a very unhappy home life and I was a very unhappy child because of it.

"My mother, in a sense—not in a sense, in absolute terms—was the more materialistic of my parents. But that's because, when my father took off, she was left with the task of supporting us. It had always been understood, when I was a child, that we would go to college. Because that was the thing to do. It was always understood that we'd get good grades. Never why. It was always understood that the thing we really needed was a little more money than what we had. And, I guess, it wasn't until very recently that I started questioning that. It wasn't until recently that I found it difficult to think of my purpose as being . . . making money.

"I'm still finding it hard to break out. But I see what I'm doing now as a compromise. I see it as putting in a certain period of time to fulfill an obligation to my past. To those, a younger generation in the family, who need a hand. I've got to, quote: 'Establish myself' in a social and materialistic way. But I also see it as a means to break out. So that I'm no longer constrained, or constrained so closely. Not to be more 'creative' because I don't think of myself as a very creative person. But to do more of the things that now, in many ways, I can't afford.

"I found that I have a distinct leaning, a feeling for—I don't quite know how to put it—for relationships with people. For understanding people, getting close to people . . . I think I have an innate talent, an innate feel for that and it gives me a great deal of pleasure. It's only very recently that I've begun to read in psychology, of which I knew nothing, and I actually sometimes think how different things would be if I had studied differently in college, if I had pursued a different career. If I only had had the presence of mind, the awareness, when I was in school, to hunt out these different paths. I didn't. My years at college were very much of a . . . I don't know what to call it, except to say that it was a limbo. I was very much an inhibited and captive person in that, I don't know, I felt I had to repress many of the yearnings and feelings; the restlessness I had, feeling that there was some greater purpose that I should commit myself to. I just wasn't aware, wasn't able to understand the things that were ticking inside of me. Nor the fact that my restlessness was really the symptom of a change.

"I can remember, when I was a child, waking up on a conversation my mother was having—as a matter of fact with my aunt Gianna—relating as to how bad things were financially. She didn't know I was awake, it was early in the morning. I guess, I always had those impressions which I . . . I even wonder now as to how much of a fundamental insecurity has always been a part of me, and how much it has influenced judgments I have made, decisions I have taken. We were always living at the margin. My mother worked as a tailor, a coatmaker, and, you know, even now I can never get that fundamental, deep-seated fear out of my mind that it's all going to collapse and come down on top of my head."

The crickets all around sounded like a hundred umpires' whistles or like a little bell that, struck once, keeps on ringing miraculously and faithfully at the same steady pitch. The planes came in long intervals now, and fireflies did their spooky thing, sparks off some invisible, infernal fire.

It had been a long day for Ruscetta. Yesterday, he had been asked to go to his company's plant in New Hampshire. There some sudden, urgent business had required him to stay up almost all night. And today, in the afternoon, back in the New York office, they had held an important meeting, which had gone quite badly. It had lasted until seven, barely giving him time to hop into a cab and launch himself into the maze of walkways and tunnels that is Penn (Central) Station. A big crowd had been milling up in front of the gate to his train and he had had to wait, and there had been the constant stream of announcements from the man in the information booth, calling out departure times and track numbers like a bingo game. Finally, the gate had opened. The air outside had been unbearably hot but, luckily, the train was new, nice, and cool inside. It accelerated through a long tunnel and shot into daylight in the middle of a heavily industrial neighborhood past old factories, square, with rows of tiny windows. The train had stopped at stations that were but a roof and a couple of posters. Gradually, there had been fewer factories and more houses, cheap, run-down, wood-frame houses and apartment buildings, infinitely ugly, offensive blocks exhaling trembling hot, wasted air through the gills of air-conditioning systems. Gradually, narrow aprons of green appeared in front of the houses and he had seen people sitting on porches. And, as the aprons got wider, a swimming pool occasionally blinked in the evening sun. Cars were waiting at the platforms now, where the train stopped, and some were very expensive. It took Ruscetta the usual hour to travel home and after the heat and the waiting he was pretty beat.

"I was always . . . always felt very much plagued by the
fact that I could never fit the pieces of my life together.
And all of a sudden, toward the end of Business School,
I realized that I was free, maybe for the first time in my
life, finally to decide what it was that I wanted. And
I realized that I had no way to make that decision.

"I was very much aware that I was preoccupied with
security—or insecurity, however you want to call it—and
that I was exposed or . . . I can't quite put it in words . . .
the fact that there really was no cushion. That there
was nothing between me and the world except myself. That
I had to accept the responsibility. Not only for myself
but for my family too. That we were in debt. That

things could be rough for a while. But, I think, being aware of all this enabled me to go beyond it. To think that . . . well, to accept the possibility that whatever I did, I might fail. And as a result not be 'successful' in traditional terms. And that in fact, after all was said and done, even that would not be unbearable . . . I could always go back to the most fundamental type of life. All that mattered was that I really lived my life. The fact that I did and my family did exist and that we had each other.

"I began to develop an appreciation for very little things. I think I began to have perceptions that I never had before. Things that I have ignored for close to twenty-five years. Things like, how pretty birds are; what fascinating things insects are and how—this is going to sound strange—the track I was in, in terms of getting through the Business School and getting a job and making money, how this track had made me aware that I appreciated and wanted things other than a life in business.

"I went through, oh, it must have been a good dozen interviews with financial institutions. Till I finally realized, you know, how stupid I sounded. Because during one interview I just woke up and listened to myself, listened to the things I said, that I repeated time and again and finally heard why they were unconvincing. Because I didn't mean them. I just . . . it really was a very funny experience. I kind of broke out of it there and decided that that was that. That I was going to have to live with the fact that I wasn't going to be a mutual-fund manager.

"I went around looking for other things and it was just about then that I saw the folks at Kirkland Bros. Shoe Company. I had heard of them through McGrady who told me some very nice things about them. So when they were at the school, I went to talk to one of their vice-presidents; we chatted for just a few minutes and he said that I should drop by and visit them in New York. We chatted again down in New York and I guess it . . . it wasn't a very well-reasoned thing. But I liked the people I met, the job sounded interesting—continually flexible, I could do whatever the hell I pleased—and we were able to negotiate a salary. So, rather quickly, as a matter of fact, we settled.

"I hate to say it but I really don't give a shit how the shoes come out looking. Shoes don't turn me on. The fact that it's a business with several hundred employees who are highly dependent on it for their livelihood means something for me. It hadn't dawned on me until I started traveling, how many people are dependent on us. Up in New Hampshire they have three hundred people whose only livelihood in that goddamned town is the Kirkland Bros. shoe factory. If Kirkland goes these guys have no jobs at all. They can go and cut wood for a while, but in terms of their basic bread and butter, Kirkland Bros. is it.

"The company is in bad shape, it's going through a very tough period, and I'm very much challenged by the need to keep it going, get it on a firm footing, and the fact that a lot of good things can come from that. I don't necessarily mean shoes, like I say, I don't give much of a shit about shoes. But the fact that a lot of jobs will be there. And that whatever is out there to grab, I can go out and grab it. Nobody is going to say: Do it or don't do it. It's up to me.

"Sometimes I think I just try to justify what I am doing. But it's truly interesting to me. I guess what is coming out of it all is that I'm able to accept uncertainty and say: 'Well, I can live with that. And work within the confines of not knowing.' Now I can quite productively focus on short-range goals—which is what I am doing—and be content with the process of gradually finding out."

9

An Unexpected End

March 24: On this day, a perfect spring day, David Rosen shot himself in his office.

He was to have started a new course with us today, LOB (Laboratory in Organizational Behavior). At eight-forty he was to have been here for the first class of the course.

It was a class to which we looked forward with apprehension. Our troubles in HBO (Human Behavior in Organizations) have not really been cleared up but instead faded away in a mutual withdrawal of forces. Indifference, a sort of compassion that sought to prevent further injury, and the inability of some concerned students to get through to Rosen had left the issues in suspension.

And so it was all here today—the questions, doubts, mistrust, hanging over our heads like a sultry Boston summer afternoon. To make things worse, there were rumblings of discontent stirred up by some of the inexplicably harsh grades which Rosen had handed out in HBO. A number of people were bitter and it seemed just a matter of time before there would be new confrontations.

But David Rosen didn't show up.

At nine o'clock McGrady, our SA representative, went to give him a call. Rosen had left his home late, McGrady said, and would be here shortly.

He didn't come.

After Rosen's class we had Finance, and halfway through Finance, McKay showed up and then Dean Kellogg. They left and came back and people looked at one another, trying to figure out what was happening. At the end of Finance, the dean turned toward the Section: "I have bad news for you," he said and his voice was shaking. "David Rosen took his life. You . . . you can go home. There will be no more classes today."

It was completely unexpected. The violent blow sent the mind spinning, tumbling out the same message over and over: "Rosen is dead. Rosen is dead. . . ."

It is peculiar how the soul protects the thin flame of consciousness against the violent gusts of emotions. How in moments of great triumph and tragedy alike, it shuts and bolts its windows, keeping the little flame in stillest darkness with nothing but a distant echo of the agitation outside.

And so it was today, as this shot resounded through Aldrich 108. No more than a faint "thump" could be heard in the shuttered, locked confines of our minds.

March 25: Professor Claffin was pale, and the white of his shirt, contrasting with his dark suit and black tie, made him look paler. His mouth was moving, straining to save him the embarrassment of having his emotions spill into the classroom. His hands, locked tightly, wrestled to keep from shooting up in futile, agitated gestures. Claffin is about Professor Rosen's age, not much more than thirty, tall, lanky, with the overly careful grooming of a high school beau.

"We will not talk about course material," he began. "I think it would be difficult for me to keep my mind on it . . ."

In the past months, Claffin was one of the people who had gotten to know Rosen better. They had started to work together as a consultant team. In fact, they had spent the last weekend together. They and their wives.

"I have seen a few short moments of his life. And so have you . . . We know little of him as he was, little of the thirty years that went before . . .

"At the school here, he was around these brilliant and sensitive people. And still nobody knew that his problems were so deep, so complex . . ."

As he talked, Claffin kept walking back and forth. There was such silence between his words, that you could hear the high, whining hiss of the air conditioner.

"David tried all his life to get people to talk to one another. And yet he himself . . . he himself couldn't talk, couldn't get through. . . ."

The quiet, like a color, a mournful soft gray, seemed to drape the room, and people, as if afraid to have somebody discover a trace of guilt in back of their eyes, were staring down, fixedly on their desk tops.

What was it that had kept David Rosen from talking? Was it that he did not talk because he could not hear? Did the tangled fabric of his mind mute all but the echoes of his own anguished voice? Was it that as a social psychologist he had the misfortune of being an expert in the very field in which he needed help?

How did he, the sensitive, almost defenseless man, get into the rough and tumble environment of the Business School? Why he, who so greatly valued human qualities, in the midst of all this counting and calculating? Was it ambition, a missionary zeal?

"We must learn from this," Professor Claffin said, "we must make sure that this sort of thing does not happen again. . . . I am willing to speak out . . . I would like to hear your views."

Nobody moved. Nobody stirred. And it wasn't because we wouldn't have wanted to speak. But everybody knew, remembered what had happened earlier, when we had tried to discuss things so intimate in front of the whole Section; what had happened with Rosen. We were afraid.

Professor Claffin must have realized. "OK . . ." he said, "OK . . ." and slowly he turned around and walked out.

"Now when they announced Rosen's death,"
KEITH KUROWSKI said that evening,
"about the first thing they said was: 'Don't feel badly and don't feel that you are responsible. Don't let the blame weigh on your shoulders.'

"And the second thing they said was: 'Here is another way where Harvard provides you with a good learning experience.' And I could have shit on the whole system and I went home and I cried.

"I think you should learn from it, there is no doubt about that. But I felt, the fact that it is a learning experience was irrelevant two hours after Dave committed suicide. To me the assistant dean was saying: 'This isn't David Rosen, your friend, teacher, a human being. This is a case. It's XYZ Corporation where there is an unhappy ending.'

"I mean, the real thing is: There *is* blame. There *should* be guilt. There *should* be feelings. But what the school did right then and there was to say that it was a case. And to me, that's consistent with the B-School outlook and philosophy. Which is good for some things. It's good for analyzing General Motor's market share. But not for analyzing Rosen. Not for the suicide of a friend."

March 28: Baker 100 is a large, rectangular lecture hall with a view of the lawn with the flagpole to the Charles River beyond. Today the flag was lowered to half-mast and inside Baker 100 you could see it flutter in and out of view in one of the last windows.

At one end of the hall there was a stage toward which

rows of seats were sloping. Center stage, there stood a vase of slender white flowers, gracefully arching into the air. On each side of the vase was a little table, covered with white cloth, on which a tall white candle was burning.

People were still coming, ushered in by Flagg and McGrady, silently sitting down, waiting. It was an incongruous mix. Mostly gray and blue suits: students of the Business School and many professors. The Section itself, sitting as a block. And, finally, like poppy in a grainfield, a sprinkling of wild-haired, bearded types—Rosen's undergraduate students from across the river.

Up front, above the candles, there were two maps of the globe; green and brown continents floating in oceans of blue. Ungainly air ducts lined the ceiling and on the long wall, across from the windows, were two giant photographs, one of a rocket riding a trail of flame, the other of white-hot steel pouring into a metal bucket. How small the earth looks on those maps, how close the continents. Yet none of us here, none of the many students and professors accustomed to hop from continent to continent, none of us had been able to reach this one disoriented man.

Even in the brief moment of reflection, we were surrounded by the images of a world that measures value in terms of dollars. Worth in terms of a balance sheet. The slender flowers, the burning candles did not fit with the rocket and the molten metal on the wall.

Whatever his reasons for joining, Rosen paid with his life for being part of all this. But, perhaps, this is a danger facing anyone who wants to play in the "big leagues." To win here you have to go all out, too far to be sure that you'll make it back safely.

Terner was reminded of a documentary he had seen, a rerun of one of the first films ever made, which showed a man getting ready to jump off the Eiffel Tower with a pair of cloth wings. The film was scratched and blurred and the people in it moved with the jerky gestures of the very early movies. But you could clearly make out the man with his wings, which were furled about him like some ceremonial robe; you could see his face, the pitiful, pleading smile; the utter incomprehension at reading in the faces of the people surrounding him that he *was* going to jump. You could see the fall, the awfully long fall, with the man's wings streaming behind him in dark ribbons and then you saw the motionless lump at the bottom of the tower.

How could it be, Terner thought, that people *did* these things? How could hopes and dreams turn into such unrelenting, killing expectation? Sitting there, in that room, Terner felt trapped; that with every hour he spent in these buildings, with every effort he made, more of his life energy was left here, in the walls, in the people, in the little scrapes made by his shoes that with millions of other scrapes had worn hollows into the stone steps; that with every hour the electric clocks spooled off, these barren walls, the faces of his Section mates became more deeply, more irrevocably part of him; that he was not just *going* to the Harvard Business School but that he *was* the Harvard Business School, and that at this moment nothing, yes nothing else mattered, and that this course on which he had set out voluntarily, uncertainly, tentatively had become an all-encompassing, consuming desire that swept him along and tore at him with piercing claws which would not let go of him until he had either reached his goal or cracked up as Rosen had. Sitting there, in that room, Terner was vaguely aware that this thing, this school, had taken complete charge of his life, only to realize that he was in it too deep to make any changes now.

Disrupting his thoughts, the door near the stage opened slowly. A girl came in, a young woman of about thirty in a bright green dress, struggling to walk upright, a man helping to steady her. Behind the girl, a group of Jewish people—the men wearing yarmulkas—followed, and then Dean Rigsby, head of the school and the deans and officials filling the front row.

The rabbi was a young, athletic man. As people rose to start the ceremony, the lecture hall chairs creaked. On his last and most private day, David Rosen was surrounded by a community of strangers, united by a faint sense of guilt, by the inbred reflexes that make people want to be polite.

A friend, a sincere friend—you could hear it—said that David had tried to link the corporate body, the body of the Business School to a heart, a throbbing heart. Then there was a flute. The lonely, thin, almost hesitant sound of a flute. It was so forlorn, so lost, so infinitely honest that you had to bite your tongue and clench your fist, to keep it from pouring out of you.

10
Lions and Christians or Something

WENDY BURGESS *reflects on the events leading up to Rosen's death*

"When I thought about it, afterward, I realized that the people I disliked, whom I had heard gossiping and saying nasty things, did not participate in the attack on Rosen. The people who led it were actually sort of dark horses. You know, I think it was that which made me feel: 'My God, even these sweet, quiet guys are seething with this kind of nasty I don't care who gets in my way . . . kind of I don't care what I say, I'll say anything because . . .'

"They weren't doing it with any malice. It was just complete obliviousness. And I felt, you know, that . . . the maggots had come out of the walls. Not only were there these . . . these vocal detractors of Rosen who were silent on that day, but were absolutely vicious in their cutting down of him outside of class. And sat there in stony silence, not participating. But all of a sudden, these, you know, these gentle creatures had come out and said: 'I hate your guts.'

"Looking back, there were very few individuals that I can honestly say I disliked. But sometimes I took out on the Section at large a kind of hostility I had for certain individuals that I felt were . . . just not nice people. They created some situations and said things in class, and they said things out of class, about other people—I think that was the thing—they were so catty. So brutally catty that I was really surprised.

"I've gone to girls' schools all my life but I never heard anything like the opinions that some of the guys had about other guys in the Section on, you know, one day's viewing.

"Perhaps it's a natural reaction to attack when you feel threatened, but that whole thing got to the point . . . you know, it gave me a kind of a turn. Even in our study group we sort of divided into the . . . the commie bastards and fascist pigs and fought it out every time something came up.

"Everybody in the Section always talked about what a close group we were and so forth, but I think, very early, I got a sense of, you know, this is no group. This is a . . . an enforced intimacy that is only making . . . is bringing out the worst in everybody. Anytime I got to the end of a day, I wanted to just run from everyone in that room and get as far away as possible and not have to see them again until the next day. And it wasn't really because anybody had done anything to me. It was just a feeling—the way everybody was reacting together. I felt the Section . . . there was something of . . . of a mob spirit in the air. People were out to do something to somebody.

"The people I talked to in the first year, a lot of people, were very, very frightened by the whole thing. I mean, even though a lot of us could joke about it and so forth, fear is a strong emotion and it has different effects on people. I think there were times when the circumstances combined in such a way as to bring out people's fear . . . in the aggressive way, in the destructive way. The whole first few months there was a lot of tension and pressure and 'this is boot camp' and 'this is serious business' and 'you've got to measure up' with very sort of unclear—it was unclear exactly what was expected of one.

"Everybody was eating up the rough, tough cream-puff stuff that McKay was dishing out and they were all in awe of him. McKay was the strong man who fulfilled their wildest dreams and nightmares of what a . . . what an executive could be brought up to be. That they could be supermen. He was an intimidating personality and he did, you know, a sort of Pavlov thing. One day he was cutting everybody down and the next day he was saying: 'Well, I'm really your friend and I'm here to help you.'

"I do not find fear a valuable motivating force. Yes, possibly to save my life or something like that. But to get people to learn? It just doesn't make sense. I don't think I really started listening to what was going on for at least the first couple of months, until, you know, the initial shock wore off. I was in a state of . . . of paralysis. I think even with all the things people had told me, I wasn't prepared for the . . . the sort of emotional reaction I had to the whole thing. You know: 'My God, what is this? We can't be *real* inside that classroom.'

"And all kinds of really funny little paranoid reactions that I never thought myself capable of came out in those early couple of months. Like that day McKay called on me and I blanked. I have never in my life, before or since, blanked like that. I just completely drew a blank. Could not think or speak. And I have no memory of what I said. Because it was just, you know, it was one's worst fears realized. The day you *really* hadn't prepared the case, he calls on you. The funny thing was that after that I still didn't read the cases. I still went to class, almost every day, having, you know, glanced at it once over breakfast. The fear . . . the fear was enough to paralyze me. But it was not enough to make me do something about it.

"I think part of it was the feeling—this sort of group feeling, the feeling that this is a mob, not a group. We are people when we're outside of class, talking to each other. And, suddenly, when we walk in there and sit down, we're all transformed. We become lions . . . lions and Christians or something."

11

Fun and Games: Round One

April 7:

It's the old "what would *you* do" routine. Only, this time the setting is going to be a lot more real. The entire first-year class will be dividing up into twenty-four corporations, three in each section. Each corporation will have three divisions, each division, two plants. Both of those plants, in addition to having to compete in the same "market," will be up against two other pairs of plants from two other corporations. So a market will be made up of six competitors, one of which is from the same corporation.

The game will start with a practice "decision move" after which there will be twelve "decision periods" covering some three simulated years. The basic organizational unit is the plant which plans, produces, and markets two or three products (depending on the decisions of plant and divisional management). For each decision period, decisions on product price, quality, advertising, promotion, product development, market research, number of employees, etc. have to be made. These decisions are recorded on a form which must be submitted at a stipulated time. The form is then fed into a computer which will simulate the market forces acting on and reacting to the decisions made. This done, the computer will print out the "results" for each market. The time available for each decision move: three hours.

Nice game. Except that this is no game. It will count as a regular course, with 20 per cent of the grade depending on how well your corporation does. With another 30 per cent coming from your immediate "superior" (a Section mate), and the remaining 50 per cent being split between the "board of directors'" (two professors') evaluation of how well the corporation is organized, and a final exam on the experience.

We've already had our first thrills, selecting the "presidents" for the Section's three corporations. After narrowing down a seemingly endless list that looked as if it included the entire Section, we chose Mark Holton, Allan McGrady, and Mike Griffith. Now, on little white file cards, the rest of us have "applied" for a "job" in one of the three corporations.

April 9: At 3:40 P.M., mimeographed sheets were handed out with the Section's names divided into Corporation 7, Corporation 15, and Corporation 23.

Although our board of directors—Professors Francis and Keeler—must have tried to balance them, each of the three corporations has a personality all of its own. McGrady's has three of the girls and the "hardliners"—the professional military in the Section.

Holton, in contrast, will be playing billiard with odd balls. He has the least clearly identifiable segment of the Section. A good part of the "foreign element": Mendoza and Calico from the Philippines; Rene Maurois, lieutenant in the French reserves; De Latour, Maurois' brilliant compatriot; Diego Arillo, the spindly civil engineer from Lima. Plus all sorts of American standouts, like Jack Singleton, who looks like a college freshman but really is a Vietnam veteran with the rank of captain.

Griffith's is probably the most "normal" of the three corporations. Mike, a cautious middle-of-the-roader, provides the neutral ground that is attracting some of the most explosively brilliant and ambitious talent of the Section: Charvis, Kandel, O'Mara, Goodwin, Parsons, Holden.

After their tumultuous first get-together, the three corporations left right away for different wings of the building, leaving behind the usual debris, candy wrappers, and scraps of note paper, on one of which, amid a flight of doodles, a Section mate left this message: A *point to remember—it's not how you play; it's whether you win or lose the goddamned game.*

WEEK OF APRIL 12–18:

The two plants of Division 1, Corporation 7, are starting out with two products each. Two-men "product teams" are assigned to each product. One of those teams—Product 1 of Plant 1 ("the northern plant")—is made up of Tom Benson, the lawyer, and Al Terner, the former journalist and creative director of an advertising agency. Here is their report on the first series of decision periods:

Saturday: Cutting back our research expenses, we've been able to limit the $150,000 loss of the practice move to a mere $25,000 in move 1. However, to cut costs further, we have found it necessary to fire 121 men from our fabrication and 91 men from our assembly departments.

What we are selling is of relatively low quality. Nonetheless, we have "inherited" a high selling price of $8.80 per unit. All of which puts us really into the hole.

Our main competitor has substantially higher quality and sells at $7.50. So, for the moment, we are trying to hold on to our market share with heavy advertising while we improve the quality and lower the price.

Monday: Our strategy seems to be saving the product but is ruining the company. In move 2 we've run up a loss of $111,000. Lowering our price from $8.80 to $8.40 has slightly increased our sales but has decreased our profit even further. We've got to come up with a great idea or there won't be anything left to have ideas about. Russ Baxter, our division manager, is talking about killing the product.

Tuesday: Two moves.

The heavy advertising expenditures—$400,000 a move —and the money we are spending on product development are beginning to pay off. Move 3 has resulted in a profit of $4,600. Nothing to be proud of but a profit nonetheless. Our price is down to $8.30, and our share of the market steady at 6 per cent.

We seem to have taken away some sales from our competitor who is still going strong at $7.50.

Move 4 has brought further improvement. According to the printouts, we are in "peak season" and the economy is looking good. Our market share has gone from 6 per cent to 8 per cent, our profit has risen to $88,800.

We are keeping an eye on all five of our competitors, but only the one mentioned earlier is a real threat. This competitor has recovered the sales we have taken away from him during the last move, but he has gotten no further.

Now success is beginning to kill us. We are running out of inventory. Benson, who works up the forecasts, is screaming for product, but we have neither the workers nor the facilities to make more of it. We shouldn't have fired all those people in move 1. The way the rules are set up, it will take at least two moves to increase production. All we can do, at the moment, is hire eight more men for our fabrication department. Which won't help a great deal, because it takes newly hired workers one move to learn their jobs. Of course, all this time, we're paying them full wages.

We are working out of an "office" on the second floor of Aldrich (which is a coffee table in one of the alcoves, facing Professor Holywell's picture across the hallway). Our team is functioning well although we argue long and with conviction before we hand in a decision sheet. Benson tends to see the future full of roses while Terner is a little wary that a frost might touch those roses. But we always end up with a reasonable compromise.

Wednesday: Our unit price is down at $7.60 and our profit has dropped with it to a loss of $69,900. This despite the fact that our market share has gone up to 10 per cent. The reason is that we are in the "off season" and that the "general economy" seems to stutter.

Our inventory is catastrophic—down to less than one move's supply. We are going all out to add facilities and people: seventy-three men in the fabrication department, seventy-two men in the assembly. Our main worry is now that we will lose a lot of customers because we can't fill their orders. We have decided to drastically cut back our advertising and promotion expenses—we hope that this will reduce demand. We have taken another twenty thousand units in sales away from our main competitor.

Thursday: Wow! $205,600 profit in move 6.

When Baxter, the divisional manager, brings in the printouts, it's like a pack of wolves ripping away at a cadaver. They can't even wait for the some fifteen feet of paper to be unfolded in the hallway. Some of our colleagues tear out their respective pieces, leaving a mess of carbon paper and duplicates.

To say that we were relieved at the results of move 6 would be a major understatement. We kept congratulating one another, jumping around like monkeys.

Wouldn't it be fantastic if two liberal-arts types like us, beat engineers like Kandel? There are signs that this is what's happening.

Our adding on people is making itself felt with respect to quality. Our "quality content" is up almost $.50 from the $3.20 with which we started out. Watch out, competitor!

Friday: A dive to the tune of minus $52,100. To make things worse, our storage houses are practically empty. To jack our price back up to $7.90 doesn't seem to have been a very bright idea. We have lost 1 per cent of our share of market while the competitor is thriving. He has added almost 40 per cent to his unit sales.

Our quality isn't increasing fast enough and our price is again too high. He is matching our advertising effort too.

You can't win them all, as the saying goes, but with ninety-five additional men for fabrication and assembly, we keep on trying.

With this move, the first round of the game is coming to a close. Now there will be a week of regular classes and a lot of soul-searching about what everybody could have done better.

12

The Revolt of the Classes

(The Week of April 12 and After, from Another Angle)

> Strike for the eight demands. Strike because you hate cops. Strike because your roommate was clubbed. Strike to stop expansion. Strike to seize control of your life. Strike to become more human. Strike to return Pain Hall scholarships. Strike because there's no poetry in your lectures. Strike because classes are a bore. Strike for power. Strike to smash the Corporation. Strike to make yourself free. Strike to abolish ROTC. Strike because they are trying to squeeze the life out of you. Strike.
>
> From a poster nailed up on the trees and walls around Harvard Yard on or about April 14

April 14, afternoon: Today the unrest and upheaval at the college finally reached our side of the river. Some ten thousand people crossed Anderson Bridge in the early afternoon, heading for the football stadium which is just on the other side of the street from the Business School. And there, where only six months ago the Harvard eleven had tied the Yalies with no time left on the clock, where alumni had paid a small fortune to see "the Game," the fur coats and silver flasks had given way to T-shirts with the red, raised fist of revolution. The crimson pennants had become banners reading "STRIKE" and the frenzied cheers of "Go Harvard" had turned into chanted slogans of quite another kind.

The meeting was opened at around three by a red beard who, from a rostrum at the closed end of the stadium, explained that democratic procedures were to be followed strictly. The microphones and amplifiers and the reporters and cameramen made everything very real, like what you saw a lot of on TV. Except that the scenes on TV usually were shrouded in tear gas, with beating and clubbing and throwing things, while here, violence seemed as far away as the clouds in the spotless sky.

After the meeting opened, all the events that had got us here were brought up again: the evening of April ninth, when a small band of SDSs and Worker Student Alliance people had taken over University Hall. The police "bust" at dawn the next morning, when state and local police in riot helmets, their billy clubs drawn, had retaken University Hall at the cost of some fifty people (including five cops) injured. The statement of President Pusey on April eleventh, defending the police action on the grounds that those who occupied University Hall "not only committed an act completely unacceptable to this community, but also critically endangered the liberty and open operations of the university." Finally the inevitable consequence of it all, the radicalization of the students; the shock of the moderate or even uninterested majority at seeing pictures of the "bust" in the evening paper.

The sun became hotter and a lot of guys began to take off their shirts, and a fellow came around who was selling "revolution cola." A plane kept flying by with a message from the local Chevy dealer. There were so many helicopters that somebody said they were bringing in the Marines.

The speakers, obviously repeating themselves, were wearing everybody down to the point where some serious business could be transacted. Somebody moved that there be a strike until the demands of the "Teaching Fellows' Proposal" were accepted by the university. The move was seconded and, right away, red-shirted ushers began to count each row's show of hands. Then, as the result was announced, the stadium became hushed. An even split! And, incredibly, on the recount, still a split!

A compromise move now called for a three-day strike. At the end of it, with the university having had time to react, the issues would be put to a vote again. But as the sun was already sinking into the uppermost bleachers, there was neither the time nor the patience left to go through another hand-raising-and-counting routine.

"All those against, say: Nay!"

A respectable uproar.

"All those in favor, say: Aye!"

The noise was so great it took some time for the sound to clear the stadium.

So this strangely distracted, yet honest afternoon has, after all, produced a result. Without gas and clubbing. Without violent overthrow of anybody. The three-day strike will give everybody a chance to think things over.

Same afternoon: All this time, while ten thousand people across the street were wondering what their world was coming to, the staff of Corporation 7 was busy figuring out ways to increase their profit.

It wasn't that they didn't know what was going on, or that they were all hostile to the ideas being debated—though it must be said, in fairness, that their political inclinations were almost uniformly toward the conservative side. If anything, it was the methods across the street, the crowd, the shouting, the red armbands that turned them off. They exhibited the mixture of disdain and fear that came from not really understanding what a crowd, an emotion are all about. They, shiny examples of achievement, had long put so many layers of discipline on top of their feelings that they had come to look on feelings as obedient and harmless servants of the will. Why didn't those people in the stadium shut up and do something about their problems? Why can't they be rational? Geez, burning the house down is no way to refurnish.

The Business School had postponed the next move of the

management-simulation game to give those who wanted to go over to the stadium a chance to do so. But few took it. Instead, the tennis courts behind Morgan were busy and incessant babble was filtering through the corporations' doors. There was talk that people at the stadium had plans to storm the Business School, and, just in case, the big stadium gate facing the school was locked. But the crowd, which finally came out of the other gates, was too spent. Nothing happened.

"Crock of shit," Tony Rush, plant manager in Corporation 7, said of the stadium crowd. Some of the stadium crowd put up posters that showed a man in tails embracing something that looked very much like the Harvard Business School. But no confrontation this time. Not yet.

Evening: Over in the Yard, Harvard Yard, where it all had begun, night ended another act of a play whose players were still trying out their roles. But after the heat and hassle of the day, the revolution still tossed and turned; it couldn't sleep.

In front of Sever Hall, a rock group named the Albatross sent sharp bursts of sound across the Yard as they tuned their instruments. Then, accompanied by annoyed and approving shouts from the dormitories, the Albatross took to the air on a hard beat, rocking away the last drops of unspent emotion.

No matter how the university will react, it has already been changed. The billy clubs at University Hall have created a new, if only short-lived, community. The bust was the last straw. The police called in by the university; the university governed by officers of big corporations; the big corporations going along with a government responsible for Vietnam; the government going along with corporations wrecking the environment; the corporations merely "giving people what they want."

Too much!

The university was the closest thing at hand. So it was the first thing to get hit. Ten thousand people, most of them too young to be more than somebody's sister or football captain, have quite nearly shut down Harvard University. The world's greatest opportunity is turning out to be: *a bribe.* If you think something is wrong, we'll make you smart enough to rationalize it; if you don't like what's going on, we can make you wealthy enough to ignore it.

For the last couple of days at least, the old trick, the old promise hasn't worked.

Even John Harvard, sitting there in dignified bronze, even he—imagine he!—is wearing the red ribbon of discontent around his monumental head.

Night: As Terner walked back home, his ears still ringing with shouts, ayes, and nays, he came to a point where a breach in a fence offered a convenient short cut over the lawn. In fact, he was already halfway into the breach when suddenly he stopped.

"What about the grass?" Looking down, he saw that others had taken advantage of the damaged fence, because there was a path trampled, a clearly visible scar, that cut right over to the nearest walkway.

"So?" Terner said to himself, "the damage is done. And, anyway, it's only grass."

But then, as he reflected a moment, he began to have second thoughts.

"Only grass?

"Isn't that what kills it? What kills the rivers, the cities, people even. Everybody saying: 'It's only grass'?

"Everybody walks by thinking: 'Anyway, the damage is done. And if I don't walk across it, the next guy will.'

"That's what kills the grass?" Terner thought. "People saying: '*It's only grass*'."

April 15: The meeting began in such orderly fashion that you wondered whether anything so organized could be urgent enough to require a get-together in the middle of a busy afternoon.

Three to four hundred M.B.A.s were there; two or three platoons of AMPs (Participants in the school's Advanced Management Program), a group of secretaries and employees and many of the faculty, including the dean of the school. A good crowd really, but underneath those pillars of Baker Library, it just didn't look like anything. On the steps before the library, two microphones were set up, one "official" for people who had statements to make on behalf of their sections; the other for people out of the crowd, who wanted to speak for themselves.

What came through was that this taking over of buildings and making of demands are no way to do business. Therefore, the invaders had a good clubbing coming. But then again, you didn't want to condemn them too much, because they are, after all, part of the Harvard family, and you don't want to give the family a bad name. Finally, a fellow made a motion that "those present" vote to condemn the use of police force by the university. To facilitate the count of hands, "those in favor please go to the left of that little truck there, and those against, please go to the right."

The AMPs, in their middle forties most of them, marched to the right almost in step.

"They shouldn't be allowed to vote!" An M.B.A. with a mustache said that because they are here only for three months, the AMPs should be denied a vote.

A guy who spoke for the AMPs said, well, if the AMPs couldn't vote, then a lot of the other people here who weren't really students *in the technical sense* shouldn't vote either.

Only students *in the technical sense* should be allowed to vote.

"In this case," the moderator who stood behind the two microphones said, "in this case it would become necessary to determine just *who* should vote and what the appropriate procedure should be." So he herewith had to call—if all those saying "aye" would please say "aye"—he had to call for another such meeting tomorrow, at the same time.

April 16: Today, at the same time, a much larger crowd assembled on the lawn in front of Aldrich. Early in the morning, trucks had unloaded stacks of folding chairs which were set up symmetrically, in blocks, each block identified by a lettered post. The setup looked as if the Boston Pops were due for an outdoor concert.

Unfortunately, by midafternoon, a heap of gray clouds had piled up on top of Aldrich. It began to rain and soon rained so hard that the lettered signposts wilted and the rain hats made of newspaper dissolved over people's heads and faces. The Business School's new attempt to help bring the revolution to an orderly conclusion would surely have ended in a washout. Except that, at the last moment, the chairman of the meeting invited everybody to continue on to Watson Ice Rink.

There we settled anew, some seven or eight hundred strong, the two halves of the crowd facing one another across the sandy rectangle that still seemed to echo the scraping of skates, the sound of armored bodies crashing against the sideboards. Easily ten motions are put before the audience: Some declaring solidarity with the rebels across the river; some opposed; some opposed to those opposed. And gradually, what had started with rounds of laughter and applause grew into a dull commotion of ever greater volume, pierced by frustrated yelps.

When finally the question of whether the Business School should join the strike is put before the crowd, Section B, like everybody else, explodes with the furor of a choked volcano. Leroi shrieks like a speared pig and Rush has to be held down to keep him from jumping a guy who has raised his fist in salute to the revolution. "The final vote," says the chairman, whom you can barely hear, "the final vote is that the Business School does not join the strike at the College and the other professional schools of Harvard and that there be no suspension of classes."

For seven and a half months now, following the dictates of the curriculum and the crushing workload, our concern has been with technique. How to solve this. How to deal with that. *How.* But now that the machinery of the Business School has come to a halt, the *why* hangs in front of us—a weird, warped mirror that bends our views of each other all out of shape, presenting us with a hateful, leery gallery of faces. Our reliable techniques no longer work; our brilliant arguments jam at the hinges. The illusion of unity we so diligently crafted is finally breaking down.

April 24: The only definite thing to come out of the previous meetings is that nothing definite had been decided. And that the way to find out how people really feel is to hold a written referendum. In that referendum, a motion to endorse the Teaching Fellows' proposal was defeated 929 to 282. A motion not to strike, however, was passed with 933 for and 374 against. (Union officials participating in the school's Trade Union Program voted 9 to 8 to strike.)

In place of the stadium proposals, the Business School voters accepted a proposal, by the Student Association that the school be requested to suspend classes for a day to hold a student-faculty symposium on "the issues now facing Harvard."

"Welcome to the Student-Faculty Symposium," the symposium program said. And the school had put up a big green tent because it didn't have a hall big enough to hold everybody.

Nathan M. Pusey, president of Harvard University, opened the morning program with a message on disruption and coercion which was an instant replay of his earlier statements and which had a lot to say about the symptoms and very little about the causes.

The real shock came in the afternoon, in the shape of Henry Norr. The soft-spoken gentleman in his dark suit was the SDS (Students for a Democratic Society) man and radical student leader. The threatening lump of emotion from the other side of the river suddenly had a face. An ordinary, self-consciously smiling face. A head that backed statements with fact and fact with reason. Reasoning, as a Business School guy noted with satisfaction, that could be taken on and handled.

He didn't scream at us and we didn't scream at him. Everybody listened closely and a lot of good questions were asked. The dialogue that everybody always talked about was there from the beginning. Because, after the University Hall bust and our interminable meetings, we were all aware of the alternatives.

Evening:

"You know, I just don't understand," Max Tuck said in that flat nasal Boston accent of his, "I'm fifteen years older than the kids across the river . . . When we went to college —sure, we felt abused here and there, but, hell, that was part of the game . . . If I had my way, those kids would be put in the Army. I'd have their hair cut.

"When I was a kid, the way I was brought up, if you did something wrong you got your ass kicked. But the kids today, you can't win if you push them around . . . Maybe parents just aren't bringing up their kids the way they used to, you know, and soon we're going to be up against our own . . . No way, you're going to win it the old way, believe me, no way."

Tim Howell, the tall marine officer, holder of three Purple Hearts, said, his clear blue eyes fixed on Max: "When I think back to my undergraduate days, it wasn't at all like this. We were thankful just for bein' able to be there . . . Nothing is perfect in this world. And there are good sides and bad and you've got to learn to live with both . . . you can't throw out everything just because there is a fault. But I guess, undergraduates don't feel that way any more."

April 25: There is a lull now. The noise has subsided, the proclamations have been torn down from the walls or were washed away by the rain. The red fist, until further notice, is put away in a drawer.

In a time, when ages have shrunk to the size of decades, another age is about to fade. The old was a cold age. Born of the Second World War. Run by a generation in search of a cause. By a generation that kept on fighting without enthusiasm, by reflex almost, for a house in suburbia, a second car, a bigger refrigerator. Cold War is what they called it. A couple of decades that distilled the experience of the prewar years into cool, functional cubes of steel and glass; that muffled the happy ballroom music and strung it out, along thin, strangely unmelodic lines, calling it cool jazz.

An age that hung its beliefs outside its windows like the national flag, which it kept waving, threateningly, in front of its children's eyes.

The old age is turning the corner. A new generation is

reaching out, cautiously trying to balance the excesses of competition by the beginnings of co-operation. After two centuries of increasingly violent independence, a new American age proclaims the dependence of man on man.

The last several days have made all of us, who lived through them, aware that there is no "right way" to right society's wrongs. For even the rightest way eventually clogs up with habit, becomes bent out of shape by individual ambition—including democracy.

If democracy is truth, then truth lies in trying.

13

Fun and Games: Round Two

A report on decision moves 8 to 13 by T. Benson and A. Terner, managers, Product 1, Division 1, Corporation 7.

April 29, Tuesday: We got a memo from our president D. Michael Griffith, which somehow was fouled up in the printing because you could only read it backside forward, by holding it against a light.

> Our Board had high praise for Division 1, which is the top performing division in Section B and among the top in the first-year class. They suggest that perhaps some of the secrets of success of Division 1 might be useful for the rest of the corporation . . .
>
> . . . I feel certain that we have what is required to bring in a remarkable performance for the last four or five moves . . . analyze our company . . . we have the talent, the experience and we have plenty of borrowing power to exploit opportunity.

Well, we have analyzed our own and the other two corporations of the Section ever since the last move. Subordinates have analyzed superiors; superiors went over subordinates, and everybody had good advice for everybody else.

In fact, it almost went too far. Because, here we are, set in a nice routine that seems to be working just fine and now they want to put added emphasis on this, more information on that—we may just become victims of our own advice. A lot of people higher up are trying all of a sudden to meddle in our business.

Observing our negative reaction to our own suggestions, we can't help but think that we are going to run into a lot of trouble being managers in the real world. Because there are going to be people just like us, tucked away in routines just like ours who don't want to be bothered.

Friday, May 2: We are hanging in there: $171,300 profit in move 8. But, unfortunately, we made this profit off ourselves. We didn't sell more. We simply spent less. We should have made $210,000 alone from cutting back our advertising.

Our quality is up to $3.90 and our price down again to $7.70. But now we have completely run out of stock. In fact, there were 2,134 units worth of orders that we couldn't fill.

We desperately need men, not apprentices working at 50 per cent efficiency, but experienced men. At first it looked as if we would get some from Rush and Holden, who, in turn, were promised them from another division in the corporation. But now Holden is saying that they are getting only forty-seven, which they need themselves, and they never really promised us any *for sure.* Only after we threatened to go to Baxter, our division manager, did they finally agree to a compromise. We now get thirteen men for fabrication and four for assembly. Far below what is needed, but at least something.

Seems like we are not the only ones having lost sales in move 8. Our competitor's really went down too. Somebody new must be biting chunks off our market.

Saturday, May 3: In true-to-life fashion, we are working Saturdays.

Move 9 was a total flop. $118,700 into the red. For one thing, Terner made a mistake in filling in the decision sheet. This rocketed our quality up to $4.02, which is likely to give our competitor a heart attack. And not just him—us as well.

Besides, we had to reinvest all the advertising money that we saved during the last round—or rather, what was left of it. Which is putting us even deeper into the hole.

To compound our troubles, the market is going to pieces and Charvis and O'Mara from our southern plant are moving in on us. They are selling their product at an uncomfortably close $6.95. We are trying to talk them out of our segment, but they are hard up for cash and therefore hard of hearing. Fortunately, they don't have the quality.

Our spirits are still high though. Benson is forecasting renewed success. So we continue to build plant and hire people something crazy. We have got another sixty-one men coming for fabrication and sixty-four for assembly. All our present workers are on overtime now.

We are slowly evolving a clear and cruel strategy for the rest of the game. We are going to use the confusion about the true quality of our product as a kind of smoke screen behind which we will build up a clearly higher quality than our competitor. Then we will drop our price down to his. This should put him where we were at the beginning. Only, by the time he has realized it the game will be over.

May 5, Monday: Move 10 still has not helped us turn the corner but we are getting there. Only lost $22,400 this time. Our quality is steadying at $3.90, which is about $.10 above our competitor's. We are ready to move in for the kill.

Move 11: (We are playing two moves today.) The slaughter is beginning. A profit of $223,700! Moreover, our quality is up at $3.97. Market share has grown by 3 per cent. Sales almost doubled. Benson is forecasting with the precision of a Swiss watch, Baxter is greatly relieved, and Rush and Holden just can't believe it.

Friday, May 9: Moves 12 and 13.

Profit of $136,000 on move 12. Market share and unit sales steady. Our price, since the last move, matches our competitor's at $7.50. His sales have dropped by 40,000 units.

The final move—No. 13—seals it. Our lucky number. We have made another $130,000. Our share of market has reached an all-time high of 13 per cent while our competitor's has dwindled further.

Benson has calculated that, over-all, we have come out something like half a million ahead. Which isn't bad for two guys who just nine months ago could barely read a slide rule.

14
The Limits of Fear

May 14: In the short period of two months, John J. Leroi has come to sample both the sweet taste of victory and the sour taste of conspiracy and near defeat. And it has happened publicly, which made his sudden rise all the more glorious and his unexpected fall all the more hard for him to take.

A month, a week, or even a day before the SA (Student Association) re-elections, which were held around the middle of March, people would have laughed into your face if you had told them that Leroi was going to be even a candidate. "We got to Leroi through the back door," says McGrady. "Everybody agreed that Leroi didn't have a chance. Well, that was the first time we agreed. I can't remember just who all was there; we had a hell of a time. We were sitting around Kandel's room and we went through the Section list again and again and all the obvious strong people who were suggested, other people, half the group, would say: 'No,' this that and the other thing, 'not him.'"

And that is how John Leroi became a candidate; and not just a candidate, he became the winning candidate. It was like being confronted with an ambitious employee whom you might not particularly like but who is making so much more of an effort than any of his rivals that, reluctantly, you promote him in their place.

It is indeed not easy to like Leroi. His ultralong sideburns, his extra wide ties with matching handkerchief in the breast pocket contrast violently with his political views, which are so far to the conservative side that, at the slightest argument, you run the risk of losing sight of him altogether. So it wasn't much of a surprise when an anonymous sheet passed through the rows today, asking for signatures to dump Leroi.

At the end of that class, Leroi stepped in front of the Section, his shaking right hand clutching the piece of paper: "Who," he wanted to know, "*who* is behind this?"

"I was really the leader behind this drive to dump Leroi, I guess," says Tony Rush. One of my best friends in the class was Duane Gilfeder and, of course, Leroi had beaten him out for SA rep. It didn't mean beans to me, the SA thing, but it meant a lot to Duane and I think that fostered it on me a little bit.

"It also got me mad how Leroi would do some things—the way he would talk about people and everything.

"So we were over at the Pub one day and, you know, decided that we were, that the group of guys there was going to dump Leroi. Anyway, the drive was started and we had kind of a secret petition going around in class. No one knew who was behind it and everything, but everyone kind of liked the idea and it got a majority at first.

"But then, when it came to the real showdown, some guys backed off. I think one was Fred, Fred Laratti. No bad feelings about that whatsoever, Fred is a great guy. But he had some—he couldn't do it to the guy.

"I found I could. When I went, you know, when the whole class was assembled and Leroi went down in front, wanted to know who was behind it, I got up and told him and told him why."

Leroi made a brave effort to defend himself against his attackers whom now at least he could see. He had done all he could, he argued with some justification, and because he had, he would not offer his resignation.

So it was decided that Leroi should leave the room and the Section would vote. With Leroi gone, several guys spoke, but it wasn't until Baxter that someone struck a chord: "I don't know what you guys think," Russ said, "but it looks to me like John got the message. We shouldn't push this too far." Laratti, too, who was one of the guys who had started it, said that he thought the thing had gone far enough, and others said pretty much the same. The vote therefore came as an anti-climax with Leroi winning, but not winning happily and not laughing but looking uncertainly at the Section filing out of 108.

May 16: Today we were given a guided tour through part of the "real world," whatever it is, that people talk about so much here at the Business School.

Our first guide was a young man, only four years out of the school, whom Professor Meehan brought in to tell us about *the Street*—Wall Street, of course. The guy wore a greenish suit and looked as if he had stepped out of a mail-order catalogue. A tight, mannered smile periodically lit his face.

"Work on the Street," the man said, "is lots of fun." And from the respectful silence you could tell that a good many people really ate this stuff up. Finance is the thing to go into these days, what with all the mergers going on, the talk of "performance," the mushrooming mutual funds—these are the heydays for the financial types, the money runners, the fund managers. "Making it on the Street isn't a matter of age and experience," the guy went on, and the relaxed even tone of his voice left no doubt that he knew what he was talking about. "You've got to know the rules. And there's a great deal of pressure, constant pressure. You've got to keep up with it, every minute of the day, every day.

"You can't be an amateur in this game," the guy said, "and if you are a talented amateur, it pays to become a professional. It pays very well indeed. Millions," the guy said, "many millions."

He kept talking of "growth stocks," of getting "on" and "off," and of untapped opportunities abroad. South Africa, for example.

"One of the tremendous advantages," the guy said, "is you can use the money and the connections. You can really do something about the problems. Social problems and so forth. You are in a position to change."

South Africa, for example?

End of tour No. 1.

The second tour was arranged by Robert Chasey III who, just before coming to the school, had finished a stint with the Navy. It consisted in the showing of a movie.

"This movie," which he arranged for the Section to see after class, "some guys in the Navy got together to make this movie, to show what it is like to fly combat missions in Vietnam. You know, what the fellows are like who fly there."

Starting with the title, you could see that something was decidedly wrong. Because the title was in fine contoured lettering. If the guys who made this were amateurs, they must have spent their childhood in Hollywood.

Chasey is a very sincere, at times almost a little bit naive, guy. This movie must have faked him too. Because all it showed was bomb-heavy fighters roaring into a beautiful purple sky and the boys singing "Red River Valley" at the bar. Nice, clean-cut boys. The kind you used to see in college year books. There was no blood, no dying, not even a single ear-shattering explosion. Nothing but purple sky, jazzy uniforms, and somewhere, beyond the edge of the screen, a place called Vietnam.

End of tour No. 2.

May 19: Although there are several qualities that single Sy out from among his peers, none is more noticeable than his manner of speech. Sy's argument has the strength, the cool elegance of a well-designed steel bridge, with each of its beams carrying and being carried, all of them adding up to a graceful and solid whole. Sy obviously selects his words with the care of a man accustomed to having them remembered.

His way of speaking reflects a polish, a series of achievements, a glamour which is hard to match: an undergraduate degree from Stanford topped by a year of study in France. Work at the prestigious Brookings Institution, interwoven with travels in Africa and Europe. And as if all this weren't enough, fate has spoiled him with handsome looks: tall, solid, with fair skin; an even face ruled by attentive eyes, which at times are hidden in the shadow of his long blond hair. The whole of it packaged in well-tailored suits, in shirts cut and patterned in the latest fashion. A wealthy father's son. A man of determination and obvious ability. Yet, because of his success, a convenient target for the envy of men of lesser fortune.

But success, while making Sy aware of his extraordinary potential, has also sharpened his sense of vulnerability, has developed in him a subtle and easy sense of humor. And so he suffers open attack and veiled insult with the same disarming magnanimity.

With all this going for him, Sy's rise first to eminence, then to pre-eminence in the Section came early and was rather swift. PBE, which like no other course depends entirely on the liveliness of our discussion, became an ideal backdrop against which Sy could display his talent. Sy became a crown prince at King McKay's court:

"At a point where everyone is uncertain in a kind of *tabula rasa* environment, experience in public life gives a person just a little bit of a head start—though for no particular reason of his own ability, just in terms of training—a fixed point.

"I had recently returned from France and had worked in Washington briefly, in a fairly high level environment. And thus, when I came to the Business School, I was still churning at quite a high rate and the problems seemed, at the initial stage, a little less challenging than they might have been had I been winding my way through the normal corporate channels that a lot of my classmates had come from. I think that my background was unusual in that regard, and if I distinguished myself from the others, it was because I came with a special amount of confidence and a feeling that I could concentrate and think as well as the rest of them and work as hard and, therefore, that I was going to hold my own."

Yet as Sy's confidence in his mastery of the Section grew, his contributions seemed to lose intensity, became mannered, were overly calculated for effect. More and more, people impatiently interrupted him. Where earlier there had been awe, there now was hissing and malicious laughter.

"I felt that I had established a certain advantage at the beginning of the year but I knew that, as the year went on, I was losing it. People no longer would turn to one or two men in the Section—and I suppose I was one of them—for advice on matters on which they could offer advice for themselves."

But Sy even faded with grace. Although people now frequently mocked him, they never questioned his basic ability. Sy, in turn, faced the mounting challenge with the serenity of one who, though out of favor with the masses, still considers himself their rightful king.

May 20: Erwinger has introduced a new habit of leaving in the middle of class to get a cup of coffee. The worse the class, the more frequent the coming and going.

It isn't just the dull classes, it's the early ones too that are showing signs of trouble. In fact, we often begin with only half the people there, the rest arriving anywhere from five to thirty minutes late; some defiantly marching in, unabashedly clunking down their briefcase; others sheepishly creeping through the barely opened door.

Hissing, which used to be our one and only source of diversion, has expanded to include a whole range of signals, from an astonished whistling to a drawn-out, swelling "Wow" to roaring laughter.

The system, it seems, is becoming its own victim. The direst threats, even grades, have lost their impact on all but a few desperate cliffhangers. We have reached a point of overkill beyond which you get nothing but stupid grins and blank stares.

Sam Maguire, who knows Steve Blotner well, says that Steve is in real trouble. "Steve," Sam says, "got caught in a spiral. You know, where you try hard and the harder you try, the worse you do.

"I just get the impression that part of Steve's problem is that he really isn't part of the Section. He takes some real doing to get through to. Yeah, and because of that, because he gets aggressive, people just won't take the time to sit down and draw him out and bring him in.

"His falling on the outside may or may not be the reason why he got into academic trouble—nobody knows.

But now that he is in trouble, the fact that he is on the outside makes it more and more difficult, I think, for him to, you know, even feel it is worthwhile."

MEMORANDUM

May 21

TO: All First Year Students
FROM: First Year Marketing Teaching Group

Since the new case we are using for the examination is slightly longer than is desirable for 4 hours (it consists of 22 pages of text and 11 pages of exhibits or 33 pages in total), we are extending the examination from 4 to 4½ hours. Therefore, the examination on Saturday will commence at 9:00 A.M. and, if students wish, they may take until 1:30 to complete it.

Kresge Hall will remain open for lunch until after the conclusion of the examination.

May 22: Yesterday was the last evening we had to struggle through three cases. Today was everybody's last chance to get caught unprepared, to boost a teetering average, to save a year of all-out effort. The exams are all that's left before summer.

For a change you were happy that Aldrich didn't have any windows, because the season has already hoisted its little green flags on the trees and bushes and the winds are blowing in the sticky air, typical of Boston.

The Section vibrated with all sorts of strangely moving, strangely contradictory feelings that exploded into sheer bedlam when Holton pulled a tiny frisbee from his briefcase. Some people were in such hysterics that tears were streaming down their cheeks. If you had walked by, outside the classroom, you would have thought that it must be a ball to go to the Harvard Business School. You would have had to know the Section as well as we did to hear the small screams of fear amid the louder laughter; the relief that soon it would be over; the almost paranoid anxiety that in the exams something might still go wrong.

There were the groans, the mock anger of near misses as the frisbee sailed back and forth across the room, and Professor Meehan almost got hit by a wild throw as he came in to start his class. "Things sure have changed around here," Meehan said with a forgiving smile. And it really seemed unbelievable, when you thought about it, how far we had come since that intimidating morning, early in September.

May 31: The drifting puffs of white appeared to be stuck up there, of late. The silky sky had become stiff and glass-like; even the sun seemed to hesitate, before dropping over the brink of the horizon. The year had come to an end little by little, like a tin toy unwinding, until with a final, unexpected lurch it halted. There were no last hurrahs, no hats thrown into the air. There were no all-night parties, no speeches, and no regrets. Here and there, a pair of shoulders rose in an extended and thankful sigh of relief, and if there was any emotion it came from knowing that you had given it all you had.

"It's over!" You kept balancing those words at the tip of the tongue, savoring them in tiniest licks to keep their sweet flavor alive as long as possible.

The end was almost too normal. After the last exam, the finance exam, the members of Section B came over into Dillon Court, their hands still sore from writing. Big Karl was there in his beige shorts, living up one last time to the image of the reliable, handcrafted German. And Parke too, chasing footballs as if his future depended on it. The girls were there.

And O'Mara, Goodwin, Erwinger, Lambeau, Parsons, Robert Chasey III—the leaders and followers, the stars, the cliff-hangers and the dark horses; the violent, the suave, the sly, the manipulated and manipulators. There were the quick exchanges of whens and wheres that precede the final handshake and then, from the distance, a last wave.

As you walked up the stairs out of Dillon Court, you no longer saw their faces but still you recognized a voice, a shout, a certain laughter. And as you looked back, before turning the corner, there was a red frisbee in the air and then a blue one, and finally, *finally*, there was the beginning of summer.

June 1: There is something particularly bitter about losing a fight just at the final bell. Luck, it seems, is more cruel and more deceiving when it is steady, when it comes in the guise of a good friend. You begin to hope where you should think. You begin to run where you should cautiously walk. You count on it. You build your plans on it. Until suddenly—it lets go.

Against all better judgment, you begin to count on luck to have a few human qualities after all. That it will allow itself to be charmed. That it can be impressed, that you can twist its arm. You begin to imagine that if you just don't give up, it will come over to your side sooner or later. No, not forever. Just for those few extra seconds, those two extra minutes, those two years you need.

James L. Manning ran out of time just as the final bell rang. Manning, twenty-two, was found last Monday at 1:15 P.M. by one of his neighbors in the dormitory. He was lying in bed, dead, having put a bullet into the right side of his head.

It happened so damned close to the end that it didn't make sense. The guy had made it. The guy had had good grades all through the second year. His last exam was over. He had a job lined up with one of the most prestigious consulting firms in the country. He had what, to a lot of people, is "everything." And yet time ran out on him just as he, the winner, was about to receive his prizes. It was that crazy, that cruel timing that made the event so painfully difficult to understand. All this tremendous effort for nothing—nothing at all.

Why?

Couldn't or shouldn't the school have done something to stop him? Isn't education supposed to tell you something about the world so that you can live in it more fully?

Yet what you see is that education kills.

True, not education alone. It has its conspirators. Blurred shadows from an even more obscure past: a father, a mother, teachers, thoughtlessness, prejudice, "friends."

But education doesn't seem to right their wrongs. It aggravates them.

And everybody has an excuse. The students that they are under pressure by the professors. The professors that they are under pressure by the promotion committee. The promotion committee that it is under pressure by the alumni. The alumni that they merely want their school to be as good as everybody else's.

All of which turns education into a perpetual and futile effort to meet other people's expectations. Into a mindless numbers game with numbers admitted, averages to be attained, the objective of which is to whittle the number of those who want to move up, down to the number that can be efficiently processed.

That kind of education is designed to eliminate people, not to improve them.

Now some people say this is exactly what is needed. Because society can only absorb so many engineers, lawyers, and professional managers. And if you educate more, you create an "academic proletariat." As if a lot of professional people didn't end up in professions different from those they studied. As if professional people were machines, of use only for work in which they were trained. As if society with all its problems weren't in such dire need of disciplined minds—no matter what their background.

But even if some measure of competition can be justified on a graduate-school level, what about those schools which provide a *general* rather than a *professional* education? Whose supposed goal is to help you adapt to the walkways, the subways, airways, tramways, the by- and highways; the buttons, dials, codes, cards, and switches which are called "an industrialized society"? What about those schools—the high schools and the colleges? Why competition here where society not only can absorb all the able bodies they produce, but where society's survival seems to depend on *everybody* becoming a graduate? Where the cost of a dropout is likely to be many times that of a graduate, considering what society is forced to spend on police, on courts of law, on welfare agencies?

Why competition here, where everybody is after the same basic information? Where it oughtn't to make the least bit of difference how and when you get the facts, just as long as you do?

And yet, even in high schools and especially in the colleges, dog eats dog. The fast, the slow; the privileged, the underprivileged. In a manner that doesn't come anywhere near the battle of equals which supposedly characterizes clean competition; it can't even be called a fight—it is a slaughter. If the goal of a general education is to integrate people into society's mainstream, why then is every effort made to eliminate them from it? Why then are people segregated into smart and stupid, meaning rich and poor, white and black, English and Italian, Christians and Jews, accentuating rather than reducing some of society's most glaring inequalities?

Or is the real reason for competition in the schools that there aren't enough of them? Not enough good ones? Then, competition is about as good a solution as war is for hunger.

Really, there is no reason in the world why the students in America's schools should be taught intense competition. But there is a wealth of reasons why they should learn the value of co-operation.

But the sad reality is that America's schools and teachers are no more immune to some of the crazy beliefs of their society than anybody else. So they keep telling you that you *have* to compete because it is good to compete, and that you must win because it is good to win. And they know no more why than you or I. You understand that the object of education is winning, not learning; that the key word is examination, not education. And that the quicker you face up to it, the better you are going to do.

You learn in school not to give a shit if the people you climb over are weak or sick or small or blind. You understand that everybody is your enemy, and you learn to fear and hate people, to live in crowded isolation for the rest of your days. But, above all, you learn never to show your weaknesses and to put up a front at all times, and you learn to hate yourself for doing it.

You do as you are told, because there is no other way you are going to make it, and you use your own seeming success to justify the pressure and fear the schools use to teach your children. You go on slugging it out and for every enemy you defeat, there are a thousand new ones, and you have neither peace nor satisfaction. And there is no progress, no relief, because there is no progress in the way in which progress is communicated.

The Business School has become accomplice to another death. The cost of our education is going up. It is at two lives now.

July 8: The intricate, informal network of communication that keeps on functioning, even over the summer, has finally given up the names of those who didn't make it. There are three of them, and you couldn't help but be surprised and saddened when you found out who they are: Steve Blotner, Len Lambeau, Frank Gustin.

Sure, they can try to console themselves by saying: "What I've learned I've learned." But after all that has happened, who cares about the learning? When it wasn't just your brains but all of you that was on trial, every day, every minute you were there. It won't be easy for them to find excuses.

"Frank particularly was in trouble," Allan McGrady says. Allan was our SA rep and he got to see their problems from very close. "It was the type of thing that . . . he cared, yet he didn't care. If that makes any sense. It was a very blasé attitude on his part that made things difficult. He wanted help, yet he was too proud or maybe too desperate to accept it when it was offered. So the work that was needed, I guess, on his part over and above the class sessions, to keep up, just wasn't forthcoming."

Whatever the explanations, the fact is, it has happened—happened to them.

Maybe that's where the message of their defeat lies. That sooner or later the same thing will happen to the rest of us. Where with all the pushing and straining there is no further way to go. Where the higher you get the harder you are going to fall. But you don't want to think about that right now, nor tomorrow, nor ever until it's too late.

15
The Lucky One

KARL HOFFMANN'S *story*

"It was the tenth of April 1958. Because the identity card which I had to carry afterward said April 10.

"I'm not quite sure at what time of the day we came into New York—I have come by boat since and my memories have become a little confused—but we saw the Statue of Liberty and the island of Manhattan with the large buildings. It's very impressive, but I can't say that I had any feelings like this is your new home, or you are leaving a home, or any feelings like that.

"My mother and I had left from Schwäbisch Hall-Hessental, which is a small village of about three thousand people in southern Germany. Schwäbisch Hall is the *Kreisstadt*—the county seat—where Hessental is a small village that is part of this county. I grew up on a farm there that belonged to distant relatives. We got to the farm in 1943 when children of school age were evacuated out of the large cities into camps run by the government. But my parents said they would not let their children go, and they decided to leave with us and that is when we moved to Hessental. I was five years old.

"Hessental is a farm community; well, there is a military airport close by and some people are involved with the airport. There are a few factories in what is considered the "newer part" of the village, but the old village is just a cluster of farmhouses. Part of it is on a hill and some of it is in the flat land, and the church is about halfway between. There are the old *Fachwerkhäuser*—the old timber-frame houses—and the *Misthaufen*—the manure piles—in front of them, and the barns and equipment sheds. There is an *Arbeitersiedlung*—a lower income development—which is about half a mile away, but it still belongs to the village. The majority of the population lives in the Arbeitersiedlung and, subsequent to the war, the expansion of the village occurred in this direction.

"The farmhouse we lived in was about thirty meters from the church, and we could look down toward the church and the village and the main thoroughfare which went this way and that way, winding into town. It was a three-story house with two of the stories being lived in and the third story under the *Giebel*—gable—being used for storage of wheat and apples which, after the harvest, the farmer would want to keep for his own use until wintertime.

"My father died in '44, shortly after we moved to Hessental, so I have just the vaguest recollections of him. He died of TB and he was away in a sanatorium when he died. The reason I remember is because of the way my mother, my sister, and I went to the funeral. The sanatorium was about thirty kilometers away, and we went there on the back of one of these wood-burning trucks which we had during the war. On the way back we took the train, but something like seven kilometers from home, the track had been bombed, and we had to walk, and it was long after midnight when we finally got home.

"My mother worked on the farm and I went to school for eight years, this was *Volksschule*, and after, at age fourteen, I started an apprenticeship as tool- and diemaker. A "die" is usually something from which something else is made. For instance, to make a coin you have to have a device to stamp the impressions. This is called a die. And if you are familiar with a lathe or milling machine—well, for either you need some sort of knife that cuts or machines. These knives—or tools as they are called—are also made by the tool- and diemaker.

"The factory where I took my apprenticeship was in Schwäbisch Hall, which is three kilometers away from Hessental. At that time they had about seven hundred people working there. They put you in a structured learning program for the first year, and after this you would be assigned to a *Geselle*, a journeyman, and would work for him two years, and in the last half year—the apprenticeship was three and a half years—you were on your own.

"As I was nearing the end of the apprenticeship, my sister was able to go to the United States on a student exchange, and she got married in America. She liked it there and I heard about the salaries and I was tempted. I wanted to go, and so it was decided that my mother and I immigrate to the United States.

"We arrived in Havre, Michigan, on a Thursday and the next Monday I went to the employment office with my brother-in-law. I had had some English in school but it was minimal; he helped me fill out this form, and the fellow there called a few people and after half an hour or so he gave me an address to go to. On Wednesday I went there and they wanted me to start right away, and I worked for them till the end of 1958, when I was laid off. They didn't get the next government contract, so they laid off the people with least seniority, and I was out of a job.

I saw an advertisement where a car manufacturer was looking for tool and diemakers, so I drove up there, to nearby Brunswick, and got the job. I worked from twelve midnight till eight in the morning because this is where the openings were. Usually, with the seniority system, the youngest men get the worst shift, and usually the midnight, or 'gravy,' shift is considered the worst. And shortly before the new models came out, actually this was as much as four or five months ahead of it, there was a lot of work preparing the new tools, and we worked overtime a lot, and then I worked from twelve midnight till twelve noon—twelve hours. And when you worked twelve hours, just about all you could do was work, go home, sleep, and go back to work.

"I worked approximately a year at that plant and in between met Uschi. I used to take out one of her girl friends and the way my wife tells it now, this girl friend said: 'There is this fellow coming over again. Why don't you meet him, too, and we all go out together?' Uschi was standing on the veranda of this girl's house, and that's how we met.

"So every weekend, I would be driving from Brunswick back to Havre, and during one of those trips I ran into my former boss who told me that he had so much work that he was again looking for people. I went back to Havre.

"In early '61 I received notice that I had to go for my physical, and for a while I thought of maybe enlisting in the Army and try to get to officer-candidate school which was one way of getting an education. I can recollect how sometimes I had a boring job—as a tool- and diemaker you have jobs where the machine does all the work all day and you just sit there, next to it, without any physical involvement. I remember how I had time to think and daydream, and I guess I came to the conclusion that there must be more to life than sitting next to a machine and being a tool- and diemaker.

"I was thinking of maybe opening up my own little tool shop, although I didn't have the capital by any means. But the more I thought about it, the more I concluded that education, additional education, was the surest road to a more successful life.

"In the meantime, Uschi and I had gotten married, and I was again working night shift to have time, during the day, to check what the possibilities were for further education. If I wanted to work full time and go to school full time, time would be the thing I would have least of. So I decided to try Griswold College, which was just fifteen minutes away, and since the only engineering they had was industrial engineering, I decided to try industrial engineering. They told me that as long as I passed a certain test, I would be allowed to take courses for credit. So I took the test and did fairly well, but I had a lot of difficulties the first semester.

"I had to be on the job by ten at night. So I would get up at eight-thirty—Uschi woke me when dinner was ready and I would eat my meal in a hurry, grab my lunch bag, and not come back till seven in the morning. By that time, Uschi would be up and we would have breakfast together. Uschi then went to work and I would go to school. I'd get through at twelve and on some days at five, and I would rush home and hit the sack till eight when Uschi woke me up again and I would go to work.

"I really had to concentrate very closely on what went on in class because I would have relatively little time to do any homework. It was tough, but you got into a routine after a while and didn't really notice it that much.

"In the meantime, I advanced on the job to shift foreman and then to toolroom foreman until, at the end, I was department head. I had the machine shop under me, which was about seventy people, and I was responsible for the daily running of it—the quoting on new jobs and all those things that go with it. I have to say that by that time, I was working day shift and was taking evening courses. I had most of the course work out of the way, I was in the last or next to last semester and had more time to work. I liked and enjoyed the responsibility, and I asked myself—how can I get more?

"One fellow there, a vice-president, said that if he were me, he would get an M.B.A. And after I checked into it, I decided that I would follow his advice. But each time you mailed out one of those applications, you had to send a check for twenty-five dollars. So I told myself, why don't I try MIT and Harvard first? All they can say is no, and then, one Saturday—I had been out washing the car—there was the acceptance letter from Harvard.

"After that, whenever I talked about it, people said: "Oh! You're going to *Harvard?*" It blew up into a big thing and I began to feel, here you are coming from a little university no one ever heard of, with a record that is just about average or a little above, and you are going out to compete against all these bright individuals from Princeton, Harvard, and Yale. And that fear persisted till the time Art Ruscetta started riding with me to the Business School. He was living out where I lived, and one day, while driving back, I told Art about it. Well, Art was just as worried and it made me think that if Art, having gone to Princeton, has similar fears, maybe there is no need to have any fears at all.

"I don't think—well, I shouldn't say Harvard didn't teach me any specific skills. Because it did. But I think the great thing—or what I would consider the more important thing—is that I will always hear a little voice saying: 'Don't just look at it from the marketing point of view, or the manufacturing point of view, or the people point of view. This is a total entity. It's a bag of worms that's intertwined.'

"In the past I would look at something and say, 'This

is obvious.' Well, Harvard told me that nothing is obvious. Not to take things at face value. Or at the most obvious first answer.

"Uschi and I left Harvard on the day of the last exam, I think it was a Friday. I actually had two examinations that day, one in the morning and one in the afternoon that ended at six. Our plane was to leave at nine. But they told us at the airport that it would be another two hours before take-off. So we had a couple of drinks in a restaurant where we sat with a real gregarious-type fellow who entertained half the room there. He kept saying: 'Aw, have another one. It's on the airline.' And by the time the airplane took off—which was around midnight—we were already flying high."

Set in a ring of wide and busy boulevards on which two rows of cars speed bumper to bumper in both directions as on a giant roller coaster, now diving into tunneled underpasses, now with their engines accelerating, roaring up into daylight, from the Place Sainctelette down Boulevard d'Anvers, going right, into the Boulevard du Régent, sharp right again, up Boulevard du Midi and Boulevard Du 9ᵉ de Ligne, feeding back into the Place Sainctelette; set in dead center of this circular stream, yet quite removed from it, is a jewel of extraordinary and overwhelming beauty. Wrapped into consecutively narrower streets that split and fork as they approach it, filtering out the grosser elements of the heavy traffic, wrapped into an entire city is La Grand-Place—the Great Square.

La Grand-Place is drenched in the smell of sauerkraut, sausage, and fried potatoes that drifts the length of it, splashing up against the gray stone of the surrounding houses. Tall, narrow houses, leaning roof against roof, each bejeweled with such laces of arches, collars of bright little windows, and gilded brooches of massed figurines as to boggle the mind.

On La Grand-Place time, its élan spent on a myriad of beaks, bows, and ringlets, is standing finally and forever still.

The music of silverware clangs from the *petites rues*, their cobblestones ringing with footsteps, their doors, as they are flung open, releasing squalls of voices and the delicious smells of heavy, buttery cooking. Silhouetted against the mellow light, in the little glass squares of the windows, heads are bent over tables and dishes, and above them the steep, triangular gables are awash in the brightest moon. Like a golden, heavily encrusted button, La Grand-Place sits on the fat belly of this city.

The night is getting on and the eaters leave. Loud, quite loud from the wine. Brussels, on a heavy stomach, is going to sleep.

Karl Hoffmann's silver-gray Mercedes turns right and right again into the Marché-aux-Herbes, clattering over cobblestones, across a little deserted square and uphill into the Rue de l'Infante Isabelle, up the Mont des Arts—the hill of the arts—passing along grimly disciplined facades of large, official-looking buildings until the hill begins to level onto Place Royale with its bronze horseman, his metal flag painted by time with a tired green.

The Mercedes swings right, away from the area of the royal palace, into the Rue de la Régence, at the end of which, about half a mile away, there looms a tall structure with two columned wings, the Palais de Justice. Just off the Palais, the Mercedes bursts onto a huge square, Place Louise, where even at this late hour, the Boulevard Waterloo and the Avenue Louise weave thick strands of traffic into one another.

Another half right turn and the Mercedes is heading down Chaussée de Charleroi, with the tram tracks glistening, and now and then the sharp clang of a bell, a tram lumbering around a bend, square, faded, yellow boxes with a large number on top and a listing of the destination.

Beyond Place Ma Champagne, the Chaussée de Charleroi becomes Avenue Bruggmann and widens considerably. Karl steps on it and the Mercedes shoots forward, with intersections becoming less numerous, the tall, flat-fronted office buildings disappearing altogether. A solid wall of two-story houses now lines the road, stretching from intersection to intersection, each house with its characteristic tall door. Another square, another couple of turns, and the Mercedes pulls over in front of a newer apartment building.

An elaborate aluminum-glass door ushers into a lobby with aluminum letter boxes sunk into the wall. There is a house telephone, and across from the letter boxes, straw flowers bathe in a beam of orange light—it's all the pomp and demonstration of well-being with which European bourgeois try to give permanence to their tenuous membership in the upper social classes.

Karl and Uschi live on the ground floor in two small rooms, adjoined by a kitchen and a bathroom. A three-seater couch takes up about a third of the living room, which is not big enough for a good-sized table. There are two modernish lamps and two glass and steel coffee tables. Karl is a little embarrassed—they only have bought the necessary, so far. Outside, a heavy rumble, then the clanging of a tram. Upstairs, the brick walls seem to amplify it; someone is practicing a romantic melody on the piano. From the light, waltzing, yet melancholy sound, it could be Chopin.

"The first month and a half on the job I was just
reading catalogues. I was trying to familiarize myself
with the products and to get an idea where we were,
what was being planned in terms of budget and strategy.
I was sitting at my desk and would study, study, and study.

"I was working for the vice-president, manufacturing;
the company, an American company, has a dozen plants
in Europe, and I dealt with six of these whenever there

were manufacturing questions. But now the vice-president I worked for is back in the U.S., and his department doesn't exist any more.

"It had become obvious in early December that there were apt to be changes. Profits were off severely and someone in New York was bound to notice. On the third of December there was an official announcement that the president of the European operation had resigned and along with him the executive vice-president in the States to whom this first man reported. Around the fifteenth, the new team arrived, and I was told there is some interest on the part of the new man—would I talk to him and see if I would like to work with him? Well, almost from the moment we sat down at the table it was clear to me that we wouldn't be able to work together; I felt there were some mistakes being made and I was very outspoken. After that, it was just a matter of deciding on mutually agreeable termination benefits, which came to seven months' pay or about $12,000, after tax.

"I now have accepted an offer from an American with a plant in Stuttgart, which fits in well with my plans. Because once a man has proven that he can run something —a plant or company—it's just a step to running something on a Pan-European scale.

"Now, as to my other ambitions, I am quite confident that I will have a decent living, an almost carefree living for the rest of my life. Not that I will live like Onassis or a playboy or anything like that. But a good middle-class existence. With an apartment or house, depending on where we are and what is available. And be able to go to the opera or play skat with the boys. Really, I have no great ambitions as far as becoming a social leader. I just kind of want to be my own man.

"Looking back on the last several years, I'm very

satisfied and I am kind of proud of myself. Not just of myself—I couldn't have done it without Uschi. She had to work. We had to borrow money. In one stretch, she didn't buy a new dress for two years in a row. So, all in all, I think Uschi and I should be proud of our accomplishment. I view it as an accomplishment, quite frankly. And it feels good.

"A lot of people, when you talk with them, say: 'Oh, you are lucky.' But I think it's being prepared for the luck. Some people sit in Schwäbisch Hall-Hessental or in Havre, Michigan, with a record as good, or better than mine, who would never think of putting in an application to Harvard. Now, is it luck? Or is it that they are not accepted at Harvard because they never made an attempt to be? I am saying, the people who usually are referred to as lucky people, I think they do something about it. They do something to help that luck along."

When he died of a heart failure on February 9, 1973, Karl Hoffmann had become general manager of a plant in northern Germany, with authority over the work of ninety people and over more machinery than the number of people would indicate. He had started a minor miracle there and his future was so obviously bright and promising that nothing could stop him, except death.

II

The Great Opportunity

SEPTEMBER TO JULY OF THE SECOND YEAR

1
Mixed Feelings

September 5: Summer was a great time. Perhaps because, after the first year, it couldn't help but be a great time. But already the papers are full of football previews and, in the streets outside the dormitories, the moving vans with their tailgates wide open dump the jumbled pieces of living rooms and bedrooms onto the hot sidewalks. Registration Day is just beyond the next weekend and with every guy you meet, the rumors multiply like little white rabbits.

There are rumors that the second year is going to be a breeze and that nobody in his right mind ever flunked out of second year at the Harvard Business School. But there also are rumors that say exactly the opposite; that everybody is going to have to work their balls off, with recruiting, the prospect of six courses in the fall and five in the spring and, of course, the research report—a kind of master's thesis required by the Business School.

There are rumors that you don't have to talk in class if you don't want to, and everybody seems to know a guy who didn't say a word all his second year.

There are people rumors, about people having had babies, people having gotten married, and about amazing things some people supposedly have done during the summer. But there are also scary rumors; that a certain professor whose course you have signed up for has a habit of nailing people to the wall; that courses for which you have registered are real backbreakers.

And before you know it, you feel the old lump in the stomach because, rumor or no rumor, the Harvard Business School just isn't the sort of place where you hang around for a year, enjoying yourself. While it may not be anything like the first, the second year is going to be no picnic.

September 12: On the surface, Registration Day was as dry and busy as its name promised. There were tables spaced throughout the hallway on the second floor of Aldrich, and there were long lines of people waiting to be processed. Groups of friends were waiting together, and as you went through the checking and rechecking, you ran into a lot of people from the Section. There were great boisterous hellos and it made you feel good to see some of these guys again, because with all the things you didn't know about the second year, here were some faces, some people you did know, and they gave you a place to start from and perhaps a place to retreat to, if the lump in your stomach got a little bit too heavy.

But if you were honest with yourself, you didn't really feel all that good even about seeing the people you liked. Because from today on, they would again become the standard against which you would have to prove yourself. Only now you knew how good some of these guys are, how hard they drive themselves, and how difficult they are to beat.

September 15, Monday: It's exactly thirty steps from the first to the second floor of Aldrich but to climb them takes an entire year. Today our class officially arrived on the second floor.

Naturally, you had been on the second floor before. When the Coke machines didn't work downstairs, or when all the alcoves were taken. But those visits had always left you feeling conspicuous and slightly silly, like being a tourist in a very foreign place. This morning seemed to change that perspective once and for all. You were looking down on them now, onto the sullen first-year crowd, as their hands brushed along the wooden railing, reaching—some timidly, some brashly—for the door into the first year.

Why, the view of downtown Boston was so much better from up here. It was a proud moment, the consummation of a triumph that had begun an instant earlier, as you had stepped out of the stream of first-year men to continue upward, taking their envious glances as a sort of grudging homage, shaking off their stares by leaping upward, lightly and happily, taking two or three steps at once.

Yet, as you reflected on the magnitude of your achievement, it was as if the snap produced by the closing of each classroom door, as if each pinnacle of the wild growth of downtown office towers punched a little hole into your inflated ego. Before you knew it, all that pride and triumph and even the sweet thoughts of revenge, had blown away with an inaudible hiss.

September 18: The mood is quite a bit more grown-up in a second-year classroom. You no longer need a prepared speech, every time you want to say something. You still *have* to speak up but in many courses, the professors are content to rely on volunteers, rather than forcing people.

The main difference is that you are no longer part of a Section. In every class it's a different gallery of faces—sometimes only twenty, sometimes a hundred or more, depending on the reputation of the professor and the popularity of the course. You meet too many people to remember more than a few exceptionally able or exceptionally obnoxious ones. The brilliant argument you just made, the next class won't know or care about, and if you blundered, in ninety minutes at most you will get a brand-new chance. Things don't sink in as they did when you always spoke before the same people. It leaves you less vulnerable; you are more of a private person now.

You're no longer in that constant state of alert that made you prepare for way-out eventualities that never occur; for enemies that exist only in your imagination. You have learned to economize your moves.

"There is no one person that can prepare a case so that he can include all possibilities or account for all possibilities," Fred Laratti says. "Someone is always going to bring up a point that you haven't considered. And that's sort of frightening because you like to have a firm base and argue from there. But I discovered, you know, not all people are absolutely brilliant at all times. Not all people are absolutely prepared at all times. And as I grow more aware of other people's strengths and weaknesses, I'm becoming, let's say, more objective about my own."

September 22: Today's BP (Business Policy) case raised a very fundamental sort of question. The "what-business-are-we-in-what-business-should-we-go-into" question. The company, a successful ski manufacturer, was wondering where they should go from here. Are they in the ski, the ski-equipment, or the sporting-goods business? How do you answer a question like that?

The class—BP is the only required class in the second year—worked out two answers. Call them the bird and the squirrel approach to business planning.

Under the *bird approach,* you start with the entire world, scanning it for opportunities to seize upon, and you try to make the best of what you will find. In this approach you resemble a bird, searching for a branch to land on, in a large tree. You will see more opportunities than you can think of; you will have an almost unlimited choice. But your decision, because you can't stay up in the air forever, is likely to be arbitrary and because arbitrary, it will be risky.

Under the *squirrel approach,* you start with yourself and your company: where you are at with the skills, the experience you have; with what you can do best. In this approach you will resemble a squirrel climbing that same large tree. But now you are starting at the trunk, from familiar territory, working your way up cautiously, tree fork by tree fork, deciding at each on the branch that suits you best. You will only have one or two alternatives to choose from at a time, but your decision, because it is made on a limited number of options, is likely to be more informed and less risky.

In contrast to the bird who makes single big decisions, the squirrel makes many small ones. The squirrel may never become aware of some of the opportunities the bird sees, but he is more likely to know where he is going.

September 23: The case in Cost Administration brought back some key MERC I terms: variable vs. fixed cost, full vs. direct cost. It was surprising how clear, how useful, those terms had become. Looked at from the distance of the second year, they all kind of fell into place.

The second year is the real opportunity at the Harvard Business School. You get to take a second look at all the stuff that has been shoved down your throat; that still turns in your stomach undigested. You have time to let the loose jumble of buzz words settle into a coherent pattern. In the first year you learn; in the second you're beginning to understand.

October 1: Justin Butterworth is one of the greatest professors at the Harvard Business School. He must be close to six feet tall. Butterworth—or JB, as he is called by those who claim the honor of having gotten to know him—has the most extraordinary reputation. He had so many people show up for his first class in the fall that they filled up the extra chairs in the rear and even the stairs down to his desk and they would have sat on the window sills if there had been windows.

Justin Butterworth's reputation is one of the few things at the Business School that you don't argue about and if you do argue, it is by repeating after everybody else how truly great the great Butterworth is.

In typical JB fashion, his first class had begun long before the first students ever got there. It was like walking in at half time, with people milling about, and Butterworth busy, filling up the blackboard, showing the class the back of his well-tailored suit and a well-trimmed, clean back of the head with its straight black, meticulously combed hair. He filled the board with neat, formally lettered instructions. He wanted you to do this and he expected you to do that. And he left no doubt that he knew what was good for you.

He has a very economical face, the great Butterworth, with no spare bulges and extra curves, but with wrinkles over some of the sharp edges like the back of a book that's been opened a great many times. His is a face that can laugh only with its mouth and he has three or four gestures that come up so regularly and expectedly that you keep seeing them as special gestures, rather than as part of added emphasis.

He never, he said, has missed a class in something like the last fifteen years (and he never missed any when some of Section B got to be his students). In brief, Butterworth's world was orderly and because of it, very easy to get bored with. So there was a lot of busy work to keep everybody jumping, and the pile of work gave many people the feeling that they were accomplishing a good deal.

It was a classic case of self-confirming prophecy. Everybody expected Butterworth to be great and rather than admit to themselves that they might be mistaken, there was no occurrence trivial enough, no pronouncement too superficial that they didn't profess to see some deep meaning in. It was strange to see this supposedly famous man mistake his faith in a couple of arbitrary answers as proof that they must be the final truth. But it was even stranger to see so many supposedly well-trained minds leave the great Butterworth with the illusion that he was right.

October 3: The war won't let the political wounds of last spring heal. Now the nationwide moratorium scheduled for October 15 is threatening to open them wider than ever, because yesterday and today, a group calling itself the Harvard Business School Vietnam Peace Committee has been circulating a petition that is going to raise a lot of conservative eyebrows:

> We, students at the Harvard Business School, oppose further United States military involvement in the war in Vietnam. Our government has shown itself time and again unwilling to extricate itself from a fight which has never been ours. It has thus demonstrated a remarkable insensitivity to the wishes of many millions of Americans representing virtually every segment of our society. This constitutes in our belief a clear abdication of governmental responsibility that seriously impairs the ability of the United States to act effectively in its domestic crisis.
>
> We therefore call upon the leaders of our private sector to marshal every resource, exercise every pressure, and implement every lawful means to make our government stop this war. We urge the leaders of industry and finance to take these steps in the long-run interest of the free enterprise system and of all Americans.
>
> (x number of) Students
> Harvard Business School
> Boston, Massachusetts

October 7: According to stories making the rounds this morning, the Peace Committee's petition has been an unexpected success. There was talk that a third of the student body signed it and that the press was informed yesterday morning.

The stories must be true because this afternoon there was an angry reaction. Copies of a telegram appeared on the bulletin boards of Aldrich:

PRESIDENT RICHARD M NIXON
THE WHITE HOUSE, WASHINGTON, D.C.

RECENTLY A SMALL GROUP OF HARVARD BUSINESS SCHOOL STUDENTS, CALLING THEMSELVES THE HARVARD BUSINESS SCHOOL VIETNAM PEACE COMMITTEE CIRCULATED A STATEMENT OF POLICY. 500 PEOPLE REPORTEDLY SIGNED THIS STATEMENT. THIS SMALL GROUP HAS TAKEN THE 500 SIGNATURES AS A MANDATE TO REPRESENT THE ENTIRE HARVARD BUSINESS SCHOOL COMMUNITY OF 2600. THIS IS WRONG.

THIS SAME SMALL GROUP GAVE THE PRESS ONLY PART OF THE STATEMENT MISREPRESENTING THEIR SELF-PROCLAIMED MANDATE.

A GREAT MAJORITY OF THE HARVARD BUSINESS SCHOOL COMMUNITY INDICATED THEIR DISAGREEMENT BY NOT SIGNING THE STATEMENT. SOME WHO DID SIGN DISAGREE WITH ITS USE. WE, REPRESENTATIVE OF THIS MAJORITY, WISH THE AMERICAN PUBLIC, THE ADMINISTRATION AND THE AMERICAN BUSINESS COMMUNITY TO KNOW THAT WE SUPPORT CURRENT EFFORTS TOWARDS PEACE IN VIETNAM.

THE COMMITTEE OF CONCERN
HARVARD BUSINESS SCHOOL

October 15, Moratorium Day: A sight to behold. Some three hundred future captains, majors, and generals of industry demonstrating in the street! They had assembled on North Harvard Street around 10 A.M., at first milling about self-consciously, looking at what everybody else would do, until groups had begun forming, growing, flowing together behind a banner reading: "Harvard 'B' for Peace."

As far as you could see, the street was filled with straight-looking types, many wearing jackets and ties, some marching stiffly as if leading troops in parade. Terner couldn't help feeling ridiculous and conspicuous in this strange procession. Here, he was learning that the way to solve problems is to solve them, and not to talk and philosophize. That you've got to discipline your thoughts, establish objectives and priorities, and develop a plan of action. Yet, here he was, not reasoning, not developing any plan of action, not doing anything but putting himself on display amid a mass of like-minded bodies. It seemed silly and primitive and unprofessional.

The people in the ranks ahead and behind were either solemn or else talking hectically, as if to block out bothersome reality. Terner, returning the stares of the people on the sidewalk, felt closely watched, almost on trial. He had fears that his presence was somehow recorded and entered into his dossier as a black mark that cast him once and for all as an "extremist" unfit to command.

But what else but this was left to do? What but to go on strike, to shut down as much as possible of America, Inc.? What could you do if the big boss didn't listen to disciplined thought? Didn't want any part of priorities? Didn't care for well-thought-out plans of action? What could you say to a man who, after years of killing and destruction without any perceptible impact, still persists in his lonely, futile ways? Who for reasons of foolish pride cannot get himself to end the agony?

Why didn't we, Terner thought in a blink of sarcasm, have any cases on *that?*

October 16: Today's *HarBus News* ("Serving the Harvard Business School Community") confirms that 508 of 1,500 M.B.A.s have signed the Peace Committee's petition. One hundred and thirty-three have signed an even more strongly worded petition which condemns the United States "for the systematic attacks against the Vietnamese people, the indiscriminate destruction of defenseless villages and the ruination of the countryside . . ." Their opposition, the signers of this second petition say, "does not lie in 'practical' arguments of economic expediency. Our opposition is rooted in our moral conviction that the war is a grave crime against humanity . . ."

October 24: The Moratorium Day controversy is ending on an almost comical note. The evening the Peace Committee had released the results of its petition, the president of the SA had called several newspapers, telling them that the signatures on the petition might not be valid, or if valid might have been obtained by devious means. The declared neutrality of the SA had lasted only until it became apparent that the Peace Committee was going to have a greater impact than expected and that it dared to carry our political squabbles outside our windowless walls. Pressured by a loose congregation of hawks and conservatives, the SA president sprung into action on behalf of what he perceived to be the school's silent majority.

Ironically, when the school's majority finally did speak up, yesterday, through the full assembly of its elected representatives, it turned against its supposed benefactor, "admonishing" the SA president for having unnecessarily extended the powers of his office.

Some silent majority!

November 7, Friday: In place of the WACs, BP reports on various aspects of corporate planning are due every second or third week. They are read by girls like the WAC readers except that the girls who read the BP reports are called BP readers. And they are due during, not at the end of, the week. So, no more Saturday deadlines; no more post-mortems at the Pub.

For two days every weekend, it's to hell with the Raston Manufacturing Company, Inc., and all the marketing, finance, and any other kind of unspeakable problems it may have.

November 7, evening:

(BEN DAVIDSON *talking*)

"Guys go to Father George or Furlinger's and I must say that I've been to Father George several times and I've been to Furlinger's a couple of times in the first year. I guess, if you did an analysis of my dating-bar habits, you'd find that they are—that the dating bar is only a necessary evil for me. I don't function too well in that kind of an environment—noisy, with the band playing and crowded. That's not the way I like to meet people. But some guys keep going. You know, they have a contingent, people like Kandel. He just loves dating bars. He goes there all the time.

"When I am with Gail we sometimes go to a place called 'Two Onions'. A lot of Business School kids go there. It's a beer-and-peanuts place, banjo music, you know, and sing-along. It's a pretty good place. And sometimes we have a party in our room. We'll invite people, some of our neighbors in the dorm, and have some wine and cheese and hot dogs. We'll give a few of those, and other people have them and invite us. Whatever you do, because there isn't much time, you appreciate every minute of it.

"So far, second year is turning out to be a diving year and . . . rightly so, I guess. We've lost some of the fun and sharing that we've had as a Section. Still, nothing like being a bachelor at the Business School. Because, you know, you are a big commodity in a great town with—in the second year—you've got time. You've got everything going for you."

November 19: Of twelve alumni classes recently surveyed by the Alumni Program Office (all of them ten or more years out):

> Half the graduates responding have a total annual income (salary plus other income) of about $30,000 or more.
>
> One out of ten has a total annual income of $70,000 or more.
>
> In ten classes, every second man is worth at least $100,000 in total assets (securities, real estate, cars, etc.).
>
> Every class has at least one millionaire.
>
> In eight classes, approximately every tenth man has become a millionaire.

These statistics may suffer from the same syndrome Professor Keeler once described typical of Business School reunions—namely, that since only the successful dare report, the number of those reporting from each class gets fewer and fewer. But even if you discount the figures by this factor, they look reassuring.

So, unless we foolishly ignore MERC I, MERC II, marketing, and all the rest of it, we can pretty much count on a comfortable life with enough cash to buy protection from the more common forms of violence, good schooling for the kids, and just the right distance to the pollution from the city.

November 25: Stripped to a couple of thumbtacks, the bulletin boards in the West End of Baker Library languish beige and barren all through the summer and early fall—an intended, wanton void, a threatening nothing sizing you up through a million sneaky little thumbtack holes. But when the leaves finally come down from the trees, other leaves go up on those boards; the white, double-spaced variety, crowded with words that are disciplined by harsh white spaces into obedient blocks of type.

There is a slow, predictable growth to these notices, beginning the first day of the school year, down on the first floor, on the board with the heading "Part-Time." Spreading upward, where the stair goes into its first right-hand turn, they appear on the boards marked "Second Year Correspondence Opportunities," creating a traffic jam that leaves no doubt that the recruiting season is about to start, that the first job offers are in.

Some of those offers are terse, unfriendly requests: "Our company has an opening for an Assistant Portfolio Manager in our Investment Department." Nothing more. Scribbled on the bottom of this message a sarcastic answer: "Thanks!"

Strange things are asked: "Must be a leader . . . honest and willing to work hard."

Great things are promised: ". . . in case of proven ability, he will gradually take over the position of general manager."

". . . opportunity to immediately contribute . . ."

". . . broad exposure to corporate structure . . ."

The money? Most offers discreetly leave that question open.

Soon the notices will grow across December to fill the wall to where the stairs go into another right-hand turn. By January they will have reached the next turn and yet another turn where the boards are divided into the five workdays of the week. "Second Year Interviews at HBS" says the caption.

The recruiting season hasn't really begun yet. But the signs of it coming are on the walls.

December 17: After the first class on the Great Loom Textile Corp., in Marketing Management II, we were dead convinced that what this company is pursuing, is a lousy marketing strategy.

Well, we come out of next day's class wondering whether their strategy isn't, after all, a good strategy. And that their financial manipulations are really helping the long-range marketing effort.

So, a couple of days ago—now this is still the series of Great Loom cases—we try a different angle. This time we look at how, to what end, Great Loom is organized. Now maybe *that* tells us something about the sort of strategy they are pursuing. But the evidence is inconclusive. Some elements indicate sound, classical marketing; others, a strong financial orientation and that this company isn't interested in marketing at all.

Three times now Professor Wilson has let the discussion take what seemed a decisive turn. And everytime that gets us back to where we started.

Well, this morning, a guy wants to know why a marketing strategy can't have a financial orientation. "You people keep saying, this strategy is financially oriented. So it can't be a marketing strategy. Well, what do you know! *What really is a marketing strategy?*"

What is it? The guy is right—what is it? Here we've been going on and on about marketing strategy, and we're passing all kinds of judgment, and it turns out we really don't know what we are talking about. The guy's question pulls the plug on the whole argument. All of a sudden, the big-talking "experts" are trying to hide behind their name cards, and the room is filled with meek and modest people wondering how they could be such fools.

It may sound crazy, but low moments like these are true highs in a Harvard Business School education. Being given a chance not just to *make* a mistake, but to *discover* and *understand* it. And by understanding it, *to become your own redeemer*. To turn a potential waste of time and energy into a dramatic, exhilarating gain of experience. And to walk away not as the fool you were but as the brilliant thinker you are.

There is the reason for Professor Wilson's fame as a case teacher; there, in fact, is the secret of the whole case method. Giving people a chance to run into any trap they care to, and not to push them in deeper through punishment; or yank them out with misguided helpfulness, before they've had a chance to figure out how to avoid having the same thing happen to them again. Helping them only where they want to be helped and, even then, only helping them to help themselves.

The difference between traditional learning and case learning is like that between eating a cream puff and having someone tell you about it. The difference is between an event and an experience. And because experiences are full and complex things, most schools and teachers never make an effort to create them. Instead they go the clean, efficient way, reducing experience to a "problem," which is nothing but a bunch of words, and an "appropriate solution," which is nothing but more words. And two weeks afterward you can't remember a thing.

To be fair, you have to admit that even with the best case, the best case teacher, and the sharpest students, a true experience in a classroom is an almost unattainable goal. Even under the best possible conditions, the thing may fall flat. It may be that the food at lunch was bad, or one of the lamps in the classroom isn't burning, or it's too hot, or too cold, or too something. Even with the case method, it's rare to have a class like today's where you didn't need to do all the scribbling in your notebook, because what you experienced is imprinted in your mind for all time.

So, more often than not, case classes struggle along, reaching many little peaks but no real climax. But, at least, they are little peaks, and not the void, flat nothing of so many lectures.

"Really, the content of what the Business School has to offer," Wendy Burgess says afterward to Al Terner, "is just distilled common sense. The idea of how to approach a problem, of weighing the alternatives, examining your environment—all these things, no matter what you do, are useful. Even in running your own life.

"I think," she says, "the two years are giving me confidence that's underneath initiating problem-solving behavior. You know, not just to question but to *need* a solution. Wanting to come to an answer. That kind of attitude has a lot of implications on how you live your life, and what you do and how you react; whether you accept your environment or whether you try to change it.

"*I* think," she says, "the two years are giving me confidence that plain old common sense can do a lot to change the world. You come out with a feeling of . . . yes, if you just want to, there is nothing you can't do."

2
Strategies for Success

The question of a job and the fact that graduation is only six months away are forcing people to think about their long-range objectives

SIDNEY O'MARA, *twenty-nine, married, B.S., M.S.E.E., University of Kansas, previous job: sales, Mersham Alloys, Inc. (four years).*

"The kind of life style I like is one in which there isn't too much structure, formality, status. You know, I don't have an eight-ply rug on the floor and all sorts of things on the wall, and I don't have mahogany furniture, and I don't dress in a Brooks Brothers suit. That's not the style of the company I'm going to work for; it's not my style.

"I'm going back to the people I worked for previously, partially out of a moral commitment, partially in return for certain remunerations, shall we say. The company is very 'free form' or whatever you want to call it. If I decided to quit and gave the reason that it just wasn't the type of work I wanted to do, I'm sure the guy I'm going to work for would understand. If I wanted to get involved politically, I probably could do so without too much static on the job.

"I mean, how much better can you really be sure of what to throw yourself into, when you've known people for four years? When you know the company intimately, know which direction to take, and what type of job you might be able to create? There aren't a heck of a lot of times in a person's life when he has that much information about something and feels good about it.

"I'll be making $18,000 a year plus fringe benefits. Which is not a terribly exorbitant amount, given New York City. I'll never get rich from the money I make in terms of salary. Very few people, I think, do. So, you know, I'll probably coast at around $18,000 to $20,000 for the next couple of years. And if I go on in a normal way of doing things, maybe I'll be a division manager or maybe a vice-president by the time I'm forty, forty-five, or fifty. And, you know, at those levels you're certainly making out. You make in the sixty-thou range. But, even there, you're not gonna really get rich off your salary.

"If I wanted to be rich, I wouldn't do some of the things I'm going to be doing. Like living in Manhattan. I most certainly don't spend money foolishly, but there is a certain strategy a person follows if he wants to accumulate money. And that's too big a price to pay. I really don't feel I can be bothered with that right now. I'm sure if I would want to get rich, I would save money and would start investing and be worried about that. Sort of these anal fixations some bankers have. I think, you know, I'm *not* oriented in that direction.

"If somebody asked where am I going to be fifty years from now, I guess I'd have to say, that beats the hell out of me. Dead, probably of pollution. I don't really know. I have always thought of myself as being very independent. I've always entertained the thought of having my own business. And it's one of the advantages of this job that it is going to afford me an opportunity to gain management experience at a very low risk. Experience I can translate later into running my own company. You know, that's my father when he left Ireland saying: 'Well, I plan to go to the United States and work there for ten years and then come back and enjoy Ireland.' He never went back.

"So, really, fifty years is a long time. It's like asking a guy when he is twelve what he wants to do when he is thirty. Not very many people still want to be a farmer when they grow up."

DAVE KEARNEY, *twenty-seven, married (two children), B.S., Carnegie Institute of Technology, M.S., Pennsylvania State, previous job: plant engineer, Willard Elevator Corp. (two years).*

"Like the typical Business School student, I want to start at the top.

"It has to be something where I am out there, at the line. I want to get a chance of running people. And it has to be something that is exceptionally challenging. I don't want to be just another nice guy. I want something I can work hard at, something that makes a lot of sense to me. But I guess I also want something where you can get some money back. You know, really win it, money-wise. Roughly twenty K plus a stock option.

"I guess I want to make it quick. I want to be able to be the head of a company at a young age. You know, working long, long hours in a big company, working up the corporate ladder slowly—I guess no Business School student really wants to do that. I don't want to wait around for five years and then take a chance. Where, when the stakes are there, the guy above me grabs them and runs.

"I don't think I have any long-range objectives beyond what I've already said. I know that sounds strange, but I think the biggest thing is flexibility. I want to be able to do what I want in fifteen years. I don't know what that'll be, but it's always been very important to me to be able to pick up at a moment's notice.

"I never thought I had any clear-cut material requirements. And I still don't, really. For example, I drive a '61 Corvair. Sometimes it occurs to me that I should be proud of driving a '61 Corvair, but sometimes it seems kind of . . . you know, a lower class type of thing. Especially my Corvair because it's all banged up.

"So, materialism doesn't bother me too much. Except that I like to wear nice clothes. I have no time schedule for anything, no schedule at all, except ASAP—As Soon as Possible."

FRANK CHARVIS, *twenty-nine, married (one child), B.S., mechanical engineering, University of Pennsylvania, previous job: marketing-executive, North American Steel Inc. (five years)*.

"Every corporate environment has some kind of personality. And the bigger the company, the harder that personality is to find. Which is why, in any kind of large company, you are better off to go in at staff level and work with the executives who run the various departments. Not so much because you have exposure to them, although that's certainly a positive aspect to it, but because you find out what's going on within the organization, where the critical needs are.

"Quite frankly, and maybe this sounds kind of dismal or black in a way, but how do you exploit situations that you run into? Some people are going to block your way like crazy. How are you gonna get around them? How are you gonna capitalize on opportunities without walking all over everybody else?

"You know, what are the ethics? Operationally speaking,

what do you do? You are gonna make bucks—*that's* what you will do. Because that's what everyone else does. Because that's what the people you're trying to impress do. No matter how long you talk about it, you're always gonna get down to the nitty-gritty reality of making bucks.

"Now whether making bucks is correct or not, it's—let's put it this way, if you're not the head of the corporation, you've got to face the reality that there is little else you can do.

"Minority employment, social responsibility—it's not bad to talk about these things. But you've got to respond to the system, otherwise you just run into a blank wall. What I'm getting at is that organizations, specially large organizations, which are merrily going along their way, making money, being quite successful; these organizations aren't gonna change for the sake of change; they aren't going to change until the pressures on them become so great that they *have* to change. And I'm not sure, if I were running something, that I wouldn't take kind of a risk-averse attitude too and say: 'Well, I'm gonna keep the status quo going, because I will make a profit and they will keep me in my position.'"

ROBERT CHASEY III, *twenty-two, bachelor, A.B., economics, Dartmouth College, no previous working experience except summer jobs.*

"I expect to have a family, and I just may wind up living in suburbia, which is something I don't find repulsive as many people do. I'm looking to fill, eventually, some sort of general management position in a large company. And when I say a profitable company, I have to qualify that because it seems to me that the role of the business firm is going through an evolutionary process. In the past there was such an emphasis on growth and capital accumulation. I don't see that as the pervading role of the corporation any more—at least, it's going to be reduced in importance.

"Prior to Business School, I was involved in the Boy Scouts, things like this—which I feel is doing my part to . . . you know, it sounds kind of corny, but to make the world a little bit a better place. I take that very, very seriously and, looking at the people coming from the Business School, I feel they had an opportunity and, consequently, they've got a responsibility. I feel that, you know, some of these people are gonna be running the world, or at least the country, and that it is their responsibility, not just to go out and make a big salary for themselves, but to try and do something for . . . I guess for the community they live in. That's kind of a general way of putting it, but it's really hard to be specific. I can't say that I want to start a minority business program or something like that. But, you know, it's important to me to feel useful. And I don't feel useful just because I have made a dollar."

FRED LARATTI, *twenty-two, bachelor, A.B., business administration, University of New Hampshire, no previous working experience other than summer jobs.*

"A job is going to be interesting if it's something where I can go and *do* something. Something I can say: 'Well, yeah, this is what I did. You can take it and throw it out the window or do anything you want. But I did it.' Something where a lot of money can be saved, a lot of improvements can be made. OK? These are things I can at least project. You know, I can say this is something to strive for.

"I could do accounting, consolidating monthly forecasts. Well, that doesn't, you know, it doesn't do anything for me. Anybody can consolidate forecasts.

"I'm not sure I'm the type who likes to sit behind a desk and, month after month, for a period of one year, two years, whatever period, and each month you find that you're doing the same thing. Different information comes in, but you're doing the same thing. You get in a groove and you do it and you do it. I don't see how you can evaluate a man doing that kind of job. I'm sure that the man's boss does evaluate him. But I don't see on what he is being evaluated. Whether he has a nice smile? I mean, this guy is doing the same thing. He is doing the same thing and after three months he gets good at it. And after three months just about everybody gets good at it. So I like things to change. I like my job, the content of my job to change. I like to see different aspects of a company.

"I'm not very good at asking the standard questions. Where am I gonna be five years from now? Who do you have to know to get ahead? Truthfully, these things don't concern me much. A job does. That I'm doing it well does. Beyond that? There are too many other things to worry about, beyond that.

"I'm pretty sure I don't want to work for a small company. A small company seems to me more of a make-it or break-it situation. Well, that's very bold and daring but I'm just not that type of guy. Maybe I'm afraid of breaking it. Maybe I need a little security. And maybe I don't think I am that good to risk everything. In a large company you don't necessarily get the titles as fast but the money is there, the benefits are there, and an opportunity to control and affect more people and more money than you'll ever see in a small company. You don't get a title but you get responsibility.

RICHARD LINDSAY, *twenty-four, bachelor, A.B., history, Amherst College, previous job: credit analyst, Massachusetts Savings & Loan Assoc.* (*one year*).

"My only point of direction derives from the fact that I am continually dissatisfied with what I have. I wish I had more time, which is sort of silly right now. And when I had enough time, earlier, I didn't have enough money. It seems that I'm always fighting something, there are always constraints somewhere.

"Material requirements? That's so situational. Because, for one thing, I'm considering going into the Peace Corps. I could see where that might be an interesting-enough experience that I wouldn't be too concerned about the standard of living. I think I could stand being poor for a time when I know that it's going to be, you know, that I'm doing it for a particular reason.

"Before I came to the Business School, I used to have some sort of a framework set up, what kind of life I wanted to lead, but I decided: There's too many variables. I don't need to chart that close a course. Because, no matter what happens to me, I always seem to end up doing something that's beneficial, that's worthwhile, and interesting. And so, when you have this kind of an experience, that's not really conducive to a lot of forward planning."

ALLAN MCGRADY, *twenty-eight, bachelor, B.S., mathematics, Yale, previous job: systems analyst, Datamesh, Inc.* (*three years*).

"At some point, I would like to take over the operation of a small, technically oriented company. I don't care whether it's electronics or machine tools or whatever. A typical small company, started by a bunch of engineers; that, because business was successful, got to a certain plateau and now has all kinds of trouble getting somebody to run it.

"One of the reasons why I want to run my own company is that, like most of us at the school, I'm not really a nine-to-fiver. And working for someone else, with certain exceptions, you almost have to be, because other people are counting on you. You got to be there. You know, your phone is ringing and you've got to pick it up and answer.

"Running your own show, particularly a smaller company, gives you the latitude to expand yourself as a person. I first came across this working for Datamesh. I was dealing with one customer, Christ, he ran a diaper service. You know, his place didn't look like it was much bigger than a one-family house. But that diaper service provided him with enough money that he spent one week at his business and two weeks on his yacht. You know, he had that thing down so cold that all he had to do was come in, every now and then, sign a few checks, call the bank, and talk to his people. Now that might be a little bizarre but it's the kind of thing I'm talking about. You never can do that, working for somebody else.

"I've been spending a lot of time, this past year, thinking about, you know: I've been breaking my back for years, no vacations and working hard and late hours. Why? Now why? Why am I doing this? All of a sudden you look back and say, I've just shot my best years!

"I think it's unnecessary to tell you *what* I would do with my extra time. I mean, right now, I might play more tennis. The key thing is—I would do whatever I want to do more of.

"Now how do I get there?

"As a first step, I'm looking for a company that has a certain amount of *esprit de corps*. A company that is excited about its product and its industry. Where I can get experience in bringing new products to the market, in the manufacturing, the finance, the pricing end of it. A cross-functional job that exposes me to a lot of areas. I am looking for an environment where I think I can be used, where I can make a contribution, and where I am needed. And when I say needed, that means on a personal as well as on a technical basis. You know, it's where I kind of enjoy the people I'm around. Now if I go into a place and, clearly, the interpersonal relationship with them is bad; if I can see that I just don't mesh with anybody, then that isn't even a candidate. All right?

"Well, once I've lined up my candidates, then money is the key factor. My strategy is to accept the highest paying offer I get, unless we're talking about just a small difference. Number one because, when the time comes for a raise, raises are normally a percentage of your base. Number two because, if you leave that company in a couple of years, you'll leave it at a higher base. And three, which I think is most important, because the more a company pays you, the less chance there is that you get a crummy job. If they are paying you twelve thousand, they can afford to let you sit in a corner for a while. If they are paying you twenty, now they start to worry about: 'What is this guy doing for us? How is he justifying that salary we're paying him?'

"The guys who try to buy me off cheap with promises, they are just going to stick me into a very routine, dirty job. And that's fine, but, you know, that's not what I want coming out of the Business School. I'm not interested in promises."

KEITH KUROWSKI, *twenty-five, bachelor, B.S., M.S., chemical engineering, Massachusetts Institute of Technology, previous job: research engineer, Lenox Pharmaceutical Corp. (one year).*

"I look at my father, I look at my mother, I look at some of my friends, and what I want out of life is a happy relationship with my wife and good children. And health and . . . you know, that's about it.

"Now you can say, well sure, do you want a house? You want three cars? But I can't answer that. I really don't know if I want a house and three cars. You can say, do you want power? I want to work hard and working hard leads to power. But I don't know if I want power in and of itself.

"I'm interested, twenty years from now, in having a challenging life. What I'm worth in the twentieth year—it hasn't occurred to me to answer that question. I heard a story about a fellow who answered by saying: 'I want to have the largest net asset base of any of my classmates.' Well, that's not my goal. Maybe it is twenty years from now, but certainly not today. I couldn't care less what the net asset base of me, relative to my classmates, is. Salaries relative to guys adjacent to me are not relevant.

"I think the way I see it now, the next couple of years, working for somebody else, I'll play the businessman's game. I'll play: maximize personal wealth, maximize earnings per share because that's the measure to use. If and when I am in business for myself, I may play that game or I may play a slightly different game, where I'll be willing to suffer a penalty because of my values, where I won't insist on earnings per share.

"I went through this same thing, you know, about what I want out of life with this friend of mine: 'Just a good wife and a family and enough money to have a little wine and cheese on the table.'

"And he says: 'What vintage wine?'"

3

The Season Opens

January 15:

Companies Pull Back From MBA Recruiting

> "We are unable to pay the salaries your candidates command . . . a temporary suspension of our special MBA recruiting efforts . . . our manpower plans indicate no need for graduate business students during 1970 . . . our recruiting requirement does not justify schedule . . ."
>
> These are reasons being received from companies—some among the biggest in America—for canceling their formal recruiting schedule this year at the Harvard Business School.
>
> "The market will definitely be down from last year," said John E. Steele, director of placement. "The question is just how much . . ."

The article in today's *HarBus News* went on to say that cancellations received so far are exceeding those of last year and that schools with a fall interviewing program report that the number of companies recruiting is down. June graduates should not be discouraged, however. "Things will be down, but not desperate," Mr. Steele, the placement director, was quoted as saying.

So there *is* some truth to the talk that had started even before Christmas, that the economic recession is catching up with the Business School; that this is the year when the rising curve of starting salaries (a median of $14,000 last year) will reach a plateau or turn down; in short, that this is *not* the year to be graduating from the Harvard Business School.

January 27: A Personnel Administration case in the form of a transcript of a tape-recorded discussion. Participants: A foreman (fifty-seven) and his boss (forty-five). Background: The foreman, a long-time, trusted and able employee isn't getting his group to put out.

What do you tell a guy in a situation like that?

The boss does his best to be objective and understanding about the foreman's shortcomings. With the result that the foreman leaves the discussion kind of shaken, not really knowing what to do.

What went wrong? Whose fault is it that the talk made things worse rather than better?

It takes us almost an hour to figure out what, in retrospect, we should have seen right away; what we should have seen months or years ago. That it isn't the man, it is his behavior that is causing problems. And that the boss is being ineffective in the discussion because he is trying to change the man instead of certain harmful aspects of the man's behavior.

There is no such thing, Professor Moxham says, as a personality trait in the abstract. Personality traits are bits and pieces of behavior. So, in situations like this, talk about *what* is wrong before you talk about *why*. Talk about the actual, practical—the operational problems. Because these you can do something about. You can do a lot to change what a guy *does;* but you can usually do little to change what he *is.* Or: The way to change what a guy is, is to change what he does.

Ben Davidson said after class that it had occurred to him, while everybody was trying to straighten out the foreman, that a lot of "politics" and people problems in a company are the result, not of capitalism or a greedy sonofabitch at the top, but the unavoidable consequence of getting a lot of different people to work together toward one and the same objective.

All of which checks squarely with experience, if you've ever been out there and have worked.

February 23:

"Hello? Is this Professor Morris' office?"

"Yes, it is. Can I help you?"

"Name is Al Terner. I'm a second-year student. I'm taking his . . . I'm taking Professor Morris' course . . ."

"Yah?"

"When is there a chance that I could come in and see him?"

"Just a sec . . . now let's see here . . . well, I don't have his calendar right here now . . ."

(A couple of secs)

"OK . . . well now. This week looks bad . . . really bad. He's leaving tomorrow and he won't be back till Thursday. Let me see . . ."

"There is no chance this week, you say? Well, see if I could earlier, because I really should . . . it's pretty urgent . . ."

"Nooooh—I'm very sorry . . . this week is out of the question. On Thursday afternoon, just after he gets back, he has this course meeting and on Friday, he usually doesn't meet with any students, his class meets that morning. Actually, the beginning of next week is quite busy too . . . would the end of next week be too late for you?"

"What about next Monday or Tuesday?"

"Very sorry. Monday he's out of town and Tuesday he's already so many students scheduled . . . You know, you're not the first one calling today."

(Embarrassed, frantic pause)

"Why don't you try catching him after class?"

"Well . . . no chance then, right?"

"I'm very sorry."

"OK . . . thanks."

It's not that the professors are trying to be mean, or anything like that. It's just that for Harvard Business School professors, as for their students, it's a rat race all the way.

Part of it is the nature of the academic job. You can't just teach. You've also got to put a couple of books on the shelf. Part of it is that in almost all basic disciplines of business administration, you've got to *do* it to understand it.

So, as a professor, you've got to square the need to teach with the need to learn. And you've got to square the need to learn with the need to practice. And, as if this weren't enough, you've got to square the money you get with the life style you have earned.

A full Business School professor, after six to ten years of having proven himself, after A.B., M.B.A., and Ph.D., makes about as much as his best and most qualified students make in their first year after graduation. An assistant professor, which is what a young Ph.D. usually starts out as, makes about half as much: $12,000 to $25,000 is the range. You wouldn't expect a fellow, going through two or three extra years of doctoral education and the agony of writing a thesis, to put up with that?

The answer is that a professor earns what he fails to earn in the classroom by working on the outside. He becomes a consultant, he has himself elected director of a company, he writes, or he teaches cases outside the school.

Teaching is by far the most tempting alternative, since it normally involves little preparation—the cases are the same as those taught in class—and bingo! the fee is $200 or $600 or even $1,000 a day. Consulting is no less lucrative, but it requires much more involvement, a lot more preparation. Which leaves being a company director as the alternative that offers least immediate rewards. Yet, in the long run, it is the most potent means for a professor to "leverage" his outside career. The job itself is largely honorific. You go to a board meeting once, twice, perhaps four times a year. You approve recommendations by the company's chief executive, you get a free meal and if you are lucky, your fee is large enough to cover your travel expenses. But what you really get is a reputation in the business community. You meet bankers, presidents, and chairmen who introduce you to more bankers, presidents, and chairmen, and if the company is of any size at all, you become a member of that confusingly intertwined fraternity of power brokers that swings the really big deals this side of what used to be the Iron Curtain.

Combine this with the salary level at the school and you begin to wonder why Professor Morris, who won't be around until Thursday, will be around at all.

The school bravely tries to keep all of this under control. There are regulations that limit the faculty's outside activities to one day a week and the new dean of the school personally keeps an eye on what his colleagues are up to, outside of class. But how can you really check on this? Should you even try to, if you are paying your assistant professors half of what their brightest students make the first year?

The real loser isn't the school, which is doing its best to keep its salaries halfway competitive, nor the student who vents his frustration on helpless secretaries. The real loser is society which forces its best teachers to sell out to the highest bidder. Because, in the case of business administration, the highest bidder is the corporation. The consumer loses, the government loses, the people lose. Check the environment, check the quality of many products and services. Check, check, check . . .

March 4: The doors of Aldrich, this afternoon, were like curtains to a stage, opening upon a sight so peaceful, light, and inviting that you almost hesitated to step outside, for fear that at the slightest movement, it would all dissolve into the bleak reality of Business School life.

The sky was a frail, distant blue—clean and clear—and beyond the bend of the Charles: Boston with its neon signs flashing nervously even at this early hour of the afternoon. The Prudential Building, square and unimaginative, poking in empty triumph at the sky. Boston—so close, yet too far, unexplored, and tempting.

The Charles, its surface trembling in a light caressing wind, breaking the sun into a zillion glittering pieces. And from the upper bend the sound of voices, shouts—the Harvard boats approaching, the fours, the eights. The rhythmic encouragements of the coxswains, all bundled up against the cool wind. The beat of the oars, a mute melody, cheerful and pleasant as this afternoon, serenading the young grass, courting the sun that dances on the spires and cupolas of Grandfather's Harvard.

The concrete and the wind, the oarsmen, the neon signs, even the bizarre pieces of trash, washed up on the Charles's shores—for a minute, for an afternoon, it all had its place, its voice, in a kind of relaxed, lazy yawn of creation.

March 12: Fred Laratti says that most of the time the reason a company's interview sheet is crowded is because of location. Because people want to take a trip and see San Francisco.

The job situation has made the *HarBus News* again. Only this time, more ominously, it was tucked away on page 8. The threat of a deteriorating job market isn't real and immediate; yet it's part of too many of our conversations to be easily ignored. Everybody talks about it, but nobody admits (at least not in public) to being worried.

"Recruiting Continues Slow; Consulting Still Popular," the title of the *HarBus* article said. It reported "feelings of frustration and anxiety" and predictions by the placement director that there will be fewer offers per person and that those that will come, will come later than they did last year.

In only one area of recruiting do there appear to be outright difficulties. The slump in the stock market has closed Wall Street—usually one of the foremost consumers of Business School graduates—to all but an ultra select few. Graduates already there are forced to lay off fellow graduates. Jobs in money management and investment banking, considered among the most glamorous in terms of money and influence, have suddenly evaporated. The standing-room-only crowds who are taking Investment Management and Institutional Investment and Investment Banking are finding themselves without a place to go.

4

Places Close to Heaven

March 5: The recruiting office is a bland room with shelves along the walls and three or four tables with plastic tops, where students can read the company literature stacked on the shelves: The annual reports, the recruiting pamphlets, and the job descriptions left by earlier generations of students. It's a small room with doors going off in every direction. A door to where you sign up for interviews. Two or three doors to cubicles where you can sit down with employers. And, of course, the doors to the women who keep everything on schedule.

8:10 A.M. The first recruiters arrive. They come in twos, gray overcoats slung over their forearms, hands gripping briefcases. They wear little, high hats. Underneath the hats they wear faces. Underneath the faces, white shirts, dark suits, and steady voices.

At times there are six or eight of them, queuing up in front of the registration desk. "Your name?" the woman checks a schedule, "here, please fill out this name tag. Your room is the alcove facing Aldrich 207. Second floor. Second alcove to the right." Quickly and obediently the double footsteps fade down the hallway.

This, then, is it. For this we have studied Newton, Freud, George Washington, MERC I, MERC II—the works.

To be a standard answer to a standard question, at a standard price.

March 6, morning: Mr. Saylor's place. Mr. Saylor is on the sixth floor, and above him there are floors and more floors, and above the floors there is an impenetrable canopy of fumes.

Below Mr. Saylor there is a small, almost anonymous entrance that has thin golden lettering over it. Inside, marble walls echo the nervous ringing of elevators and the intermeshing rhythms of a multitude of clicking heels.

When you step off the elevator, on the sixth floor, you walk into a white wall that forms a long, narrow room, a windowless room with two brown doors that are flush with the wall, as though part of it. A plush, obliging carpet runs the length of the room. At one end there is a plush, obliging sofa and a little table with a sampling of last month's magazines. At the other end there is a desk with a pair of inquisitive eyes, and between the desk and the sofa, Mexican-type clay figures smile from the wall.

It is quiet. So quiet that you drum your fingers to your own heartbeat until, suddenly ringing, another elevator spills its load into the room and for a brief, tumultuous instant, there is the sound of footsteps, the blows of the brown doors closing, and again nothing—the pair of eyes, the sofa, the beating of your heart. Until an elevator slides open again, displaying its wares as in a showcase, twenty or so absorbed, impatient, indifferent faces. And shuts and is gone, and again, silence.

Now and then one of the brown doors opens, releasing a human shape that, like some celestial body, heads straight and steady, with seemingly inevitable motion, for the other door wherein it vanishes.

There you sit, on that flattering sofa, having said that you wish to see Mr. Saylor. But Mr. Saylor, I'm very sorry, is on the phone, and again there is silence.

Somewhere, behind one of these doors, is Mr. Saylor and probably he too, somewhere, sometime ago, was sitting in a room like this one, waiting to see another Mr. Saylor, hidden behind doors like these, waiting in the company of a pair of eyes, for the end of a long telephone call.

Afternoon: Mr. Taylor's place. Mr. Taylor is on the twenty-eighth floor of a building that is still quite new and quite white. Taylor works behind a wall of glass, thirty stories high. A giant mirror showing glassy fronts, reflecting fronts, reflected in fronts in infinite succession.

In the elevator lights flash as it moves up until the light reads "Executive Offices." Mr. Taylor's floor. Not many elevators stop there and those that do leave you to a respectful silence. To a room of well-bred materials, with panels of exotic wood covering the walls and suave black leather on the chairs; heavy chairs that swivel to the wall, where the room becomes all glass, from ceiling to bottom, giving out onto a sight that leaves you gasping. For now you are high enough to look down on the forms, on misshapen piles of stone and steel, on the green and unexpected presence of a park. Right in front of you, blocking part of what you might see of the park, there floats a sort of Florentine palazzo stacked on top of one of the buildings, a candle on a tall cake. And above the palazzo, a jet, trailing a streak of black smoke, disappears into the haze.

Somewhere in this semidarkness, in the built-in twilight of the room, is not the usual miniskirt but an elderly lady with painted cheeks and a dazzling array of curls, and a young, tall, and taciturn black who seems to be her only source of diversion.

And the elderly lady, you are not quite sure. Is she talking to the bouquet of long-stemmed white flowers that waste in the canned air? Suddenly she laughs. "The president, he said," she giggles, "why, he said, I sure would like to live in one of those new penthouses over there, but," oh can she giggle, "but—but I told him," hehehehee, "I told him—why, you probably can't," heheheee, "you probably can't afford it . . ." Only very gradually does her giggling subside.

"Mr. Taylor isn't back yet," the lady says, and there are more black streaks as one after another, in regular intervals, jets head for the horizon.

The dirty light seems to drip from a couple of trophies mounted on the wall, and the lady, disconnectedly, absent-mindedly, talks to the young black.

5

Here the Blasé Sonofabitch Comes

March 13: "Erwinger must be having his first interview," Professor Latimore said at the beginning of Sales Management. That's how obvious Erwinger looked.

Now Erwinger usually is the quiet, self-confident type who likes to blend in with the surroundings and be noticed only when he decides to be noticed. But today, with that blue suit that looked so infrequently worn that you thought you were seeing the coat-hanger creases, with the wild waves of blond hair calmed by greasy kid stuff, and a faint-yellow silk tie splashed over the steel-blue shirt, he was the very cliché of the smart, blatantly eligible bachelor about to marry a rich company.

It's a characteristic of the interviewing season that a good many people are going through a good deal of trouble to package themselves. Beards, sweaters, and other demonstrations of independence quietly, and at times forever, disappear on the day of the first interview. For a few strong individuals, it may be only a tactical measure, a gesture of politesse. But many, in spite of their garish ties, look like they're going to their own funeral. It's the end of an adventure. A sudden hard landing after a timid flight of the imagination.

The barriers that we have taken two years to wear down are going up again. It's back to Brooks Brothers.

Same morning: Personnel Administration brought back an old friend, Douglas McGregor's theories "X" and "Y."* The fact that in dealing with people you can assume that they are basically stupid and lazy and will move only if forced (theory "X"); or that they are basically willing and eager—qualities which resist force but might surrender to a friendly pat on the back (theory "Y").

Since we talked about this, sometime late in the first year, two new characters have been added to our collection of basic B-School types: The "hard-X-er" and the "theory-Y-er"; the law-and-order type and the bleeding heart.

We must be getting more mature or more realistic or whatever you want to call it, because today, the hard-X-ers and the theory-Y-ers carefully avoided the kind of ideological clash we had the first year. Everybody more or less agreed that the more competent, the more motivated people are, the more you can be theory-Y; and the more their drive has been blunted, the more resigned they are, the more you have to be hard-X. Which implies that theory X is no solution. Because the more hard-X you are, the more resigned people become, and the more resigned they become, the more hard-X you have to be.

"OK," Mike Daks said afterward at the Pub, "but how
do you motivate anybody these days? How do you get
commitment? You know, they are growing up with
a lot of their physical needs satisfied. They have good
housing, they take a pretty good income for granted.
And industry is going to need them. It's going to need
them in management roles; it's going to need them in a
lot of other places where somebody has to make decisions

* Douglas McGregor, *The Human Side of Enterprise*, published by the McGraw-Hill Book Co., Inc., 1960.

and take the initiative. And I don't think that industry with its 'bottom line' incentives is going to attract these people.

"They are going to say: 'Goddamn, we already *have* enough money. What the hell do we need more for?' Look at the hippies. A lot of them are college students doing jobs as leather craftsmen and things like that, where they have control over their work, rather than doing some stupid little thing where they can see neither beginning nor end.

"I don't think that overtime, all kinds of increased wages are really going to be an incentive. Even in labor unions. Wages don't mean all that much. I don't think they mean that much at all. I think it's more of a need to feel that they are having an influence on the system. I sense a whole different kind of motivation coming. We will, somehow, have to create opportunities for these people. But have we ever thought about how?"

March 20 (*spring recess*): Through all the confident talk about the future, the rumble of the rumor mill can be heard louder and louder. The gears that haven't had any real stuff to grind on for over a week today were fed new gobs of hearsay and speculation by the *Wall Street Journal:*

B-School Blues
Demand for Graduates
With MBAs Declines
And Salary Rise Slows

Their Propensity to Job Hop
Big Wage Targets Cited
Along With Economy's Lag

Some executives say, the graduates demand more money than they're worth and these executives say they simply won't pay the premium any more. Others assert, the young men they hire often stick around only long enough to learn the business and then head elsewhere, often to a smaller company, where they get a larger say. Still others maintain, some MBAs think they're smarter than they are and rub too many colleagues the wrong way.

Whatever the reason for the diminished enthusiasm for MBAs, the result is clear. Not only are there fewer people bidding for MBAs, but also those who are still interested in hiring them, are offering little more than last year. . . .

Sounds like the bad turn in the economy is giving a lot of people their chance to prove that all the talk and publicity the M.B.A.s got in the past is a lot of bullshit, and that the M.B.A.s are just people, like everyone else.

"OK," SIDNEY O'MARA said, "so no one is going to work at starvation wages. So you're economically independent —relieved of the economic factor in making the choice. And you know you've got that. You are sitting on it and everyone thinks: 'Aha! The halo effect! Here the blasé sonofabitch comes.'"

April 3: When we got back from spring break, summer seemed so close you could almost see it on the other side of the river. But now, after two weeks of classes, it seems further than the furthest dream. The discussion on the Black Rose Cosmetics Corp. was led by second stringers, and Terner was looking at the clock so frequently that he became convinced it was broken. Its hands didn't seem to move.

At first he kind of enjoyed the drifting and letting go and not being able, or wanting, to do anything about it. But the thin red hand, ticking off the seconds, made him increasingly restless because he could literally *see* his life go by. The troublesome thing about it was that this happened not just now but happened yesterday and four years ago and tomorrow. And, it seemed, he and most of the people he knew were always waiting for the end of something to come so that something better could begin, which really always turned out to be just another wait too. It was this way with high school and with college and with all the springs and falls and winters and rainstorms and beautiful days which he had watched from behind windows, except that now it was a job he was waiting for.

In fact, Terner thought he could already see out of the next window and the window after that; he could see himself heading for something which, at first, was a mere line, a thin line leading from one end of the horizon to the other, growing wider as he approached, growing to the size of a narrow ribbon.

A mountain range perhaps, Terner thought. But as he got closer, he recognized that it wasn't a mountain range. For although it had peaks and depressions, these were evenly spaced like the teeth of a zipper. A crazy, endless zipper holding together the up and down of the horizon.

Getting closer still, Terner began to hear voices—the kind of low murmur, pierced by occasional shrieks and high pitches of laughter, that comes off large crowds. Terner now began to distinguish shapes, tall shapes brilliantly lit, and he was amazed to see what seemed to be a single building bathed in intense bluish light that made its white facade so white it hurt the eyes. Terner observed that the building wasn't tall —three stories at most—with its wings losing themselves to both sides in the distance. And every two blocks or so, the compact wall-like front of the building was adorned by a tower, two floors taller, crowned by a shiny spire.

Very near now, the building had a door with its two heavy wings open and there was a long line of people waiting. They were neatly lined up in twos, although many seemed to have come singly, and they were chatting quietly, introducing themselves to one another.

Terner, who was very tired, waited and he couldn't afterward remember just how long he had waited, but he knew it was a long, long time. But now it was his turn to enter and he saw that inside the building everything, even the air ducts on the ceiling, was laid out in wood that wasn't really wood, but made of plastic. On the walls, wherever there was an inch of free space, there were paintings: paintings depicting Venice, paintings of children with freckles, paintings of clowns, and paintings of sail ships braving glassy waves.

It was Terner's turn to step in front of a desk on which there were two phones and behind which there was a man in a black tuxedo. The man, an older man, was very busy with his phones, but finally he looked up briefly, busily taking stock of Terner in his uneventful gray suit, somewhat rumpled from the voyage.

"How many?" the man asked, "how many in your party?"

"One," Terner replied.

"It will be awhile, sir," the man said mechanically. "Would you mind going upstairs to wait in our lounge?"

The lounge upstairs was quite narrow, or so it seemed, of undeterminable length and crowded with people. And all along the wall was a bar with flickering lights that were meant to look like gas lamps but really were electric. There were many little tables at which people sat in twos or singly. And here, too, everything that looked like wood was plastic. Terner took a table near the window and, as he sipped his drink, speakers skillfully hidden in the ceiling sprinkled him with sweet, infinitely monotonous music.

But every so often the music stopped, and there was the voice of the man at the desk: "Mr. So-and-so, please. Party of one. Mr. So-and-so, sir, your table is ready and waiting, sir. Mr. So-and-so, please, your table is ready. Please take your time."

And again sweet music and again a name and again the music.

And Terner waited and it seemed to him, yes, after some

time, it seemed to him that the man at the next table, the woman and the man had sort of crumpled, slid down onto the table and into their chairs.

And again the man in the tuxedo: "Mr. and Mrs. So-and-so, please. Your table is ready and waiting."

And suddenly now Terner saw it. Saw that the eyes in the man at the next table were gone, saw the white skull, how the skull suddenly, gently rolled over the edge of the table and with a hollow, wooden thud splintered on the ground.

6
A Lot of Talk

(Sales Talk)

Fred Laratti:

"There was another guy from New York. The guy looked like a doll. He was dressed up in the latest suit and had long, long hair. He didn't have any information about his firm or the job or anything. But there wasn't a speck on his shoes.

"Now I realize that the people who sent him up weren't going to hire anybody this year. He was just there to hold the bag."

Frank Charvis:

"There were divisions who resented the fact that this one division was trying to pull in people from the Harvard Business School and paying them outlandish salaries and was pulling them in at this high level.

"Several guys did go through the process of talking to people within this division and by the time I came along —I was one of the last people to come through—a few people in the other divisions were asking: 'Hey, what's going on here?' You know, 'Ship us one of these guys. We wanna talk with him too.'

"So they shipped me over to a marketing manager who was like second in command; in fact, he was a vice-president or something, and he was a real hatchet man. He was a young, hard-nosed, crude guy who had fought his way up—I would say he was in his middle thirties —he had this very good job and he tried to, I think he was basically trying to find out: 'What kind of stuff are these guys made of?' He had the idea that we were basically prima donnas and corporate bullshitters. I had said in my résumé that I am interested in marketing, so he asks me: 'What do you think of a job in sales?'

"I said: 'Well, no immediate interest in that.'

" 'Why not? What's wrong with sales?'

"I gave the kind of reply you give: 'Well, I don't feel I could contribute as meaningfully in sales as I could in some other function where I can use a lot of my background and recent experience, recent academic experience.'

"He says: 'What do you mean, your academ . . . ? What do you mean, what's all this crap?'

"The gist of what this guy said to me was: 'One thing is gonna make or break this company and this division, and this one thing is sales.'

" 'Well, hell,' he said to me, 'you can't be a good manager unless you're a good salesman.' And whether he really believed it or not, I wasn't sure. But he pounded his fist on the table and got all excited.

"I said: 'Oh . . . I disagree.'

"You know, 'Why do you disagree?' He got very riled up but then, quite suddenly, he came down to ground zero. 'Well,' he said, 'let's not use this high-class vocabulary. All this stuff about 'co-ordinating' and words like that, goddamnit! That's a lot of bullshit. Let's talk about people and making bucks and profit. And what you want to get out of this company.'

"He said: 'You guys are just out to exploit the company.

What makes you think you are worth eighteen grand?'

"I had some solid logic behind why I was worth eighteen, but I said: 'I never said anything about eighteen grand. How did you ever come to that?'

"He points out: 'Oh, it's here, in somebody else's evaluation, that they're gonna have to pay you at least eighteen grand.'

"I said: 'If you want to talk in crude terms, fine. But this isn't my vocabulary. I talk the way I'm most comfortable and if that's too high for you, let me know.'

"That took him back a little and he said: 'Basically, I get a lot of people that come through with good educational backgrounds, but they don't know the first steps; they don't have any self-concept of themselves. They think they can do this and that but really aren't sure. They end up going, you know, going aground on the thing, getting washed ashore. They get screwed up as time goes on.'

"He came down to offer me a job before even the people I had come to see had a chance to talk to me."

JAMES ERWINGER:

"I ran into a guy from Globotec, Inc., who, I think, was a little younger than me. And he was on this Globotec rotating program where he goes here for two weeks and there for two weeks and all I could think of was that the guy was kept twirling.

"He had gone to the Business School but I just thought: 'Gee—I know more about electronics than he does. I know more about marketing than he does. And I know more about Globotec than he does.'

"So I thought, it was silly talking to the guy. I thought, he shoulda been talking to me."

FRED LARATTI:

"Well, they were sort of in a hysterical state. They had just started to turn the company around, they had gotten a new chairman and a new management . . . it was supposed to be a very hush-hush thing; they were really hot to get some sort of 'whiz kids' in.

"So we were sitting around in one of the dormitories—it was Dillon Lounge I believe—the three of us had gone there one evening around seven-thirty, and we sat around the table all hunched over and this guy comes in; he was going to put together a team, three or four people, and place us in this company, and we were gonna change the company and we were gonna make profits with a lot of hatchets—chop people's heads off . . .

"And he was going through these organization charts, telling us this, that, and the other, telling us who is good, who is bad; he was telling us more than we thought was necessary and even good to do. And I'm not gonna forget that; it was just so strange to see this guy who talked like he was from the Secret Service and was gonna hire us to pull off this really heavy plot."

KEITH KUROWSKI:

"He says: 'Gee, I see you're an engineer and you're not in engineering any more. Now could you explain that a little bit?'

"I said: 'Yes, I worked as an engineer and I saw that, you know, the potential for . . . for remuneration was limited. You really weren't paid enough. Although I found the work challenging and interesting, I thought that long term

—seeing older engineers—it probably wouldn't be worthwhile.'

"And he said: 'What did I hear you say? Did I hear you say money?'

"I said: 'Yeah, essentially that's what I'm saying—money.'

"He said: '*Money!* You said the magic word. That's it! That's what we want, money!'

"And in a sense, that was literally part of the appeal, most of the appeal Wall Street had for me. But I thought, it's funny for this fellow to come and say money out loud. You know, to me money is a dirty word. In the back of my mind it's a big motivator and all that, but it's a dirty word and you don't want to admit thinking about it, to people.

"And here this fellow is reaching his hand out, across the table, and he says: 'money!' "

RUSS BAXTER:

"The offices of the president and of the partners were on, I guess, the forty-sixth floor. It was magnificent offices. The first partner I met was about 888 years old. He wore a big vest, he had a big stomach and he had this black-gold watch chain with about three or four loops in the strands.

"You know, I was going in for a job interview with this old man and what do we talk about? He mentioned something about being in certain parts of Wyoming and I said: 'Oh, there's good fishing up there. Did you know that?' And, by God, he started talking about fishing, and we talked fishing for three quarters of an hour as a job interview.

"It was a tremendous . . . a tremendous way to get to know somebody, to see how he socializes.

"You know, this company which was the staid, conservative old company; it wasn't one of the wheeler-dealer, go-go companies and, you know, you're gonna have to socialize in order to be competent in that kind of environment. *That* is the required skill."

KEITH KUROWSKI:

"We went for lunch; that was about five people, and everybody ordered milk.

"I ordered hot tea because that's what I order for lunch. I enjoy hot tea. Sometimes I order milk too. But I thought, this time I wouldn't, in the sense that they all did.

"The first guy says milk. The second guy says milk. The third guy says milk. And I say hot tea. Whereas, really, the cool thing to do was to order milk and be one of the boys.

"But I'm setting myself up as different. I guess, at this time I was getting to feel good, I don't know why—it was a good interview, everything was progressing relatively well. I said: 'It's interesting how you all ordered milk,' kind of commenting on the fact that, you know: 'Isn't there one guy among you that has guts enough to order something different? Is that how you play? One guy orders something so everybody orders the same thing . . . is this how you run your lives? Is this what it's like to live in this environment, that you play "follow the leader"?'

"And the response was something to the extent: 'Well, Keith, if you really like milk, you drink milk and you don't care what your buddies, what people, think.' He interpreted my question to mean: 'Milk is for children, so how come you guys are drinking milk?' And he says: 'I'm drinking milk!' And my real question was: 'How come nobody here has enough guts to order something different?'

"Well, he told me, he missed my point, but I don't think he missed it. And another guy kind of quieted him down and we got by the milk issue."

HANK SCHWARTZ:

"This was at the Business School. Actually, it was in one of the rooms at the placement office. And I ask him a little bit about the company and he is saying: 'Yes, well, Wall Street is huh a very huhh challenging huhhh fast huhhhh moving huhhhhhh fascinating huhhhhhhhhhhhhhhhhhhhhhhhhhhhh . . .'

"His head got lower and lower and his voice got lower; he fell forward and started to doze off to sleep."

KEITH KUROWSKI:

"I was taking Interpersonal Behavior, and we were studying the Rogerian technique of interviewing, where you are non-evaluative. You just say: 'Oh? . . . geez! . . . I see, I see . . .' You don't burst the bubble.

"Essentially, I sat there and I had three or four quick questions to ask him like: 'What's the nature of the job? What's the nature of the people you interact with? What's the potential for salary in the future?' And that was it. I didn't want to know anything else.

"He answered these questions one, two, three, and then I said to him: 'What are *you* doing here in the company?' He is the manager of a couple of branches in the New England area. So I said: 'How do *you* like the job?'

"We were in a library, it was soft and quiet; it was a small library, the size of a living room; chairs, rugs, desks, everything was very luxurious and . . . I don't remember, we talked for something like two hours about his job. And about him as a person and the challenges *he* was facing.

"One of his challenges was that he had to fire people. And he didn't know how to do it. And we talked about how it affected him personally, and what his feelings were, and what techniques he used to make it easier on the people that were being fired.

"He talked about the fact that he has no friends here and socially, he wasn't really well accepted. He talked about the fact that he is Jewish and that he is the first Jewish person in the organization . . . He talked about very personal things.

"You know, at one point, it was really interesting, he said: 'Hey, what are we doing here? Gee . . . let me ask you . . .' He had my résumé in his hand and he asked me another question, and I talked a little bit more, but then I went back to him and asked more questions.

"Well, when I left, we walked out together and he was . . . he was like a very good friend. We had established a strong rapport between us. You know, I would say that man was very vulnerable and apprehensive, but I had established trust.

"It was around the middle of March or early March; it was early in the interviewing season. But I really felt I was learning something . . . something very important about listening to people."

PETER PARSONS:

"So we're sitting at lunch, these two fellows are talking to each other—Mr. K. and Mr. O. Mr. K. has paid no attention to me, I'm a nothing. I'm not even sure that Mr. K. knew why he was having lunch with Mr. O., namely to meet *me.* It was just like I wasn't there, you know, and they are talking to each other, and Mr. K. is saying something about: 'You know, we're having trouble with our new sales managers. We acquired these outlets and we're running into real difficulties.'

"So I leaned over and I said: 'Oh! You mean, you're having trouble with company X's managers? The company you just acquired about three months ago?'

"Well now, he almost fell off his chair. Because I wasn't supposed to know who company X was. But since I had read up on everything the company had done in the last six months—I had about fifteen pages of material—I knew very well who company X was.

"For the whole rest of the meal, Mr. K. didn't talk to Mr. O. He asked who I was, what my goals were in business, why I was interested in his company, how I heard about it, what I wanted to do there . . .

" 'Well,' he said when we finished lunch, 'you come with me.' I had driven to lunch with Mr. O. Now I drove back in *his* car. It was a totally different story."

KEITH KUROWSKI:

"The interview was 30 minutes and he talked about the company for 29.6 minutes. And he asked me nothing about myself, who I was, why I was interested in the company, what my goals were. All he did was talk about the company and I said: 'Yeah, yeah,' and it didn't bother me a hell of a lot except that I wondered why they hadn't sent me a recording."

7
Kind of a . . . a White Elephant

(WENDY BURGESS *talking*)

"My parents didn't know I had applied until just before I was accepted, and once they got over the initial shock, they were proud and happy. There were occasional giggles at cocktail parties of older friends of my parents, but most men—at least on the surface—were congratulatory. You know, they would say: 'Hey, great . . . good . . . fantastic!' I actually, at that time, was quite naive in assuming that all this resistance to women in business was a figment of some uptight woman's imagination.

"I probably would have come around to applying sooner or later. But, somehow, my friends looked with a raised eyebrow at business school. I felt a traitor to a whole group of people that I had come to know and discuss things with, and I felt very much that I would be going into an environment where I was there for different reasons than other people were. And not because I'm a woman but because the kind of job I wanted would be different. I mean, when I went to the Business School, I . . . I was going because I wanted to change the world. Not because I wanted to make a lot of money in the stock market.

"I still saw myself as a journalist and as a social scientist. You know, my father was in business and didn't like it and I just never thought of *that* as something I would be good at. Writing was what I could do. And I assumed that whatever I did as a career, it would involve writing in some way.

"I guess the change happened slowly while I was in Europe. Before I even got down to deciding what I was going to do when I graduated from Smith, an uncle of mine—a great Hispanophile—offered me a year in Europe. So I took him up on it. I traveled the Mediterranean countries, and in the course of the two years—I stayed in Madrid another year—I worked and studied. But gradually the thing palled. I don't know if you've ever done little or nothing for any long period of time; you begin to quarrel with yourself and to get impatient to do something. Something that's moving in some direction, rather than just sort of improving yourself on all fronts at once.

"I started thinking about concrete alternatives and, somehow, the idea of sitting in a quiet little corner and working my way up the ladder to be senior writer did not appeal. So I went to school for a couple of months to get back into what was going on in this country. I started meeting city planners, economists, all kinds of people like that, and I finally decided to go to work for the city of Cleveland, to sort of get in at the bottom of what looked like an interesting field: government administration, urban renewal, and the whole bag of environment changing, which had grown up in my absence. And so that led pretty directly to applying to business school, because—compared to city planning school—it seemed like an exciting, stimulating, you know, even dramatic experience. It would be something that would not leave me unchanged.

"I had been trained not on action but on careful consideration of all the alternatives, writing up history essays where you culled a little out from everything and didn't come to any particular conclusion. Which is, I think, what liberal arts education in this country consists of. You know, a joy in reflection; a joy in searching for the truth rather than saying: 'All right, we've got something to do. Let's go do it.'

"And this is something I had to learn a lot about, you know, to go out there and fight, to defend myself. This isn't something you are called upon to do very often, as a woman. In thinking about my career, the kinds of jobs I will be in and the kinds of attitudes I'm going to run into, I had to start thinking of behaving in ways women are encouraged not to. Or, rather, I should say, rewarded for not behaving like. It's a process of education and, I guess, I never regarded ignorance as a good thing. It's sad to know that the world is big and ugly out there, but I've been brought up that ignoring it won't make the ugly things go away.

"I think the big difference with me and with a lot of the girls at the Business School—we talked about this a couple of times—our fathers were very important in our lives. They always sort of expected us to think for ourselves. You know, not fight for ourselves maybe, but to think for ourselves. They expected us to do things. And I think that a male authority figure still has a bit of . . . of mystique for me.

"To me, the traditional woman is kind of a . . . a white elephant. I really don't think there is going to be much of a market for her in the years ahead. I don't even know that there ever was one. It's something that I didn't have, you know—being feminine was never portrayed to me in my family as anything special or different, although my mother and father certainly fit the classic pattern in many ways. But I wasn't brought up to think of myself, to think of that as being a major portion of my identity. Even when I was younger—before I really thought much about what I was going to do with my life—femininity, to me, was the phony kind of things I saw a few girls do. You know, flirtatious behavior, doing sneaky, lying little things to get men to ask them out. I never thought of femininity as an entity that could be lost, gained, or that even existed, except in novels.

"I think any woman who tries—any woman or any man who tries—to be several different things at once would get screwed up very quickly. But I think if you have a single concept of who you are and what you are, regardless of whether it conforms to any stereotypes in the culture, you'll be OK. You know, it doesn't upset me to do things that are . . . I don't feel guilty about doing things that are stereotyped to be masculine. It was never drummed into me, as a child, that I must not do certain things because they are unladylike. No one ever spoke to me that way. They subtly may have encouraged me to do certain kinds of things, but I don't have any great feeling about: "This is masculine behavior" and "This is feminine behavior."

"There are men I know who aren't very . . . who don't fight, who are very . . . you know, who take the prerogative of being male very naturally and it's very much part of their identity, but who aren't really aggressive people at all, either intellectually or physically, and whom I think of as being very male.

"In fact, the extreme differentiation of roles—along sex lines and along many other lines too—is among the most unattractive, dysfunctional aspects of our culture. That there have to be roles. That there have to be class distinctions. It's a debilitating thing. It says that people born into a certain situation have to behave in certain ways. And that's unnatural, in that I don't think it allows people to develop . . . develop their own thing, their own great potential.

"In certain ways, perhaps, it is helpful to divide up the work load. To assign certain tasks, certain roles, to certain people. Because it's difficult for a society to function with everybody thinking of nothing but how to fulfill themselves to the greatest possible extent. But you can go overboard on this kind of thing, trying to organize society around a very rigid set of roles, where each person is what he or she is from the beginning, and you don't have people striving to break out of their mold. I want to try and move in the direction of a very mobile society. A true democracy in a psychological, cultural sense. And I don't really think that this small step of . . . of blurring masculine, feminine roles is going to be anywhere near the last one, the one that really tears society apart.

"I think we could go a lot further toward blurring a lot of roles, types that we have in our culture—even beyond the ones that are attached to race and different social backgrounds—to different religions, different groups from different countries.

"But changing people's attitudes is a much longer range thing. You'll never do away with these sorts of class distinctions entirely, because parents are always going to want their kids to live up to something. Whether it's to be masculine or to be feminine, or to be, you know, a great President or a great football player—there is always something that's going to screw the kid up somehow. But the less pressures there are, the better chance we'll have to find something that really fits and works.

"I don't believe everybody will be alike just because there is less emphasis on this masculine-feminine thing. You know, what defines diversity? I don't think it's necessary that people be divided into whites and blacks, or men and women or . . . Europeans and Americans. They can be diverse in other ways too. Along many, many different dimensions. And the male and female are still going to be there. It's not going to disappear. But I don't think it has any implications for such things as occupation. You may say: 'All right, but there is a difference in psychology!' Maybe, but who knows? Who knows what's learned and what's inherited anyway?

"And it seems to me that the effects of this polarization are especially severe on children; in forcing them to relate to one parent and not the other, in being 'overmothered' and 'underfathered,' because of the way in which the old division of labor works. The fact that the men have to work long hours and be away from the home so much is bad for family life, for men, for women, and for the economy. You know, if everybody weren't tagged—it's obviously never going to come to that—but if we move in that direction, I think people would be just as diverse. And they would still be males and females. But their little roles would be less narrow and less confining than they are now.

"It really didn't occur to me that it was a big thing for the guys at the Business School that we were there. And that many of them had strong feelings of fear or disapproval. Not all of them, but that it was really there, this bogeyman that I always thought of as a lot of talk; it's not real. They are not really that uptight. But a lot of them are.

"The single girls found it very hard to have a normal sort of social life. Either they were treated like one of the guys, which would be fine except that they wanted to be invited out like any other girls. Not necessarily that they wanted a boy friend out of them, but, you know, when the guys went out together on Saturday night, they wanted to be asked along, even if just as one of the group. And that never happened. They found that the guys had trouble dealing with them in that way.

"It seemed to be one of two extremes. Either the girls didn't go out at all or they formed one very close alliance that was either a boy friend or a husband. The guys really didn't—didn't know what to make of them. You know, they tended to assume that because there was a great confusion in *their* minds about just how to treat you, that there had to be a great confusion in *your* mind about who you were.

"If you hadn't been thinking much about your Section's reaction to you; if, as in most cases, you just hadn't wanted to see any of the . . . the hostility that was there—the big shock came when it got time to look for a job. If you were single, the recruiters were worried that you might get married and move to another city; if you were married, they were worried that you might get pregnant and leave the job. You couldn't win.

"One guy I talked to, the first thing he said to me, he looked at my résumé, goes through my education, my jobs, and then at the bottom, under 'personal,' I said that I had studied and worked in Europe for two years, spoke fluent French and Spanish, and a couple of things like that. But I hadn't put down the jobs and degrees I got in Europe because it was so far back and it wasn't really relevant to any job I might take.

"He said: 'Well, I assume from this you were married between 1965 and 1967.' And I said, you know: 'Married?' In retrospect, what I should have said: 'It's none of your damned business.'

"I said: 'Well, it's right here, on the bottom of the thing; I was in Europe.'

" 'Well, what did you do over there?' You know, right away assuming that I was trying to hide something, and that, obviously, I must have had an unhappy marriage or something.

"Well, in another interview I ran into this guy who wanted to make sure I wasn't, you know, 'radical.' He said: 'Do you think it will be a problem' and so forth, 'being a woman in a consulting firm?'

"I said: 'Well, I have worked for a firm; they were worried about their clients and the people I was to get information from not trusting me.' But that I found people were, in fact, more than willing to talk to me and tell me about their problems and pet projects, and that my employer had been happy too. As far as I could see, it wasn't much of a problem. But that in a very few cases it *was* a problem. So I guess, I would have to be prepared to put up with it, should the occasion arise.

"I said that I thought, in practice, a lot of this turns out less of a problem than it seems. In fact, I could remember having real arguments with guys on a theoretical basis, but when we got down to nuts and bolts, we worked together just fine. Emotions become a lot less important when there is a lot of work ahead of you.

"He kept asking questions around it, wanting to see whether I would get defensive. You know, they don't want a woman who is going to get upset or offended easily, just as they don't want to get a black who is going to complain if he doesn't get a front-office window. The companies that have decided: 'All right, this year we will take our token.' They want to make sure, they get a nice, docile token.

"What made me particularly angry was the attitude: 'Well, girlie, you have to prove to me that you're serious about this.' Damnit, I've gone through two years of Harvard Business School. I've spent so much money and grief, and you think I'm not serious?"

8
A Body With Many Heads

April 8: The scene was all too familiar. First the police and then the dean and then, a couple of hours later—when people were having dinner—the little black wagon came. There were two men in the wagon with a two-wheeled cart—the kind used to move heavy crates up and down staircases—they took the cart into one of the wings of the dorm, and when they came out, there was this thing strapped to the cart. Something the size and shape of a bag of golf clubs, only taller maybe—wrapped in dark tarpaulin.

They moved it quickly, and one of the men jumped and opened the rear of the wagon and they swung the cart around and lifted it in. The wagon was plain black, with no markings, and it drove away in a hurry.

That's how James Hinman left his first year at the Harvard Business School—dead of poison.

This is the third guy now, leaving like that, without knowing, without caring, where he is going to be five or a hundred or a couple of thousand years from now.

God knows how many times you have been told that competition is the American way and the only way; how you have heard it from lecterns and pulpits, and how you have almost come to believe it. And then you see a little cart wheel away what could have been a lifetime of laughter and tenderness and bright ideas. Suddenly you see the problems of it, the cost, and you wonder whether there *really* is no other way.

Because, when you come down to it, all competition is, is

behavior. A piece of behavior that builds on the need of individuals to be faster, cleverer, richer than the next guy. And, undeniably, this need to be unequal is of great value to society. Because one way of getting things done is to get everybody to outdo each other.

So society encourages that kind of behavior by reward structures where the guy who ends up fastest or smartest gets everything, the others nothing. Suddenly it forgets that people have needs other than wanting to be unequal. That some groups and types of people, that everybody at certain times in his life, want very much to be *like,* not unlike, other types or groups of people. That progress doesn't just depend on people setting new and higher standards, but that, just as often, progress is a matter of attaining existing standards consistently.

Everybody forgets that despite its undeniable advantages competition is a wasteful process. That every winner comes at the cost of a hundred, a thousand, a hundred thousand losers. And that one ought to consider the cost of it, before one starts advocating indiscriminate competition.

And this is where the American society is at; it talks of *competition* as if it had never heard the word "co-operation." It refuses to see that too much pressure doesn't move people; it kills them. Instead, everybody pushes and pushes each other, and they call the other a lazy bastard, if one of them happens to break down.

No, Coach—winning isn't everything. It's only a thing.

April 12, Sunday: As nearly as one can make out from the sometimes ambiguous wording and the confusing array of corporate titles, the last November-December issue of the alumni *Bulletin* reports three hundred and fifty-one major alumni promotions: twelve new chairmen of the board; three vice-chairmen; twenty-nine company directors; fifteen partners or associates; twenty-one owners and founders of their own business; sixty presidents, chief executive officers, general managers or managing directors; ninety-five vice-presidents of all denominations (executive, senior, group, division, etc.); fifteen directors of marketing, finance, production, corporate development, etc.; nineteen treasurers, assistant treasurers, comptrollers, and assistant comptrollers; seventy-two division, department, and regional managers; seven assistants to and three appointments by the President of the United States.

The most recent, the January-February issue, reports four hundred and ten major promotions: eleven chairmen; two vice-chairmen; thirty-six directors; ten partners and associates; twenty-four new owners; seventy-seven presidents and chief executives; one hundred and sixteen VPs; thirty operating directors; eighteen treasurers, comptrollers, and assistants thereof; eighty-two division and department managers; three presidential appointments, and one new lieutenant general.

But the picture we get of the alumni isn't just made in the *Bulletin* or in *Business Week* or *Forbes* or the *Wall Street Journal;* it is made in the classroom as well. All you've got to do is pick up one of your cases, and chances are that one of the first people you are introduced to will be described with the discreetly obvious flourish of being "a graduate of a well-known Eastern Business School."

The phrase must have started as a genuine expression of false modesty that well became a winner like the Harvard Business School. But in a time that has seen the likes of Muhammad Ali and Joe Namath do away with the phony business of passing the wolf off as the lamb's best friend, in such a time, false modesty has lost its false grace. And so, in more recent cases, Business School graduates are introduced straightforward as Business School graduates, at times even with their real name and the year when they got their M.B.A.

But the bit about the "well-known Eastern Business School" lingers on as a sort of self-conscious joke; as a slogan on a crimson pennant that you can buy at the newsstand in Kresge; as a way of laughing the apparent enormousness of the place down to bearable proportions. Because, after two years of seeing these fellows in your cases, you become convinced that a Harvard Business School graduate is a mister or a sir in a wall-to-wall leather chair, gazing through the proverbial fiftieth-floor window while juggling the pieces of his corporation's future. Or a white knight on a jet plane, arriving just in time to snatch the company from the jaws of imminent disaster.

As if to prove that all this is for real, some professors bring in the grads you read about in the cases. Like the boy wonder who told a second-year marketing class how he had gone out, with a couple of Section mates, and had made his old man's fast-food business take off faster than you could say "Hi, there." Or the two brothers whose family-owned, large retailing chain—heaven help—is drowning them in cash.

It's like Alma Mater is always reminding you, unintentionally perhaps, of how well her other sons are doing. And the whole bit is so crushingly impressive that you become unsure whether this M.B.A. of yours is going to be a just and great reward or a verdict of everlasting damnation that forces you to battle all the giants business folklore can muster and that, if you don't end up the winner, you aren't worth the proud title of Graduate of the Harvard Business School.

April 13: For two years now, we have been told that you've got to be good to people, because if you're good, they will work harder. And if they work harder, you will make a profit.

For two years it has been: You've got to make a better

product because, with a better product, you will make a greater profit.

What if they had told the story the other way around?

What if they had told us: You've got to make a profit because if you don't make a profit, you can't build offices that are pleasant to be in. Without profit you can't pay decent wages. Without profit you can't satisfy a lot of the needs of your employees.

What if they had told us: You've got to make a profit because, without a profit, you will never be able to develop a better product.

The profit would still be made. People would still get decent wages. Most employers would still make an effort to improve their products as they do now.

Still—you would have a whole new ball game.

April 15: In connection with Earth Day and the ecology movement, a case on water pollution in BP. Subject: the Charles River. Question: What would *you* do?

Answer: Why should I do something? *Everybody* is polluting the river: the communities, businesses, the people who run their boats up and down it, the people along the banks who throw in empty beer cans.

Greed, selfishness, and the blind pursuit of one's own personal advantage isn't something you, I, or even businessmen have invented. Businessmen are merely going along with it a little more effectively than everyone else. Like everyone else, *they* want the higher salary, the faster boat, the better-looking babe. If *they* are greedy, if *they* destroy the environment, they are merely doing what everyone, from kindergarten up, has taught them to do. They are what they were educated to be, and the community deserves them, even if it can no longer afford them.

For some reason, everybody seems to believe that it is

"natural," an inalterable fact of life, that the individual and his needs should always come first. But just because the idea comes easily doesn't mean it's right, or even that it is better. There is no reason on earth, why the *community* couldn't come first—the greatest good of the greatest number of people, or some sort of thing like that. If in our society the individual comes first, it is because we have decided that he should come first. We have let him put himself first.

Now letting everybody do his own thing wouldn't be so bad, if there weren't all this technology, the machines and weapons. Because, if you just let people take, they will take those too. And suddenly they are no longer nice old men, or ladies in tennis shoes, or young dynamic executives, but an unbelievably powerful threat to the survival of the community.

It isn't greed that is dangerous. It's greed armed with the technology our society has developed.

Empty talk? People, individuals, don't really go that far? They aren't that greedy? Well, if the robber barons of the turn of the century, if the slums and the pollution aren't proof enough, what is?

Still some people claim that there is a great fortunate accident in the affairs of men that causes the interest of all to be best looked after, by each looking after himself. Unbridled self-interest is an accident, all right, but not the fortunate kind some people are claiming it to be.

Seeing the damage the early industrialists did to the community, someone sooner or later had to ask: Why? Why should individuals be given such power? Why should they, why shouldn't the community be in control of the new technology? Looked at this way, communism is a necessary (although perhaps unnecessarily violent) reaction to the extreme individualism born of the Industrial Revolution.

The individualists—who are falsely called capitalists—assumed that people are born basically equal and that some degree of inequality is a powerful motivator and therefore a desirable goal; because of this, they insisted on competition as the most economical behavior. Someone had to ask: Isn't it just as reasonable to assume that people are born basically unequal? That some degree of equality is a powerful motivator and therefore a desirable goal? That co-operation is the most economical behavior?

Fortunately, it is finally becoming obvious that neither communism nor individualism, neither total sharing nor total egotism is the answer. They merely define the problem. They are the limits within which solutions will have to be found.

The extreme individualist side will have to start from the fact that precisely because it is individualist, precisely because it wants to permit a certain healthy dose of selfishness, it can no longer afford the slums, the discriminated minorities, an environment going to the dogs. Industrial societies have become such delicate machines that the failure of one cog can stop it all. So each of its citizens has to start applying the same energy, the same resources that he applies to his own needs, to satisfy certain minimum needs of all.

But who is going to start? Can you ask the guy who is dumping stuff into the river to sacrifice some of *his* profit to clean up? Can you, in effect, ask him to let the competition get ahead? Can a single player change the rules of the game?

The answer is that only the community can change them. Only if the majority backs them, are you going to get new rules and a different, a fairer sort of game.

But rules—that's legislation! That's bureaucracy! Red tape! Enforcers and corruption!

As if MERC I, MERC II, Finance, Marketing, as if what we have learned about administering a business could not also be used to administer the needs of a nation. Figuring out what people want—this isn't just a problem of marketing, this is the bread and butter of every politician. Foreign relations—as if large multinational corporations didn't have to worry about them too. Profit—as if the President of a nation could ignore questions of budget any more than the president of a corporation; as if to the president of a big corporation the sheer survival of his cumbersome organization weren't just as, or even more, important than making a profit; especially where many smaller companies, where whole industries, where entire countries even depend on his corporation's survival. Or are you so cynical as to suggest that the survival of several hundred thousand people—which is about what a very large corporation numbers—weighs any lighter on a man's shoulder than the survival of one, two, a hundred million people? So, really, what is the difference between running General Motors and running the U.S.A.?

April 16: Some fifty years of offensive and defensive campaigns have worked over his forehead and cheeks and the area around the mouth and have left it furrowed like a field, crisscrossed by a system of infantry trenches. His pants, slipping off the stomach, show a patch of shirt like tattered regimental colors. The tie of indefinite origin is tucked into a jacket on which the rubbing against the blackboard has left streaks of white.

Even his language is worn. His sentences are driven by corny innuendoes, his examples minted in cheap clichés.

But although the wear and the fighting are written all over him, his will has not been touched; rather, strengthened by adversity, he attacks—attacks at all times, under all circumstances, and the more tenuous his position the more relentless his fight.

He teaches business in its basics. Simple rules that work even in the midst of carnage. He urges you to go out into the field with the troops. He forces you to look into the white of the enemy's eye. He leads you so close, the old soldier, that you become much too busy surviving to ever ask what you're fighting for, or why.

May 5, morning:

"The case says they are selling mostly cash registers. They are selling them to mom-and-pop stores and only a . . ." Terner tried his best to keep his thoughts on what was going on in class, but he just couldn't. *I can't believe it,* he kept thinking, *I just cannot believe it. I mean, this is crazy. It says, the soldiers say, it was because of snipers. But the students say*—No, *no—it isn't, there wasn't . . .*

"So, assume it's mostly cash registers. Well, the company is doing just fine as they are, with specialized salesmen at branch level."

Why?, Terner thought. *How come? Those kids can't have been a real threat. Not against bayonets and tear gas—not against those formations.*

"The case says their sales force is one of the best in the industry. These guys know what they are doing. For those mom-and-pop stores you've got to have salesmen who know everything there is to know about cash registers."

What are we doing? What are we doing on a day like this? Who, for heaven's sake? Who did it? Not the Guard—the Guard in a way. But the President, he says he knew when he ordered the Army into Cambodia. He knew there was going to be trouble. And still he went ahead with it . . . Cambodia . . . Kent State . . . one more war. Just one tiny little war more . . .

"Yes, the cash registers . . . the class . . ."

It isn't us. It's far away in Vietnam and in Ohio.

"And, anyhow, they do sell some very large clients. These clients don't just want cash registers. They want a whole data-processing system with accounting machines, registers, computers, all hooked together."

What are we doing? Why don't we stop? Why do we go on with this as if nothing had happened?

"Yes, sir, a systems-sales force, too. Located at headquarters. For the very large clients."

You can count on us—country, world, humanity. But later on, don't you see we're busy right now? Later, OK? And, anyhow, how far do you want to go?

"Indeed, sir, right, they should go to two sales forces. One specializing on cash registers at the local level, the other a systems group. This would indeed strengthen . . . this would . . ."

Fire!

"Hello, can you hear me? I was saying it would work just fine. Hello? Can you hear . . . ? Hello?"

Fiiiiiiiiiiiiiiiiiierrrrrrrr!

2 P.M.: The sun, the crowd on the steps of Baker Library, the war—it was like an instant replay of the events a year before.

Only this time the crowd was three or four times as large. This time it didn't take many meetings to figure out where the meeting stood. When it ended, about an hour later, the coming Tuesday was declared an "open day," to be used for political action and discussion; the following resolution was adopted and money was collected to place it as an ad in the *Wall Street Journal:*

> *Resolution by Certain Students, Faculty and Employees of Harvard Business School*
>
> We condemn the administration of President Nixon for its view of mankind and the American community which:
>
> 1. Perceives the anxiety and turmoil in our midst as the work of "bums" or "effete snobs";
>
> 2. Fails to acknowledge that legitimate doubt exists about the ability of black Americans and other depressed groups to obtain justice;

3. Is unwilling to move for a transformation of American society in accordance with the goals of maximum fulfillment for each human being and harmony between mankind and nature.

In particular and most urgently we call for an end to the escalation of the war in Southeast Asia and for the withdrawal of American forces from that region. In the United States we demand an end to the use of blind force as a means to resolve legitimate disagreement.

May 6: Convened this afternoon, the faculty backed the call for an open day on which the new crisis can be discussed. The decision on whether or not to cancel classes, however, is left to the conscience of the individual instructor.

The number of action groups and committees seems to be growing by the hour. One, made up of faculty and students, is putting together a program for Tuesday. Others are establishing contacts with the National Guard and police to prevent further violence; still others have gone to Washington and New York to get members of Congress and influential businessmen to press Nixon to end the war. The surprising thing is how smoothly and effectively everybody is working together. In place of the SA, which this time is staying out of the picture completely, a body calling itself the HBS Student Group provides a network of communication through which the various groups—irrespective of their programs and views—can inform one another and the school of what they are doing.

This, everybody seems to agree, is no time for business as usual.

May 12, Tuesday: Most professors had either canceled or rescheduled their classes, and the few who did meet did so early in the morning so to be done by nine-thirty when, with a speech by a pro-peace congressman, the "Education Program" on the war, Cambodia, and the shootings at Kent State began.

In spite, or maybe because, of the topic, it turned out to be a rather quiet, reflective day with groups of students and faculty patiently trying to disentangle muddled strands of argument. The day, the last couple of days, really, were just so many more symptoms of the fact that the United States has contracted a vicious, tropical disease in the jungles of Southeast Asia; a disease that leaves the body politic unimpaired in its outward appearance but in sudden, ever more frequent and more violent seizures, shakes and convulses it down to the last inconsequential little cell. The longer the disease is allowed to go uncured, the higher its debilitating peaks, the lower the troughs of blues and depression that precede the next phase of seeming recovery.

It all reached another depressing low today, with the outrage having spent itself, giving way to the sickening realization that the protest and even the deaths at Kent State haven't brought the United States one step closer to cure. Except maybe that they have driven the dangerously impulsive man—impulsive despite all the hollow jargon of "options" and "contingencies"—the spiteful, bitter man at the White House one step further into unlistening isolation.

It is one of the tragedies of democracy that it is unwittingly sabotaged by those—the near poor, the almost well-off—who stand to benefit the most from it. By those who fear the degradations of their past too much to risk what little they have become on a more promising future. By that silent, sullen majority whose anxieties are all too easily exploited by men like Mr. Nixon.

Yet, in spite of the over-all futility of the situation, the Business School, by this latest series of convulsions, has been driven another irreversible step from its conservative neutrality to face up to the issues of the day. After forty years of gradual and mild change in political weather the Business School, with members of its own student body and faculty, has been thrown straight into the eye of the storm.

> Of the Class of 1930, which graduated forty years ago, 7 per cent are Democrats, 80 per cent are Republicans and 11 per cent are Independents.
>
> Of the Class of 1950, which graduated twenty years ago, 15 per cent are Democrats, 65 per cent are Republicans and 12 per cent are Independents.
>
> Of the Class of 1969, which graduated one year ago, 32 per cent are Democrats, 45 per cent are Republicans and 22 per cent are "none," "other," or "uncertain."
>
> In the Class of 1949, 68 per cent at the time of their graduation said that "Yes," communism is a serious threat to the United States. By the time the Class of 1969 graduated, that percentage had dropped to 25 per cent.

In their *Bulletin #3*, issued yesterday, the chairman of the HBS Student Group describes the change this way:

> It is plain to us that faculty, staff and students have joined together in a way that, as far as we know, is unprecedented in the history of HBS. We feel that the faculty and many of the staff are participating wholeheartedly with students in a variety of actions that have in common a serious determination to bring about rapid changes in American society, especially within the business segment.

In matters political, at least, the student body at the Harvard Business School, if it ever was a body, has grown a great many different heads.

May 16, Saturday: You don't know should you call it a beginning or an end because the two kind of melt into one another, with talk of jobs and new places easing the grip of the second year, and graduation only a couple of weeks away.

Final exams are starting on Monday, and so the members of what used to be Section B decided to hold their farewell picnic today, using the last moments of relative quiet. It was a lucky decision because the day was warm and sunny, and almost everybody dropped by with wife, children, and lunch baskets. The picnic was held on Robert Chasey III's family estate, a place which is rolled out, like a soft, silky rug atop one of the hills outside Boston. There were several short trees dotting the lawn, and through the gaps in their leaves you could see the heads of the men swaying in and out of view, and bits of blankets, curls, and cribs—the women sitting in little circles.

People drifted through the afternoon like so many snips of paper dropped onto slow-moving water, touching and staying, separating and coming together again in an inexhaustible array of patterns.

Still, there was no longer the desperate happiness of some of our earlier gatherings. With much of the strain off, the teetering social structure of the Section had collapsed during the second year, like a tent whose ropes are thrown loose. And so, fittingly, there was no clear-cut end to our last picnic but a gradual breaking up. Partly because you had really nothing more to say to a lot of people and partly because, with others, there were all these things you had always meant to say and do. You just walked away, thinking about when and how you might go to see the nice ones again, about letters to be written, and how this is no end but merely another beginning.

June 9: This month's issue of *True* has the following to say about the Harvard Business School:

> The B-School is, in fact, a sort of grandfather mill, in the sense that it turns out more captains of industry, more patriarchs of the business establishment, than any other institution. Among its 33,000 alumni are 3,300 board chairmen and presidents of major corporations and uncounted (by Harvard) thousands of

> senior partners and vice-presidents—not to mention generals and admirals, senators and congressmen, and such world movers as former Secretary of Defense Robert S. McNamara . . .

You read this and similar things which keep appearing in the papers, and you ask the alumni office about it, and you get a flurry of polite excuses. The true extent of the alumni's power remains a jealously guarded secret, hidden in the vault-like cellar of Alumni Center. There, in the care of discreet custodians, some 33,000 file cards are stored in large steel tubs, rotating at the touch of a button with a soft, nasal whirr, straight from the sound track of a science-fiction movie.

In part, this hush-hush must stem from an understandable desire to protect the privacy of the alumni. Much more likely, it has its origins in something comparable to a rich man's reluctance to reveal the true size of his fortune, for fear that this makes him an easy target for envy and all sorts of unwelcome curiosity.

Because if you check into the situation, if, for example, you go through the 500 largest industrial corporations listed in last month's *Fortune*, you find that one out of eleven of them—45 in all—are run by a Harvard M.B.A. This figure becomes even more impressive if you include among the alumni also the graduates of the management training programs and those who attended without getting a degree. Then about one in seven of the top 500 have a Harvard chairman or president.

Harvard's share of the nation's most powerful executives is extraordinary by any standards, but compared with some of its best-known rivals, there is no contest. The runner-up to Harvard's 45 is the University of Chicago Business School with 5; Stanford with 4; MIT, New York University, and the University of Michigan's business schools with 2 each.

Some of the Harvard dominance can be explained by the fact that it is the United States' oldest *graduate* school of business administration (it was founded in 1908), and that it has consistently produced the largest graduating classes: Some 25,000 M.B.A.s, as opposed to 8,100 by Chicago, 6,900 by Wharton, 5,700 by Columbia, and 5,400 by Stanford. Yet, together, these last four schools have produced as many M.B.A.s as Harvard, but only 9 of them (as opposed to Harvard's 45) have made it to the top of one of *Fortune*'s 500.

It's quite clear now why the school isn't too eager to talk about the reach and influence of its graduates, because if you are so obviously No. 1, you know that everyone is after you, and you don't want to encourage them to try even harder.

June 11, Commencement Day: Now that graduation has finally come around, at least half of the Section is at work or on vacation. Two weeks, especially two weeks of vacation, were too much to be wasted on a ceremony and a piece of paper.

The glamorous part of the ceremony was held, over in the Yard, on the green between Memorial Church and Widener Library. A large stage had been erected on the steps of Memorial Church, which was filled to the edge with robed dignitaries and marshals in gray top hats. Facing them, in the hot sun, were the degree candidates, many wearing white armbands for peace, instead of robes, one carrying a flag of the Viet Cong. And all around, parents and relatives crowded the green.

It was a very mixed ceremony, because soon, a group of young blacks from the slums downriver, behind the university, interrupted everything, sending the colorful robes of the dignitaries flying back and forth across the stage, in hurried consultation. The blacks, in jeans and freaky shirts, through a bullhorn—the mikes they seized were turned off in a hurry—demanded that the university stop moving into their neighborhood, tearing down houses, and evicting people.

After some sort of compromise was achieved and the blacks

had left, there were the scheduled speeches, at the end of which the president of the university got up, reciting a formula for all the people receiving advanced degrees and a formula for all the people receiving bachelor degrees, and because the negotiations with the blacks had taken up quite a bit of time, that ended the ceremony.

The Business School graduates now went back, across the river, to actually receive their degrees at their own school. The ceremony was inside Kresge, and though only about half the graduates were there, they and their relatives filled the building all the way back to the door. There was an immense line waiting for food and an immense line waiting for degrees, with some people deciding that it was too long for the food and to get their degree first, and others deciding that it was too long for the degree and to get their food first.

The place was hot and happy. As you approached the table with the degrees, all kinds of people started shaking your hand, the assistant dean, the dean's wife, and, finally, there was the dean himself with a friendly handshake and a crimson envelope, as a lot of flash bulbs put a zing into your eye.

It was the kind of day that left you with a montage of half-defined pictures all crowded into one another, no one of them really dominant or memorable, but all of them together forming an experience too pleasant to be quickly forgotten. But now that it's over, the world, which had shrunk to the size of a classroom, has suddenly expanded again, like a window opened onto a crisp morning. How could it all have been so much to us, how could it have hurt so much at times —so . . . so little a place?

After being "up" for so long, the pendulum of our feelings is swinging toward a relaxed, indifferent "down."

July 20: For what it's worth, the job hunt has yielded a first verdict on Section B. On the whole, the prophets of doom proved to be false prophets. On the whole, the predictors of cutbacks in HBS recruiting and lowered salaries were definitely gazing into the wrong crystal ball. In the case of some Section mates, however, even a Harvard Business School diploma wasn't big enough to hide an inexperienced or irresolute man.

By the time the final set of exams came around, all but fifteen names on the Section list were followed by a company name. And of those still blank, four were getting ready to start their own businesses and ten others had at least one firm offer or promising lead. Only one really had found nothing, and he hadn't found anything because he didn't know what he was looking for.

The starting salaries range from $13,000 to a high of $25,000. The median starting salary for the entire class is $15,000, up $1,000 from the year before.

In spite of its reported wretched condition, ten Section mates have landed jobs in the stock-brokerage and investment-banking business. Four of them on Wall Street.

Five have gone into consulting.

One has been invited to become an assistant's assistant at the White House.

Two have joined civil branches of the armed forces because they were drafted. Another draftee voluntarily chose the Department of Defense. One each was drafted by the Army, Navy, and Air Force.

One man is with the Department of Health, Education and Welfare. Two work for their respective state governments—one in Kentucky, the other in Idaho.

Two have become lecturers on business administration.

One is working for a company that makes yachts.

Four are pursuing professional military careers in the Navy and Air Force.

One owns part of a going concern.

One is in Honolulu.

Two have been drafted by the French Army.

Four have joined large banks.

Four have jumped back into the lap of alma mater as research assistants and/or doctoral students.

The rest are spread over a large variety of manufacturing and service companies that range from gasoline to air transportation, from wood to broadcasting, from diesel engines to department stores.

9
The Culture Hero

(JACOB SOKOLOVSKY *talking*)

"Different things make different people afraid. And strange situations, even if they are harmless, can make you afraid, though when you think back, it seems odd that you could have been so frightened.

"That particular time we had flown out to a base on a cross-country training mission—there were four airplanes—and the idea was to fly back at night. It was to be my first night-solo mission. I don't remember exactly, I think mine was the second airplane to take off, and everything went normally. It was quite dark. Everything was going smoothly until, I don't know, at about thirty thousand feet, one of my engines started acting up.

"This base we had just taken off from was to the south. I think it was actually only a thirty-minute flight from our home base, but since we were supposed to fly for an hour and a half, I was flying north and then I was going to turn and fly west and then turn again and fly south—kind of fly around three sides of a rectangle.

"So I was heading up into—I think it must have been Oklahoma—where there were no cities, very few radio and navigational aids. After about five or ten minutes—I was getting rather far away—I was supposed to tune in to a station out in front of me. And when I tuned to this station—nothing happened. The instrument I was supposed to guide myself by was circular and had a needle on it. The needle just rotated. It wasn't locking on to anything. It wasn't pointing anywhere. It was just going around in circles.

"It caught me off guard. We always trained for emergencies, and there was no single thing that could go wrong which we weren't somewhat prepared for. But one of my two engines had already gone wrong. And I was going, perhaps five hundred miles an hour, not knowing exactly where, without the use of the instrument to get myself back with. Being up there, at night, I started having all kinds of fears.

"You can't crash-land a jet airplane. I mean, you can't just put it down on a field or something. You have to have a runway. And we had a very strong instinct not to lose the plane. I can't really describe it. I mean, I wasn't afraid of ejecting . . . but I was terribly afraid of having to go back and face the other student pilots, having lost a million-and-a-half-dollar airplane.

"I called immediately on the radio, saying: 'Fort Hobbsville Center, this is Beercan three-four.' 'Beercan' is a student code name, and they finally caught on and gave me a direction. Soon I could see the lights of our home base on the horizon because the town nearby is quite a big town and at night, from 42,000 feet, you can see it a hundred miles away.

"As I found out later, the station I was trying to tune in on, wasn't transmitting that night. So there was nothing whatsoever the matter with my instrument. But I just panicked. Nobody *knew* I had panicked—it wasn't a major thing. But, I mean, I knew how I felt. And I felt very silly about it afterward.

"I guess the risk involved in learning to fly a jet airplane was one of the major factors that attracted me to it.

It's really that different cultures have different ways of becoming a man. But somehow you always have to pick some difficult task. Something which proves that you are a cool guy, you know, that you have guts or whatever. I don't know whether that explains it—probably there was also an aspect of being on one's own. I mean, our culture keeps young people down a lot. We're held in enforced adolescence for a protracted period, and you seldom have a chance to test yourself. You're always overly protected in everything. If you go boating, you have to obey Coast Guard regulations; if you want to climb a mountain you have to go with a group; if you want to go scuba diving, you have to use the 'buddy system.' Flying seemed one of the few ways that you could really be alone and put yourself in a situation where you couldn't just shrug and wait for somebody to help you out, if you got into trouble.

"My family in New York was always fantastically impressed with my intelligence and the fact that I was going to boarding schools, relatively good boarding schools. To me that always seemed ridiculous because, although I liked to study and read, somehow the greatest satisfaction never came from school. I got through Harvard undergraduate doing ridiculously little work. And although I was under pressure during exam periods because I had done so little work, I never felt threatened, really threatened in school. So the idea of doing something I viewed as being difficult; something which other people viewed as being difficult; something which would be a . . . a real test had a lot of attraction for me.

"It's a romantic, it's definitely not a rational thing. The best pilots I knew in the Air Force couldn't really explain why it is that they want to get up there in an airplane. You speak to a mountain climber: 'What the hell do you want to get to the top of that ridge for?

Why do you risk your life scaling rock faces?' I will say that I was not really a natural pilot. I have the feeling that if I had ever been put into an extremely difficult flying situation . . . I guess what I want to say: To be a really excellent pilot you have to live and breathe flying a particular airplane. You have to be able to do the most important things automatically. It has to become instinctual. And in order to have that depth of feeling about a thing, you have to have tremendously deep involvement.

"I never had that kind of involvement; I never had that deep a feeling about anything, really. I come from a somewhat broken home. My mother became ill and was hospitalized permanently when I was less than a year old. My family felt—my father and my aunt didn't feel they could take care of me properly, so they sent me away to boarding school at the age of five. And I went to a school which was run by very independent, very outdoors, very intellectual, very culturally tuned in, very alive people. Whereas my family in New York was relatively timid. Afraid of having their apartment broken into. Afraid of losing their money. Afraid of wars. Just worried, worried people.

"The man who ran the school was really the typical, universal Renaissance man. He was a carpenter. He made musical instruments which he played. He was an artist in photography. He was extremely well read and tremendously imaginative. And I would go home to New York where the people were kind of uncreative, unimaginative. I really didn't want to be, well, like my father. And yet my father had control of me in various ways, particularly through money. I mean even at this early age it was very easy to make the comparison between, on the one hand, these people at the school who were relatively afraid of nothing and who did everything, and these other people, my blood relatives, who did nothing and seemed to be afraid of everything.

"I would come home from school, where I had been sleeping out in a tent in the middle of winter—sometimes it would be ten below zero Fahrenheit—and I would go home to New York where it wasn't very cold, and immediately my aunt and my father would be harping at me about putting on my galoshes and wearing a T-shirt and putting on a scarf and not going out without a hat. Even to a child, this was a ridiculous comparison.

"However, your family is your family and they leave some kind of mark on you. And, I guess, I always have wondered to what extent I was what I didn't want to be and had to prove to myself that in spite of the fact that my family were people who have been what I call 'beaten by life,' I didn't want to have to suffer their fate just because I was born of their blood.

"At the school I was constantly pushed into being independent. Maybe there wouldn't be anybody to play with, and I would go into the house where I could be with other people, but Martha, the wife of the man who ran the school, would scold me in a friendly fashion and say: 'Why don't you go outside? Get out of the house. Don't hang around. Go out and do something.' In New York my family were all continually pulling together. Continually trying to huddle into little groups to protect themselves.

"It worked out that the only time the family would get together were these climactic occasions—whether it was money or somebody was sick—which seemed ridiculous to me. If somebody would die or somebody would be in the hospital, we'd go there and everybody would arrive. People you didn't even know. And everybody would say: 'Oh, this is Morris' boy, Jacob.' And I'd look up and I'd see all these people and I had no idea who the hell they were. And they were all looking down as if they knew exactly who I was. But, in fact, they had no idea who I was. They just knew that I was Morris' boy, Jacob. Ever since, I've had a skeptical attitude about families that are always proselytizing this idea that blood is thicker than water.

"That's as well as I can sum up the strange combination of influences that pushed me into the Air Force.

"Well, from the very beginning, the military as an environment seemed ridiculous. At Harvard—and I suspect everywhere else—ROTC is a total farce. Some of the things they tried to tell us were out and out lies. And yet they didn't seem to know it. And, I thought, maybe when I got out into the real Air Force, it would be different. But it wasn't. Right from the beginning it seemed like a kind of fraternity. To start with, there was hazing and there were a lot of silly traditions. There was a lot of group pressure put on you, to fit the Air Force military way of life.

"Through all of my growing up and learning to perceive the world, there was this kind of a . . . a slight double-image effect. I mean I would read the papers and the history books and I would say to myself: 'The world really can't be as crazy as these events seem.' Intelligent people, leaders, responsible world powers—they can't possibly do some of the stupid things I see them doing. People were writing about military strategy, about 'pre-emptive strikes' and 'mega-kill.' Yet, somehow I couldn't really believe that it was out there. But when I got into the Air Force, it seemed . . . it seemed worse. I mean, it seemed even more unreal than the newspapers. The people who were supposed to be 'the big guys,' the grown-ups, the ones responsible, the fighters, the officers—somehow they seemed very childish and immature.

"And this continually amazed me. I would live, when I was in SAC [Strategic Air Command], I would live day in and day out on alert with seventy or eighty men, and maybe sixty of them were officers. They were crew members on the B 52s; some were majors and colonels—people who had been in World War II—with distinguished military records. And what do you suppose they did out there, while they were waiting for World War III? They played poker. Everybody played poker, and they would get tremendously involved in these damned poker games.

"It took me five years in the Air Force to finally figure out that that's the way the world really is. And that this is why the crazy things are happening. And that you couldn't, for example, expect anything more of Richard Nixon, just because he is President than you could expect of my aircraft commander, who was demoted to copilot, after ten years, for having showed up one day so drunk that the crew refused to fly with him.

"Suffice it to say that for the last three of my five years in the Air Force I thought of almost nothing but getting out. I briefly considered becoming a doctor, but the education just seemed too long. I didn't really want to go back to school for that long a time. I mean, being in such limbo socially and having no freedom, since you don't have an income; being constantly evaluated and re-evaluated; cramming your head with more and more things while forgetting more and more—that never really appealed to me.

"So I thought of all the various kinds of graduate schools I could go to that wouldn't be too long, but would still give me some kind of credibility and leverage. I felt that if I'm going to live my life in America and I'm not going to be a bohemian or an artist, I have to have some way of presenting myself. I read somewhere that in America, what you do is what you are. To do little is to be little. And to do nothing is to be nothing. If you haven't got a job, a professional position, you're extremely unlikely to have any social status whatsoever.

"Well, Business School seemed like the quickest way to solve my problem. I wanted to stay in Boston. I was involved with a woman, I had an apartment, I had friends here. And so, in fact, I only applied to Sloan and Harvard. But I wasn't accepted at Sloan and, at first, I wasn't accepted at Harvard. If I'm telling my life, I really should tell that one because it was kind of ironic.

"It happened that the day on which the acceptances were to be received in Boston was a Friday. But on Friday I didn't hear. So I went over to the Business School to find out and, finally, I got to talk to this young guy. And it was very weird, because I went into this office and he had my file out and he said: 'Well, this is the letter you got.'

"I said: 'Well, this is interesting. I . . . I got 94 on the test and I've been a SAC-B-52-pilot-nuclear-weapons-captain-culture hero. Why aren't you accepting me?' I thought at least I could find out what was wrong with me so I could perhaps plan my next strategy differently.

"So we get into conversation and it . . . it . . . it just drifted. It was a very weird kind of conversation because I kept asking him: 'Why haven't you accepted me? Here I am, an intelligent guy. An Ivy Leaguer, Harvard College graduate, and so forth.' But I wasn't getting any answers out of him. He was asking me questions, and I must admit they were kind of interesting: 'Here you got out of Harvard. You majored in literature. You went into the Air Force. And now you say you want to go into business . . . why?'

"I looked on this guy as a contemporary, as a peer. I figured he was some assistant to the assistant they had shoved in my direction to push me off. So I said: 'Well, you're about my age . . . do *you* have any idea where *you* are going to be in five or ten years? What are *you* doing here?' And we both got rather involved and the conversation went very, very far afield. And after an hour he turned to me and said: 'Look,' he looked at his watch, 'I've got another appointment now. I'll tell you what I'll do. I'll accept you if you'll tell me that you'll come. I'll go back to the Admissions Committee and ask them to accept you. But I want to know, before I make that effort, whether you will come.' I . . . I walked out of his office kind of stunned. I actually—I couldn't believe it. It was so unreal.

"It wasn't that I was determined to be a particular sort of businessman; that I was going to get a business education no matter what. My idea was that I would *probably* become a businessman, *if* I was able to go to Harvard Business.

"I guess, I'm an elitist at heart. It has to do with the idea that—damnit—you can't ever stand still. Security comes from moving forward; no matter how comfortable you are, where you are. You've got to be a specialist. And once you are a specialist, you have to get recognized in your specialty. The peer group gets smaller and smaller, but there's always some group of people looking over your shoulder; there is always a better place to be. 'Up, up,' I think, is the key proposition.

"And this is really a stupid thing. Because mature people shouldn't give so much of a shit about what other people think. I mean, real satisfaction should be based upon whether you enjoy whatever you're doing. But, in fact, that's not the way it is with me; and it isn't the way it is with other people. That's what I'm talking about when I say 'elitism.' It's part of the American educational experience. It was bred into me and I resent it. But if I'm going to be a businessman, by God, I want to be a *Harvard* businessman.

"Well, now I *am*, and I'm relieved the two years are over. Perhaps it was the best way to force people to learn quickly. But it was typically American. It's efficient. It gets the job done. But it's kind of inhuman. The whole David Rosen thing. I'm sure some people thought that I became excessively impressed by the David Rosen thing. Which I wasn't. I don't think I was touched by it nearly as much as a lot of people. But it did become—it became a paradigm for me of the whole experience. It was the culmination of all the worst things about the Harvard Business School.

"It probably happens only once in every three or four years that a David Rosen type incident comes along. Where the thing really runs out of control. Where a lot . . . where really too much hostility—more than can be borne—is focused on a really weak individual. But the fact that it can happen is built into the system. I mean, once you put together a group like that and you give them material where there are no set, right answers, you create a situation which has considerable potential for getting out of control. Because you're asking some very powerful people to test themselves against each other and against the group; people who don't always care too much whose blood is shed. Once they get involved they're striking out in all directions and then . . . anything can happen.

"Somehow the Rosen thing summed up what was very real about the situation. The emotional strength of the whole thing. The extent to which everybody's feelings really were . . . being manipulated and driven against each other. I was constantly wincing at the things that were going on in class. I still have visions of Jane intensely embarrassed, practically in tears; or visions of Gilfeder giving these emotional, emotional talks with a trembling voice; or visions of that guy Stahl who got wiped out in class and went into the Army, and Steve Blotner who got demolished and never talked again. And, you know, Sy Goodwin flattening that Indian guy who came to talk about the automobile business on Black Power Day. And just—I saw these people suffering real blows, from which they might never altogether recover.

"For these reasons I didn't like it. And I didn't think it was an adequate reflection of the real world. Because I don't think that the stress, even in business, is that great. I'm sure people don't want to live at that feverish pitch forever. And for these reasons I don't care if I ever meet again, you know, half the people in our Section. It was depressing that there were so many guys who, at least to my sense, were so wrongheaded; who are going to be so goddamned effective and energetic in perpetuating just exactly the sorts of things that I would like to see eradicated by fire. The whole money thing, the song: 'Hey Mr. Businessman, money can't buy you love . . .' The whole thing the current youth culture has against materialism, capitalism. You know, power serving its own ends.

"The depth of the rationalizations businessmen go through to justify increasing their own power! At such obvious expense to the people! Call it dirty pool or power politics—call it what the hell you want. But, in fact, it's clear to me—now more than ever—that people who are trained to think this way, to increase power, to sell more goods, to increase efficiency, to make more profits—people who are trained to concentrate on these ends are simultaneously trained to de-emphasize all kinds of human values.

"It's not by accident that we have riots in the cities and slums, and that we have starvation in the midst of the richest country in the world. And it's not just by accident that we get involved in Vietnam wars. It's kind of a . . . a mass insanity. And you have people who are called 'sane' continually promoting these insanities. And arguing why they should be continued. And it seems to me that there are too many people at the Business School who are going to do just that. They'll be out there, fighting for their company, and they'll be convinced that they're doing the American thing. That they won't win unless it's right that they should win; that right will prevail, and that whatever prevails is right.

"There is a tremendous homogeneity of these . . . these feelings and attitudes. When the chips are down and everybody is forced to stand up and be counted, the Business School is a very groupy place and people really hesitate to set themselves apart.

"Fortunately, I was pretty lucky in terms of roommates. Frank and I always seemed to get involved in these damned arguments which sometimes would last half the night, but maybe because of that, because in a jovial way we emphasized our differences, we became very good friends. Having gone to boarding schools and always having lived with other people, I must have had a hundred roommates in my life, and I didn't always have an opportunity to choose them. In fact, coming from an unsettled sort of background, never having lived in a house of my own, in a house where there was any kind of home atmosphere at all, never even having my own room—you know, I got used to it but I always had this image that things, somehow, ought to be better. That there ought to be a place where I could put my things and come back and have them in the same particular place.

"Well, in the summer between the first and the second year at the Business School, I met a guy who was importing these prefabricated Norwegian houses. He made certain 'come-ons' to me and I made certain 'come-ons' to him, and the upshot of it was that I agreed to build one of his houses and build one relatively quickly. I was going to move into it that September. I thought that because of the prefab I would get it done quickly and would have a cheap house to live in for the second year of school. I thought that if I were able to sell even as few as three or four of these houses on the side, I would end up with a very cheap place of my own. It seemed like I had everything to gain and very little to lose.

"So I went ahead with it and it took almost exactly one year and a fantastic investment of my own personal time to get the house built. I found this piece of land, a relatively large piece of property with a lot of trees, a good stand of rather tall pines, perhaps a hundred feet tall. The house is completely surrounded by them and they keep the sun off, so it doesn't get too hot in the summer. You can always hear them, every time there is a little breeze.

"I've never had any feelings of anxiety about living by myself; as a matter of fact, I rather like it, but sometimes it gets a little lonely. But you can get lonely living in an apartment in a big city. And I have enough friends—enough good friends—that within any hour of the night and day, I can lure someone down to my place or go up to Boston.

"At any rate, the house wasn't finished until July, and during the entire second year at the school I was continually sticking my fingers into the dike, as far as the house was concerned. There was a problem with the pipes freezing, and getting the house so it would be at least wintertight and wouldn't be hurt by the cold and snow. There were piles of boxes and sawdust and tools and wooden sawhorses, and you could scarcely walk across the living-room floor in daylight without breaking your neck or cutting your leg off on some tool. And if you went outdoors, you were in danger of sinking up to your waist in mud—which I literally once did, right up to my belt in mud, and I thought it was going to go over my head. Cars were getting stuck and the electricity would fail—it was really depressing. The whole house just seemed one continual, long problem which never got solved.

"At the same time my social life was rather unsettled. I separated from one girl whom I was rather involved with, and that was an unhappy ending; and then I got involved with two other women in relatively unsatisfactory ways—every conceivable aspect of my life during that year was very, very unsettled. It wasn't until June, July—the Business School having ended—that I got everything together again, the way I had originally hoped to have it by the previous September.

"One day at the end of July, around four in the afternoon, I tried to call a couple of friends, and everybody was out of town. It seemed everybody I knew had left. Well, at eight-thirty that night I was on a plane to Europe, and I stayed there for six weeks and saw a lot of old friends and really had a good time. I traveled the major jumps by plane and the rest of the time I hitchhiked. I hitchhiked from Rome to Capri and from Capri—actually from Vesuvius, from the top of Vesuvius—to St. Tropez, and back to Nice.

"Now what?

"I came back and looked at my house and decided that with a perspective of six weeks it actually looked better than good. It really looked beautiful. And I thought that I would be an idiot to leave this beautiful place. And I still have my friends in Boston. And Boston is really as good as anywhere in the United States and better than most. So why shouldn't I stay here?

"My present strategy is to find a job in Boston. I have no specific career goal in mind. I would like to have some money in the bank. I would like to be able to change my occupation every several years. And, if I wanted, to start my own business. But right now I need income to support my house, to pay my current debts, and to start acquiring capital, to give me a springboard from which to start my own venture.

"At the Business School Placement Office they said that it's the wrong time of the year, and at the Alumni Placement Office they showed me the open positions which didn't look too attractive.

"So then I placed the ad.

England one-bank
pany, is searching
lan/Auditor to de-
ional audits of a
uter operation (GE
le will design and
omputerized audit
id evaluate opera-
is.
, complete with sal-
nd requirements is
'all Street Journal
portunity Employer

REIGHT
MISSION
SALESMEN
llent opportunities
experienced men &
namic growth com-

power planning, mgmt. develop., compensation, employment & benefits. Exp. includes single and multi-plant labor negotiations. Currently employed by top U.S. corp., 20 yrs. exp., college & law degrees. Willing to relocate.
Box J-468, The Wall Street Journal

Creative Resourceful Harvard MBA ex-AF pilot seeks unusual job stimulating environment, interesting future, money not prime factor. Prefer Boston area but will consider interesting offers worldwide. Reply: Box J-472, The Wall Street Journal

MGR. SYSTEMS PLANNING MS Solid exp. large mfg. including heavy "hands-on" systems design, programming, operations. Strong exposure to cost control and accounting techniques. Earning $20,000 Robert Half Personnel 140 Federal St. Boston, Mass. 423-6440

MARKETING EXECUTIVE, 33, American & French nationality. 10 years marketing management experience with French & American

City.

SECURITIES ANAL
Rep. manager portf
duction. Writes bril
reports, reg. S.E.C.
advisor.
Box M-925, The Wall

POSITIONS WAN

CARETAKER—
For Lodge, Island
Marina or
Location or Salary
A. L. BEEN
825 E. Little
Norfolk, Va.
(703) 588

MERGER VICTIM—
grad with strong sa
seeks opportunity
where intelligence
can best be applied

"I had seen ads like that in places like the New York *Times* and the *Wall Street Journal*. I remember one in particular: 'Ex marine officer seeks adventure.' I mean, a lot of people read the New York *Times* and a lot of people read the *Wall Street Journal*, and it figures that there might just be somebody out there who needs somebody to smuggle gold out of Kasiriland. The point is, I believe people *do* have these experiences, and the idea appeals to me to do something completely different from time to time. And since this is an in-between time in my life—I'm finished up with one set of environments: school, my house, a girl friend—I am relatively free, and I know that sooner or later I am going to be involved in something more long range; it seems like now is the time to throw myself up for anything."

III
The Real World

AUGUST TO DECEMBER AFTER GRADUATION

August 5, Cambridge, Massachusetts: "Operator? I'd like to speak to Mr. Laratti, please . . ."

"His extension, sir?"

"I'm sorry, I don't . . ."

"I'll give you the records division, sir." Click.

A long, long time of ringing.

"Records. Can I help you?"

"I'm trying to locate a man by the name of Fred Laratti, he is . . ."

"What's that? Ted what?"

"Fred . . . with an F like Florence . . ."

"How do you spell his last name?"

One minute. Two. Several minutes.

"We don't have anyone with that name in our records, sir."

"Listen, he must . . . he just joined recently . . . at the beginning of June, I believe . . . Could you try?"

"Can you hold?"

Click. Silence. A lot of static.

"He isn't a transfer, is he?"

"No—I don't believe so . . . believe he's just joined recently—for the first time . . ."

"Sorry, there's no one by that name, sir. He is in Heavy Turbines, you're sure of that, sir? He couldn't be in Light Turbines or in Switches?"

"He's an electrical engineer, as far as I know . . ."

"A what, sir?"

"Oh, a . . . could you check with Light Turbines, please, maybe he is there . . . Laratti . . . Fred Laratti is the name . . ."

Click.

"Transfer this call to 8774, please."

"8774?"

"That's right."

Click.

"Can you hold, sir? The line is busy."

Click.

"Hello?"

"Operator, could you connect me with Mr. Laratti . . . Fred Laratti . . . he *must* be on your list; he's been working for you now for two months . . ."

"Sorry, sir. I've no one by that name on my list here. I'll give you Personnel."

"Operator! Hello, operator! . . ."

Click.

"Personnel?"

"Hello? Could you please give me the extension for Fred Laratti? . . . yes, Fred—with an F . . ."

"Can you hold a minute, please?"

Click.

"How long has this Mr. Laratti been with us, sir?"

"About two months . . . since June . . ."

"Do you know what department he is working for? Sales? This is a big division here."

"No . . . no, I don't . . ."

Static.

"Well, he isn't with Light Turbines then. Have you checked Heavy Turbines or Switches? We only keep records of Light Turbines here."

"But he's just been hired . . . this June he was hired from the Harvard Business School. This is the address he gave . . . is there anybody who might know? He must be some kind of trainee . . ."

"Let me give you Mr. Goodhue. He does the professional recruiting. Maybe he can help you."

Click.

"Goodhue."

"Mr. Goodhue? I'm looking for a Mr. Laratti. He just graduated from the Business School—the Harvard Business School—and you hired him . . ."

"What did you say his name was? Loretti?"

Static.

"No—haven't got anyone by that name. Did you check with Diesels? And with Systems? We do the recruiting for Turbines and Switches here."

Click.

Once and for all: Click.

Maybe they could have helped at Diesels, and, who knows, perhaps they might have known something at Systems. But, as it is, Laratti is gone into the corporation, launched onto some mysterious orbit which, so we can only hope, one day will pop him onto the corporate stage like a Fourth of July firecracker, where he will light the scene as a brilliant vice-president or even executive vice-president or, who can tell, as the chief himself.

August 10, New York City: Peter Parsons has to time his arrival at the Seventy-eighth Street station very precisely. If he gets there at five to eight, there is plenty of room on the Seventh Avenue express; but if he gets there at eight or a minute after, as he did today, it's one god-awful jam. Unless you are used to the trip the way Parsons is by now, it would seem bad news one way or the other. The yellow New York air, irritating as it may be up in the streets, at least it's moved around by the cabs and buses. But downstairs, in the subway stations, it just lies rotting, filled with brake dust from the trains and with exhaust flowing down from above. It's a morgue with rows of loose and limp bodies waiting to be hauled away, having the pitiful rest of their zap squeezed out of them by the crush of the too many bodies inside the cars, suffering the most fiendish collection of shrieks, squeals, clunks, and rattles of which inanimate matter is capable.

All of this is in store for Parsons this morning, as his express jerks toward the southernmost tip of Manhattan with non-stop stations suddenly flaring up in a blur of rusty steel columns and white tiles; unheard-of places like Fulton, Canal, and Spring streets. And Parsons and his briefcase in the midst of all this, in another country from his plush apartment uptown, with the doorman doing the honors at the house's entrance.

The Seventh Avenue express jerks and rattles, and you never imagined that Manhattan could be that long until, finally, the whistling brakes grind the train to a halt among a maze of black steel uprights with thin white letters saying: Wall Street. And out he goes, pushed upward by scrambling bodies, out into a narrow street which, as the street sign confirms, is Wall Street.

The Street is an especially narrow trough with gray walls and every variety of pillar glued to, set in front of, and generally used to dress up the dull facades. Many of the buildings have huge American flags hanging lifelessly over the hustle below, and there are so many flags and the street is so narrow that the flags completely block your view. Reaching above the flags, hopelessly dominated by the much taller financial buildings, the lonely soot-blackened spire of a cathedral closes off the far end of the Street.

And all along it, and all around in the area, immense black limousines with yawning chauffeurs leaning against the doors and hoods—lives wasted in waiting; lives wasted anyhow, maybe, but lives wasted conspicuously here, for the sake of two rides a day. As a backdrop to it all, in elegant and expensive understatement, the inconspicuous names of the world's biggest banks and brokerage houses. Banks and more banks and somewhere, at a corner, the big Board—the New

York Stock Exchange—and just behind the cathedral, the Curb—the American Stock Exchange.

In thick, sudden gushes the subways pump in the morning crowd until, at four-thirty in the afternoon, the human reservoir, filled to the brim, opens its floodgates and out they come—wahoooooo!—here they come, whirling around limousines and armored cars, flowing back into the subway stations.

All during the day Parsons is upstairs on a fifteenth floor, just off the Street, at a place in which the ground floor is two stories tall, with gilded plasterwork lining the arches of the ceiling. On the fifteenth floor, a plain wooden door opens on three or four large rooms which lead, without doors, one into the other. Passing through them, Parsons no longer even sees the graphs of all magnitudes covering entire walls, some showing large humps, others recording a seemingly infinite succession of tiny wiggles.

It's in the farthest of these rooms, in the farthest corner, that Parsons has his desk, on which there is a viewing apparatus giving the latest stock-market quotations.

The ring of a phone breaks the busy silence, and there is a fragment of a sentence wrapped in mild surprise: "They aren't going to put the five million into? . . . No? Do you want me to . . ." And as the receiver is placed back on the phone the silence is abruptly restored, the people—most of them in their middle twenties or early thirties—go on reading and writing.

The heart, the real heart, of the place is two floors below. An ultra-plush setup, sporting delicate Chinese vases a-bloom with plastic flowers; a hallway furnished with dark-stained, low chests whose brass mountings blink in the soft light; a middle thing between a chapel and somebody's living room—the entrée to the bosses' offices and their private dining room.

"I came down to Wall Street because the alleys are paved with gold down here. This is supposed to be the ultimate in personal leverage. And if I can learn to play this game well, I'm going to make a lot of money. It would be nice if the United States were set up so that a guy with my talents could go out and help people. But I think it's futile right now. Especially in my position. You've got to be strong to be able to be nice.

"So, right now, what I'm thinking about is making money. If you want to make a lot of money, you're not going to make it as a securities analyst, which is what I am now. The best you can make as an analyst is maybe $40,000 or $50,000 a year. And you're not going to make a lot of money in a hurry if you're making $40,000 or $50,000 a year. What you've got to do is to get into money management; you've got to get that initial 'pie,' a couple of hundred thousand dollars. And people will give it to you, if you can turn it over at 40 per cent or 50 per cent annually.

"Say a guy wants to put a million dollars into the stock market, and say I get 20 per cent of what I make for him on that money. If I can make 50 per cent a year, I make $500,000 for him the first year. The next year I make him $750,000—on top of the $500,000. So the first year I get 20 per cent of $500,000, which is $100,000. Then, the next year, that $100,000 would become $150,000 because I've increased it, along with the guy's money, by 50 per cent. Plus I would get 20 per cent of the $750,000 I made for the guy, which would be $140,000. In two years I would have made $290,000.

"So, for the moment, it's very important to me to stand out as a good analyst. Because if I'm recognized, I might be able to run money for the people I'm with now. That was one of the things that attracted me to them.

Or, if that doesn't come through, I'll try to become assistant money manager at a big fund.

"It would be nice if I could say that my justification for playing the stock market is that I like it more than anything else. But there isn't much of anything I don't like. It would be nice if I could say that a lot of it isn't just a big game. But, in fact, a lot of it *is*. It just happens to be a game where the stakes can be incredibly high.

"In theory, the function of the stock market is to allocate money to commercial ventures. It's a place where people can buy a share in a company and the company, by selling that share, gets money with which it can do business. In theory also, the better that company's prospects for the future—the greater its projected earnings—the more people will pay to have a share of that future.

"Now, in actual fact, in the long run, shares of stock *do* move according to a company's prospects. But by talking about the long run, you're talking about months, sometimes even years. In the short run, however, the people who play the swings in the market don't pay any attention to the companies whose stocks they are buying. Whether they pollute the air, whether they make ammunition, or even what their earnings trend is. They just know when a stock is gonna move. They may be a personal friend of the president of the company or of the company's investment banker. They know before somebody else knows. So they buy low and sell high. Or they sell high and buy low. And that's all they do. They buy and sell, and they make an incredible amount of money.

"Take what's happened to the software companies.* During the last rise of the stock market, one company's

* Software companies write computer programs.

stock has doubled; another's has tripled; I know of one company whose earnings trend is actually down and its stock has quadrupled. It's true, the demand for software is going to be almost sensational. But the earnings projected are very low, and if you know the software industry, it's almost impossible for them to go any higher. But that doesn't make any difference to the people playing the stock market.

"You could, of course, try to have banks do what the stock market does. You could have a clerk with one of those eyeshades figure out what the value of a company, what the price of a share in it should be. But then, you know, this guy is open to pressure and corruption. And if the government were to set stock prices, the government is just people too. It's the same problem as trying to set the price for some consumer product. Everybody wants to know what the price of oysters should be. What should the price of oysters be? You couldn't, by any stretch of the imagination, set the prices for all the consumer products in New York City. So you don't try. You just let private enterprise—supply and demand—take care of it. And even less could you put a price tag on all the companies in the United States, on what a share in them should be worth. So you let the stock market do it. You accept that there is a market for stocks just like there is a fish market.

"From the social aspect it's kind of sad that there should be no better, no more efficient, no more objective way to allocate money for private ventures. But what I'm thinking about, right now, is making money. And I'm not, you know, worrying too much about the social aspect. Because it's going to take everything I've got to establish a reputation as a good analyst and potential money manager. And then, one day, a guy will come and say:

'Look, I've got five million dollars. Will you run it for me?' "

August 11, New York City: Even by New York standards, the garment district on mid-Manhattan's West Side is a pretty busy place. Trucks, parked bumper to bumper, line its streets, and the sidewalks are cluttered with tiers of cardboard shipping boxes, around which blacks and Puerto Ricans run an obstacle course, pushing tall clothes racks mounted on screeching wheels. A row of open doors spews out crews carrying, pulling crates and racks, with the empty racks being squealed back into the buildings, whose second- and third-story windows display, in brightest neon, the signatures of ribbon and yarn manufacturers, of knitting mills, and apparel houses. Shouts of twisted English and Spanish burst in the air—it's crowded and hurried and now, in early August, it's as hot as a restaurant kitchen.

On a regular work day, like today, you find Ben Davidson five floors above all this, corner of Eighth Avenue and Thirty-seventh Street, in an unmemorable, strictly businesslike building. The building blends in with the other places there which, with their large doors and bright windows, seem to be in between office buildings and storage houses. Davidson's office, cool and carpeted, is a great relief from the street, and the rug and the air conditioner, the large window, and the desk with the glass plate announce right away that you have entered the office of someone who is someone—at least in terms of the local hierarchy.

"I was the boss's son then, and I am the boss's son now. The M.B.A. hasn't changed a thing. Same attitudes.

"You just never know where you are. You never know how close what people are saying to you comes to the truth. Some people will 'yes' you and some people will 'no' you; some will be deferential and some will be rude. But you never know; are they talking to you as their boss or as their boss's son? You never know what motivates people to do what they do.

"We deal with salesmen here, and salesmen will make the boss's life difficult no matter who the boss is. A salesman is out for his customer and, therefore, when he tells you something, you must understand that he is thinking about it in the context of his customer. These guys will try to put a lot of pressure on me to do one thing or another. You know, they are talking that the quality is bad, they tell me that the prices are too high, they tell me the terms are no good, and they tell me delivery is too slow. And if I believe all this, then I have to believe we have a lousy business. A lot of what these guys are telling me—they aren't doing it to push me around because I am the boss's son. They are pushing me around because I am the boss.

"On the whole, I've found that everybody here is willing to let me assume the power. They are willing to trust me and co-operate with me. Because I am their future. If they are going to fight me, then we're just going to be running around like a cat chasing his tail. So it seems to me that everyone here has decided to co-operate and be honest and level with me to as large a degree as they can. Which is, I think, to an acceptable degree.

"Unfortunately, my relationship with my father is not—it's different now than it was two years ago. My father is very strong, very independent, and he can be a very difficult man in that things which didn't make an impression on me two years ago now are very difficult to take. And I had to bring it out—it has come into open conflict—and we're trying to deal with it in a rational way. But you can't deal with a problem like this in a rational way. So, you know, most of the burden is on me, and it's real, and it comes down to what, a lot of times, we discussed at school: that the human part of business is the real challenge we face. And here is the perfect example."

August 13, New York City: It was one of those days when the lengthy, unnecessarily complicated explanations of the weather man become major news. When you look up his prognosis with the same worried haste that you look up the latest quotations from the stock market. It was the type of day on which the news of the weather wiped out your hopes just as thoroughly as the news of the stock market has done in recent weeks.

The New York papers were advising people to stay indoors because the air outside had become so hot and humid and fouled by the traffic that it burned your eyes and throat and was pronounced unsafe for breathing. And because people did as they were told, and turned on their fans and air conditioners, there was danger that the overload would blow the city's electric circuits, and TV and the papers were urging people to turn off extra lights and elevators.

This is why it was dark on the ground floor of the building in which Mel Kandel works. They had turned off all the lights except for what was necessary to direct the mob that was pouring from the elevators. And the few bulbs that were on, like a couple of lost sunrays, set off flashes of white on the shirts and collars that passed underneath them. The evening rush-hour crowd was in progress inside the building's revolving doors and in many thin streams flowed into the thickening crowd that ran along the sidewalk.

Kandel stepped out on the west side of the building, and the air hit him, wrapped around him like a smelly, wet rag, threatening to suffocate him. Immediately, sweat began to run down his neck and his back and stained the front of his shirt. He had a good fifteen minutes ahead, from Fifth over to Eighth Avenue. Some people almost ran to get out of this hot and heavy hell, cursing the traffic lights that prolonged their suffering, until over at the Port Authority Bus Terminal, the stream of people again split, funneled into up-and-down moving staircases.

Kandel rode the staircases all the way to the fourth floor and just barely got one of the last seats on the bus. It was nice and cool inside, in spite of all the people. There was a jerk as the driver put the engine into gear and the bus, picking up speed, broke into daylight, four floors above the jammed streets, the cabs weaving in and out of traffic and parking lots, full of brightly blue-orange and red suburban buses.

The bus swung down the ramp through tight turns that pushed Kandel against the man in the next seat, and slowed as it wedged into the honking mess of cars that were trying to organize into two lines as they headed for Lincoln Tunnel. Once inside the tunnel, the bus whipped along, and the white tile walls seemed no more than a couple of inches away, and because they were so close, you got the feeling that the bus was really moving.

After the tunnel, the bus climbed up on the ledge overlooking the Hudson River, and you could see long barge trains pushed by tiny tugs, and beyond the barges, on the other side of the Hudson, the jagged Manhattan skyline slowly flattened as the bus moved up along the river. The view was really sensational and a lot of new apartment buildings crowded the ledge. The buildings had fancy names like "River View Park" and "Altamont Gardens," and you could easily understand how a guy could put up with working in Manhattan if, in the evenings, he could come home to a place like this. Because, from here, the skyscrapers bunched about midtown with their million lights looked exceedingly daring. In their varying height they were like pipes of an organ, their harsh, angular outlines blending into a rich, almost religious chord.

Manhattan was close enough so that you could see the grand and beautiful things about the island; too far to hear the constant complaints of the horns, the wail of the ambulances.

Kandel could still roughly make out his office building, right in the thick of it, about a block from Rockefeller Plaza. It's just beyond the excited, polyglot chatter of the tourists, the unexpected parasols of the Café Promenade, which, like a flicker of compassion, are thrown in with the gnashing of teeth, the calculating helpless indifference that is New York City.

The building's smog-blackened face rises to forty or fifty floors with an elegant red canopy shadowing its main entrance. But the pomp definitely ends outside Kandel's office. The room has little that would make it a desirable place to be, not even a window. Instead, it dozes in a monotonous hum of grays and washed-out greens, which is drowned out, in irregular intervals, by the rumble of the elevator passing the seventeenth floor. It's a makeshift place with a tall steel closet in a corner on top of which a couple of old typewriters accumulate dust. Sitting at his desk, Kandel turns his back on a colleague, facing the dimly lit far end of the room. His desk is large but plain, with a heavily padded chair which has one of its vinyl-covered armrests repaired with Scotch tape. It is in these rather Spartan circumstances that Mel Kandel is preparing his ascent toward the vertigious heights, the glittering, lofty top of Multinational Holding Company, one of the largest corporations in the world.

"I'm called a staff auditor and as staff auditor, I make $16,200 a year. I am supposed to watch over the general interest of Multinational. Right now, I'm involved in a review of Multinational's Corporate

Services, which is a commitment of about 165 people: purchasing, security, telephone, mailroom, secretarial, travel, office maintenance, and so on.

"Today I was working in the Office Maintenance Group, within Corporate Services. I got over there about nine-fifteen and looked at some of the contractual arrangements we have, related to the maintenance of our office machines; whom we have them with and how much business is involved in each. One thing I noticed was that we have a maintenance agreement that says we pay $38 a year for every typewriter; and I noticed that this supplier bills us in January for that whole year of service. Well now, we're giving up this money—$50,000 or so—in January. So I said, since this service is performed over the whole year, why don't we pay for it in July and we'll get to keep our money for six months longer—for whatever that's worth at 6 per cent or 7 per cent.

"This took most of the morning, and in the afternoon I got into looking at another contractual agreement we have with a building contractor. He supplies us with laborers—carpenters, electricians, foremen—to carry out some of the maintenance work that needs to be done in the building. We've had a relationship with this contractor for twenty-five years, and I was looking at some of the billings, just really trying to get a feel.

"Well, all the time I'm doing this, I'm in the office of the five people who handle maintenance agreements. I'm there, I'm thumbing through these bills, and at the same time I'm observing the people. I'm looking at what they are doing. I want to see how these people operate. Are they busy? Is there any way to improve what they are doing? I'm looking at their boss. He controls a hell of a lot of money. I have to be cognizant of what this man is doing. This is part of it. In the back of my mind I'm keeping a record of what I see. Because, eventually, I'm going to get into the actual operation of this group. I am going to sit down with each individual and ask: 'What is it you're doing?' But today now, I'm observing. I'm getting a background on them so that when I do talk to them, I can ask the right questions.

"Well, I'm looking at this contractor—we probably do close to a million dollars' worth of business with this man—and I see that sometimes he's got what he calls 'wall washers,' and sometimes he's got regular laborers. But the regular laborers are here all the time. We give them an office and they are down in the building doing maintenance. I thought: Now wouldn't it be possible to take some of our permanent laborers and let them wash walls? What are these regular laborers doing anyway? And, sure enough, I look at the damn thing and two of the wall washers we're also paying for under another agreement as laborers. Now they can't be doing two things at the same time. They are either washing walls or they are doing maintenance. I would estimate there is probably $30,000 involved here. This is what I did today, I scheduled off the wall washers.

"No one told me specifically to review the contracts. What they said was: 'Look, review everything you think is important. Review the people. Review the money spent. Review their supervision. Rereview their productivity.' I use my imagination.

"But resistance is tremendous. Take Corporate Services—that division is built on relationships which have developed over many years. It has become sluggard and uncreative. We are recommending to reorganize it, and that is going to affect a lot of lives and a lot of ways of doing things. Typewriter maintenance and wall washers may sound trivial, but in the context of our total organization, such problems become very important.

The audit of Corporate Services alone is going to be a recommendation of some two million dollars in cost savings.

"But no matter how we're going to word it, to the manager of Corporate Services our recommendation is going to say that he has done a lousy job. And naturally he is resisting. He is resisting because he thinks he's got some power. Not he himself but someone higher up; he's got contacts. And we think we've got some power; and we've got people who can bring some influence to bear on this question. It isn't a matter of who is right; it's who's got the power. And a lot of times the support is not because our facts are 100 per cent correct, but because some guy likes what we're doing. Or he likes the individuals. Or he thinks, politically speaking, he should back us. And right now, politically speaking, it's going to be favorable for some big guy to back us because of the slump in the economy—see?"

August 19, Cambridge, Massachusetts: After little more than two months, the sort of thing is emerging that McKay, talking early in our first year, had bluntly called a "Mafia." Members of former Section B are meeting at airports, on planes, on international assignments in places such as Paris, London, and Manila. The rumors flow continuously from office to office, often free of charge over company WATS lines. And at least two men—Karl Hoffmann and Dick Lindsay—have been hired away from their first jobs by companies and on recommendation of other Section mates.

Whatever you want to call it, this pattern—which McKay had held up to us as one of the great benefits of Harvard Business—isn't of the phony luncheon-club variety. In fact, if knowing the right people was your game at the school, you were in for two very lonely years. Because even if there had been nothing but millionaires, two years are just too long for flattery not to turn stale; for a guy not to become aware that he is being manipulated. The game was what, rather than whom, you knew.

Plus, with about 40 per cent of the class on some form of financial aid, there simply weren't enough "right" people to go around. And those who did have the right names or stocks made a point of not mentioning them. Like in boot camp, unless you are some sort of superstar, you don't want to be known for anything except doing your duty.

Whatever it is and whatever it is based on, McKay was right: The thing exists and it is working. Because in business, as in everything else, even seemingly reasonable conclusions are often based on very unreasonable assumptions; and the most careful predictions are many times anchored in quite unpredictable personalities. That's where knowing these guys is going to make a lot of difference.

September 8, Salisbury, Massachusetts: After all that grand second-year talk of "distinctive competence," "critical resource," and "multileveled strategy," it comes as kind of a shock to see someone work in a factory. In a place with a high wire fence, a guardhouse, and narrow-windowed walls, to which a large American flag gives the appearance of a fort, a sort of outpost in the first line of defense of American capitalism.

There are several large buildings behind the fence—all of the red-brick variety—but some obviously newer, with larger windows and some connected with tunnel-like covered bridges. The buildings aren't tall, two or three floors at most, but are very long, and because of their length they make the plant look large.

Behind one of the buildings, but still inside the fence, there is a parking area with white squares marked off and a few of the squares—those closest to the wall—are marked with a name. "F. W. Charvis" it says in one square, meaning that Frank Charvis is an officer of the company and, as such, entitled to a personal parking space and a large office with a view.

The office is large indeed, but it's still white and bare with the only color coming from eight or nine orange chairs, arranged in U formation around a long table. In fact, the only remarkable thing about the room, aside from its size, is the view, which scene, like so many ribbons, is strung across its far end: a ribbon of browns, grays, and greens for the town with its houses veiled in blue, late afternoon shadows, a ribbon of transparent blue for the sea beyond, a ribbon of white for the haze blurring the edge of the sea, and a ribbon of a yet paler blue for the sky. Like a coat of arms, this strangely symmetrical tableau is adorned with the white steeple of a church, and much closer, on one of the flat roofs of the factory, the American flag wrestles the wind. The main thoroughfares with their billboards, their gas stations, and greasy spoons; the shabby houses of the town's Portuguese section are discreetly hidden by the trees. It's a picture of quiet and order, of fresh white paint covering what you can see of old facades.

A typical factory in a typical Yankee town with a typically well-groomed young executive sitting behind a typically large desk.

"My official title is business and technical planner, and I'll go so far as to say that my salary is past the teens, into the twenties. The company here is very large, a couple of hundred million dollars in sales anyway, and within the company there are departments, and each department is completely autonomous, has its own business, and makes its own products.

"Up to now, there hasn't been any strategic, any over-all corporate planning done. There has been product planning on the departmental level, you know; what products should we be making to serve the market for the next two or three years, but nothing has been going on to put the whole company together and say: 'What is our corporate goal?'

"Co-ordinating the activities of the departments so there is a cohesive strategy—that's really the function I'm filling. It's the old story of a very decentralized operation evolving toward more centralized decision making, and this is creating a lot of human problems. I've made trips to other parts of the country where some of these departments are and people, indirectly and some quite directly, have expressed concern about what I will be doing and what's going to happen to their jobs.

"This is the kind of company with a lot of long-service employees. They're up against a very fast changing technology and market place, and some of them are having a hard time to change with it. The fellow who runs the company is the youngest president they've ever had—extremely aggressive and very, very intelligent. He is going to be looking for people with a lot of savvy, and there is no doubt in my mind that the people who are going to survive are the kind who are up-to-date on things and aren't just hanging on to their jobs.

"There isn't a lot of open conflict. It's not the kind of thing where everybody is bucking everybody. It's more subtle. But I'm sensitive to that, and I'm trying to make peace with all departments before I do very much.

"One thing I may have to do—and I have done this on a small scale already—is to recommend discontinuing programs. Programs that some people are very involved in. But I look at it from the viewpoint that discontinuing these programs, in the end, will make us more successful, create more jobs, more opportunities. And I think everybody should carry their own load, and the people I'm talking about affecting are not the people in the factory—there's going to be things for them to make one way or the other—but the management people. Anyway, I haven't really reached the point yet where I can make or break anybody's career."

September 11, Cambridge, Massachusetts: Stanley Macht and his wife, Gladys, have their origins written on them like a flashy "seven cents off" label on a package of toothpaste. He is tall and serious and has his hair combed back in a wave. He wears slacks that narrow at the bottom and pointed shoes, and she is just a little too blond to be believable.

Gladys is a very nice, bubbly girl, while he is all business. He said a lot of useful things in class—kind of curt, but polite—and went around with a group of no-nonsense people. "We are going where the money is," Gladys had said, and after the last exam they had left abruptly, without wasting a day.

It was by sheer accident that Terner ran into Stanley, and if he hadn't been alerted by the sheen of Gladys' little curls, through the expensive, tinted glass, he probably would never have known that he was looking at them. Stanley was at the wheel of this unbelievable machine of a light tan with the windows up and the air conditioning going. Terner waved and they waved, and it was a phenomenally long, very wide, eye popper of a car.

Stanley's polite grimace still couldn't pass for a smile, and Gladys, exuberant as ever, waved with both arms, her curls flying. The car lit up in the sun like a giant lump of gold and vanished in a cloud of dust as Stanley gave it the pedal.

Gladys and Stanley obviously have arrived. But judging from the time it took them to get there, the place can't have been too far away.

September 25, Zürich, Switzerland: "If I may say so," the distinguished member said, "we have had a very bad acceptance rate." There was a vague threat in his looking intently at his cigar.

"Why is it that only one or two men from our country are accepted every year?" Thoughtfully he turned the cigar on his lower lip. "Let me tell you why, gentlemen," he said, "they don't know how to evaluate our applicants. They do not know what the grades mean. And I say—*we ought to tell them what those grades mean.*"

He let himself sink against the high back of his chair as his words hung in the air over the emptied dishes like a neon sign. One member drew tense little circles on the tablecloth with the back of his thumbnail, and the other four or five, sitting at the far end of the table, didn't seem to be looking anywhere in particular at all.

The members nearer the speaker—quite a bit younger, most of them—stared gravely at their plates or obediently followed the remarks of the distinguished member, who was seated strategically in the center.

With a dramatic lurch forward, the distinguished member resumed his monologue. "You might be interested to know," he said, "how the Japanese Club has solved this problem.

"Very simple." He grimaced as he sucked his cold cigar. "Very simple, gentlemen. They review every and all applicants. They take a good look at the fellows. And so far—you might be *interested* in this—so far nobody they backed failed to get accepted."

Murmured approval from the farther half of the table.

"What I am proposing, therefore," he said, "is that we *help* the school. I say: We ought to do that work for them. We help them a lot if *we* review the Swiss applicants."

There followed concurring comments from the farther and diplomatic silence from the nearer half of the table. The president of the club, a heavy-set man, sweated profusely. "I will get back to you on this," he said. Then, at the hour of two, the monthly luncheon of the Zürich Harvard Club (plain Harvard sounds better than Harvard Business School) ended.

So they, the farther end of the table, the inner circle who dutifully invited but didn't welcome the younger graduates; who refused to share even their first names; they are going to decide who goes to Harvard Business School, who shares in its prestige and influence. Terner stretched his cramped legs. Help the school—that had to be the most ridiculous remark since McKay told us not to come in without a coat and tie.

October 2, Boston, Massachusetts:

(Sam Maguire *talking*)

"I've always had an inclination to be an inventor, and this was just another idea I had. On a trip out to Chicago, my wife neglected to pack my neckties. So, after I checked into what the price for a necktie was on the market, the thought occurred to me that there should be some way to make a throwaway tie.

"The first thought, of course, was paper. I wrote to a few companies, got some sample materials, and made some prototypes—cut them out, glued them together, ironed them where necessary. I decided they looked good enough, so I continued to get as many different materials as I could and continued experimenting with the design. I eventually came up with non-woven textiles—both polyester and rayon—that worked pretty well.

"I then went around talking to material suppliers, to advertising specialty dealers who handle this kind of thing, to retailers to get their reaction to the prototypes, to manufacturers to see what would work. Essentially, there is no machinery on the market at this point designed to make this tie. However, it would be a fairly simple machine. So I don't think that is an insurmountable problem. The critical problem is whether the concept will sell on the market place.

"I've been trying to sell the tie as an advertising specialty item. It would be sort of a giveaway thing, at conventions where you would want to advertise an idea or a product or a candidate's name. You could buy a few thousand and then have people wear them around. That's what I've been working at, this summer, but I haven't sold any yet.

"I'm trying to build some kind of sales record before I go after capital. Because one of the main problems for someone starting out on a new venture is the lack of capital. And I'm no different from anyone else on that. In fact, I'm greatly in debt now, at the end of school, and getting money is a real problem.

"My idea would be to subcontract all the manufacturing, which means I could get to the market without investing in equipment. But there is nothing to subcontract if you haven't made some sales.

"On the whole, the amount of problems has been very discouraging, but just a couple of weeks ago the Swanson thing happened. One of their materials suppliers, whom I had contacted, offered to act as a go-between. I leaped at the idea because Swanson is one of the largest manufacturers of synthetic fibers in the world, and I'm far more likely to succeed if I can go to the market in a big way.

"I'm discussing several options with the Swanson people, and under all of them I would get a percentage of sales or profit. And if the thing is set up as a separate company, I would get part of the new company, with the provision that at the end of a certain period they would repurchase my shares at a multiple of earnings.

"But right now, what I am pushing them to do, is to hire me as a consultant and give me a couple of people to work with to prepare production and marketing, then do a test market and decide whether to go or no-go. I'm pretty optimistic they will try this because their expense would be nominal and the potential returns are attractive."

October 5, New York City:

(Art Ruscetta *talking*)

"I report to the vice-president in charge of finance. And I guess he is a lot of problems for me. I can't respect him really because, after knowing him for a couple of months, he is a bit of a dolt. Not that I don't think he's clever in some ways, but I think, over-all, he is a dolt. And it pisses me off that he is making more money than I am, when I don't think he gets anything done.

"He'll come in, in the morning, and literally, for an hour and a half, he'll call up his friends around the city and bullshit. And I guess it wouldn't gripe me as much as it does, except that I feel the company is in such dire need of organizational talent, of people who ostensibly are of his caliber, lending a hand that every minute this guy spends bullshitting is a minute preciously needed elsewhere.

"I know I'm being very uncharitable and many times I've wanted to sit him down and say: 'Now look, Larry, for Chrissake . . .' But how do I go about explaining to him that I feel he is a dolt?

"I was up in New Hampshire again last week, and I came back to New York on Monday because we were supposed to have a meeting with the plant manager from up there and discuss his forecasts and budgets. But he never showed up, which pissed off my boss. So I went back to New Hampshire to help.

"Originally, I was supposed to report directly to the plant manager up there, to be his right-hand man in straightening out his figures. But the situation was kind of queer because he had a girl in the office that he had a very personal relationship with, and this severely clouded his judgment.

"She was a young girl in her early forties, hard driving —boy!—phenomenally hard driving. Physically an extremely beautiful girl. But hard as hell. She had come with Tom from another shoe manufacturer, had worked with him right from the beginning, and that was used as justification, I think, the fact that she had done everything for a long period of time, to say that her work was meritorious, which, in fact, it wasn't. It was just plain shitty. She was in, way over her head. And she was interfering with everybody else's work because she couldn't handle her own.

"I had been up there off and on and had, by allowing myself to withhold opinions, by not telling that I saw how it really was, had neither served him—Tom—nor the company.

"So I went up there on Tuesday and shot from the hip, both barrels. I muscled my way into areas where she was responsible and which, I felt, were vitally important and she was neglecting. In my presence she assured Tom that there was nothing to worry about, that things were OK—and that's what did it. That was the thing that triggered it. The top just blew off and I let him know everything I was feeling. And I guess I gave it to him strongly enough that he—either he was impressed by the change in me from the week before, or else what I said made sense. Anyway, I think he felt that what I said was not necessarily mine alone but came from New York, and this made him sit up and take notice.

"I corralled Frances, pulled her over to the side—mind you, all of this was cordial, up until that point—and started to talk to her about her work, and she hit the ceiling. She said she quit and walked out and went into Tom's office, and they holed up for about a half hour, talking. And very rapidly, right there, it dawned on me that if I sat back and said I was sorry, she—as she had done before—would walk back in and take over, and the same bullshit would go on. I had to put up or shut up.

"So I decided to leap into the breach. While she was in there, talking to Tom, I moved in and took control of her office and started organizing the work, and when she emerged, she saw me busily at it, and I guess that cemented it. She grabbed her stuff and walked out.

"I caught a little bit of shit from Tom, but by that evening, he had accepted it and he didn't ask her to come back.

"We've been working on his budget for the last two days, which meant that I've been leaving work at eleven o'clock at night and starting at five-thirty in the morning. And because of all this, I had to wear the same shirt two days in a row and wear the same suit for three days and spilled lunch on my tie."

October 6, New York City: Draped in its swirling, early-morning, rush-hour crowds, New York City has the appearance of an expensively dressed lady whose make-up has been halfway washed away by the heat and excitement of a night of revelry and whose carefully composed exterior is quite out of trim. Forty-second Street, even at this early hour, with its block-to-block cinemas, hamburger stands, and porno joints, is dressed in vulgar and bright neon garlands, beckoning the sullen stream of commuters that flows from the Port Authority Bus Terminal. Yet the bodies pass without so much as noticing the lewd invitations, extended to them from the canopies of the movie houses which, like gluttonous tongues, hang out over the sidewalk.

Times Square nearby, with the glittery ribbon of Broadway fluttering uptown, is stuffed with automobiles, venting its indigestion in squeaking, screaming horns and shrill police whistles. The city, limp from the sleepless night, is getting another infusion of activity.

Somewhere underneath Seventh Avenue, packed into a subway car, Sidney O'Mara, quietly and resignedly, with a couple of elbows stuck in his chest and the sharp edges of a briefcase banging his shins, awaits his release into that square piece of daylight that is the street exit. Going half a block west from there, through a Gothic arch heavy with figurines, and up fourteen floors in an air-conditioned elevator, he reaches his office. It comes complete with a waist-high bureau, a generous wooden desk, two chairs, a panoramic view of a cemetery, half a window's worth of Hudson River, a full coffee pot, and half a secretary.

"As with most companies, we have been experiencing lower profits, higher costs, and a great deal of uncertainty about the future. So what I've been asked to do is look at ways in which we can cut costs, improve profitability —in general, sort of restore the health we enjoyed in '66 and '67.

"What happened the last couple of days is pretty typical. I got up at five yesterday, was out at JFK Airport at seven and in Pittsburgh at eight. A fellow met me at the airport, and we drove to the plant where I spent the next eight hours discussing how we're gonna cut cost, what people we're gonna cut, if we have to, the advisibility of reducing salaries vs. cutting people . . .

"Some of the people we were talking about, I knew; some I had worked for earlier, before I went to Harvard, and it was a very personal thing, I mean, a very difficult thing to discuss, let alone trying to come to any decision. There are forty people in the research lab, and they are thinking of laying off three or four. But this is a catastrophic occurrence in our company, because no one has been let off in the last fifteen or twenty years, except for lack of performance. This is the one thing our management always preached: job security. And here we find ourselves in a position where we might have to cut people. We haven't had a union in our Pittsburgh plant, and when people find out there is no security in lean times, and that they are not the highest paid even when times are good—you know, there is going to be a tendency to organize.

"And also the people aspect. A lot of the supervisors who told their people that there is security in their jobs now might have to go back on their word. It's a very agonizing thing to discuss and discuss in a non-emotional way, and after it people felt—they felt kind of bad.

"I went back to the hotel and made myself a sandwich. I had a period of two hours in which I wrote up what I had done during the day, and then a fellow wanted to talk to me, a young guy who has been working on a new project. He came over at nine o'clock, and we sat down and had a beer until one in the morning. He described some of the frustrations he is having on the job and how—here we are in an economic recession and he has ideas about what products to sell, etc. He went on and on and it was very interesting. I sympathized with him 100 per cent, but it was getting to be past one o'clock in the morning.

"At seven today I got up and a fellow picked me up at the hotel. I was at the plant at eight and talked to the production people about some problems they are having, and I took down a bunch of notes on what they thought should be done and what new products they felt we ought to go into.

"I then talked to the people in the cost group about certain costs on a new product which, I felt, we should determine on a variable vs. fixed or full cost basis and I got them to agree to certain figures which, I suggested, might be ball-park figures. And by that time it was almost noon, and I went back to discuss the layoff thing, pointing up other possibilities we may want to try, and then was driven to the airport and was delayed on my one-ten flight until two, and was back in New York in the office at four.

"And in all this, I'm trying to find means to help reverse the present trends and lift morale, which is just lousy, it's crappy. No one identifies with anything. No one feels as though his efforts are worthwhile. These aren't the feelings people used to have in this company and, I mean, the state of the economy is sort of a given; there is nothing you can do to change that. But other things you can change, and that's what I talked about with the sales manager.

"I sort of felt like a jar of vaseline; kind of slipping around all day, adding lubricant to the machinery."

October 8, Wasatch, Wyoming:

(Russ Baxter *talking*)

"Right around town, there is an area called Wasatch Flats. It's an irrigated farming area and it looks very much like Iowa, it's so flat. However, it's only ten square miles, and then the land rapidly changes to mountains that go right up to seven thousand feet.

"Wasatch is a Wyoming farming community. The people in town are all involved in agriculture. This is in the way of small stores who sell their goods to the farmers. And there's the elevators and the people who sell feed to the ranchers, people who sell seed and process seed for the farmers.

"The pay scale and the standard of living out here are much lower than in the East. So the pay isn't much. But they have a lot of pride and work very hard, and they are very friendly people. True conservatives. You know, they don't like government at all. They don't even have a state income tax—none at all.

"I have an apartment right now, but I'll be living in a house, a nice three-bedroom house—as nice as it can be—which rents for $105 a month, including all the utilities. I get up fairly early in the mornings, oh, probably around a quarter after six, and go down to have a quick breakfast. At the Cowboy Cafe they make the best doughnuts you ever had. Gee! They're tremendous. It's just a little cafe in town; almost all the businessmen, a lot of the ranchers, surprisingly, come in here, have breakfast, and chat with each other before going to work. Great folksy, friendly type atmosphere.

"I have a couple of doughnuts, and pick up my mail, and

then I drive to work—it's about seventeen miles or so. I think it's only been cloudy one morning since I've been here. Beautiful sun, it's very low in humidity, so in the summer, the heat isn't too bad.

"The ranch is built at the base of the mountains. They surround it, and they're quite rugged and rocky and have Ponderosa pine on them. The woods are full of elk, deer, antelope, bear, and turkey, and we have a river flowing through the ranch which is full of trout. You come into the ranch and it's about a mile off the main highway. He's got a big sign out there that says 'Double T Ranch,' and he's got this picket-wood-type fencing; it's very expensive, it looks very showy, and you come in and have a lot of cattle on both sides, on these lush, irrigated pastures.

"The buildings are all painted red. He has an old red farmhouse there that the cow foreman and his family stay in, and several barns. They are all painted red, and he has a real nice lawn with big cottonwood trees—they're huge—and in this area is the office building. Inside and out, the office building is just like a barn. The interior walls are covered with the wood off an old barn; there are a lot of antiques around, and it's pleasant and air-conditioned.

"You can look out the window and the sun shines all the time. I look past the original ranch building, built about a hundred and fifty years ago. It's a stone building, and then, past that, I can see the cow foreman's house. Beyond him, we have a big pasture, and about half the time it's horses and about half the time it's cattle. And it's really kind of neat to see those horses there, at ease. The cowboys will ride 'em an evening and the next morning and will turn them loose for the afternoon. They shift horses like that and the horses get a little frisky and race around.

"Every now and then, a calf will get out of the fence, and those of us in the office will run over and try to get him back in.

"I usually start the day reading my *Wall Street Journal*, which is two days' late, and the Denver *Post*, which is one day late, before I get into the main part of my job, into the planning: which crops to plant this year, what our capital requirements are gonna be in terms of new machinery, feed requirements for the cattle, whether to go with circular sprinklers, or the square type or contour. And throughout the day, the cattle foreman and the farm foreman will be coming in, and they both have their problems, hundred of little problems every day.

"One of the accountants and I—he likes the outdoors as I do—we make it a point at lunchtime to go outside a little while. We might be goin' out and grab a handful of carrots out of the field and feed them to a horse. There is a hospital for sick animals on the ranch, and we might go in and check on the patients they have. I think it's important to have a feel for what's happening, to keep the pulse—so we talk to the cowboys and we talk to the farm help, and it's a very friendly, informal atmosphere.

"In the afternoon it's the same type thing. We've had irrigation experts, range consultants, nutritional consultants come in, and we've been presenting our problems, and I do a lot of talking with them. A lot of machinery people too—we're investigating what different types of machinery can do for us, how much they cost, and what the service is going to be. I guess I work till about six every night. Sometimes later. Some nights I work very late, and I've been working Saturdays too. The boss uses Saturdays and Sundays to catch up on everything that's been happening, and I go in and we chat, philosophize sometimes, about what we should do, and what everybody else is doing, and how it looks for the future.

"The fellow who runs the farm is a very well-to-do guy; he is a multimillionaire. He is very smart, and he is a little different, very different in fact from the people around here. I like the kind of life he has, and I want to have a ranch like that, someday, even if it's not my primary business. I guess I want the independence. And I don't think living in a big city is healthy. You know, when I go into a gas station, I don't like some guy snarling at me. I'd just as soon go in and say hello and know the fellow, and he is givin' me service and I'm givin' him trade, and he smiles, wipes my windshield off, and everything is fine.

"I guess you deprive yourself of some things living in a small community like this, and I've had some hard thoughts these last months, saying: 'Do I want this for the rest of my life?' But, you know, what are the alternatives? I'm an electrical engineer, and I just can't get too excited any more about transistors, computers, and everything. Whereas, when I go outside here, I can see those cattle. I can touch 'em and smell 'em. I can look at those cows and . . . it means something. I can see a big field of corn grow, and I can see it change every day, and I can see what we're doing to that corn, and I like what I see."

November 16, Cambridge, Massachusetts: Today, Tony Rush in a light-gray suit, a white button-down, and a wide, boldly patterned tie that added a stroke of dash to his otherwise conservative appearance, was back at the Business School, looking for a job. He was five months older, two jobs wiser, and his learning experience, it was obvious, hadn't ended with Harvard Business.

He had left in June for what had looked like a very promising opportunity. The project involved four hundred acres outside a large city in Nevada and a man with a plan to turn them into an upper-class residential community, complete with shops and recreational facilities. Tony and two friends of his were to have managed the building and selling of the development, with the understanding that, if the thing took off, they were to be cut in as partners.

As it turned out, the project never made it off the ground. The man who had hired them got into financial trouble, and Tony and his friends were forced to bail out. The experience cost Tony one of his friends and a good deal in potential earnings. It was the middle of August by now, and Tony celebrated his first home-coming to the Business School by using the Alumni Placement Office. As a result of the contacts he was able to make there, he flew out to Chicago and down to Washington, and the offers he got ranged from $12,000 to a promise of $30,000, which was an opening for a real estate salesman.

The company Tony finally joined was in Vermont, and the salary he accepted was exactly half the $30,000. But the firm—a real estate firm—had reached a point in its development that offered a lot of potential. It had signed a contract to manage a large new vacation area and now was looking for a fourth man for its management team to help it face the new challenge. With his strong interest in real estate and his brand-new Harvard M.B.A., Tony seemed exactly what the firm needed.

The Human Behavior faculty would have been proud of the way in which Tony started his new job, because he decided, he says, "to keep a low profile." That decision, however, was not so much the result of any classroom insights as it was of necessity—his immediate subordinates were about ten years ahead of him, both in age and experience. To compound his problems, Tony was eager to prove himself in more ways than he had time for, and as for the low profile, circumstances soon combined to make it seem much too low for a man of his stature and ability.

Tony discovered that his two fellow managers weren't just the boss's associates, they were the boss's personal friends as well. And being the newcomer in the team, Tony experienced certain difficulties when it came to wanting a word with the boss. Tony concluded that under the circumstances, "offense was the best defense," and that if he couldn't by peaceful means have the kind of access to the boss which he thought his due, it would have to be over the dead body of whoever blocked his way. In practical terms, that meant the body of the boss's closest friend and associate.

Whether by intention or default—the exact circumstances were never entirely clear—the boss allowed one associate to maneuver himself into a position where, in effect, he ran the company's day-to-day operations. Point-blank, Tony refused to go along with the change. What at first had been belittled as a "difference of opinion" now escalated into an open confrontation which, because it was out in the open, involved a challenge not merely to the two men's ambitions but to their pride as well. The struggle had reached a point where it could only be settled by a clear, public verdict that was bound to save one reputation at the cost of the other.

The outcome was never in doubt. The boss's verdict came two weeks ago; Tony remembers very clearly, it was three o'clock on a Friday afternoon when he was told he had to be let go.

November 24, Chicago, Illinois: His pad is in one of those turn-of-the-century buildings with a lot of shoe-box-sized rooms piled on top of one another, connected by a narrow, steep hallway, which is no more than a glorified crack in the wall, splitting the building from top to bottom.

Kurowski's place is a sort of indoor campground squeezed in underneath the roof, improvised, haphazardly thrown together with unfinished boards and bricks and even items picked up on the street. It's a four-room apartment he shares with a chum from college and a casual, wildly different assortment of girls who seem to drift in and out at all kinds of crazy hours. The talk is haphazard as the place—like the gossipy, friendly little noises of anchored boats, flirting with a harbor's harmless waves.

Kurowski's bed is a mattress on a six-dollar frame. A battered chest of drawers, overflowing with clothes, retches out of a corner, and downstairs, a heavy motorcycle is locked with a heavy chain. The imported sports car, parked two blocks away, runs on its second engine. And Kurowski himself, around his pad, always in jeans and a sport shirt—the shirt in summer unbuttoned to the belt.

Twenty minutes away, Kurowski in a three-piece suit. Twenty minutes away and twenty floors up, Kurowski's office, square and bare, with a view through tall, narrow windows on downtown Chicago, on Lake Michigan flattened by one of the winter's first colds. The sun, quite late and red over the jarring shapes of the city. The step-shaped towers of the twenties, receding as they rise. The glassy new rectangles, the deep furrows—the streets—already filled with night. An iron skeleton, extremely tall, nearby—a tower being built by cranes hooked into the sky. And not too far off, a couple of chimneys—industrial areas overrun, engulfed by the city—flying black flags of smoke.

"The moral of this story is that American business is after a dollar and that ethical issues, as I see them, aren't addressed by American businessmen.

"I went out with another consultant from our firm and we went to see a major client. The company is one of the largest in the United States. They manufacture a product which is sold in many markets. Well, the Robinson-Patman Act—an anti-trust act—says: 'Thou shalt not price a product differently for different purchasers, if the product is the same product.' But this company follows what I think the fellow termed 'Opportunity pricing.' You price for as much as you can get. And if market A is willing to pay more than market B, you differentiate the product very slightly, insignificantly, so as to avoid problems with the law—which isn't closely on your back anyway—and you get a different price from market A than from market B.

"Well, I represent our consulting firm and if this client's objective is to maximize dollars, I have to recommend: 'Yes, you continue pricing differently to market A and to market B.' I have to say things that I personally am not happy saying.

"I walk through the fellow's plant, there is one black, and I might have seen maybe a hundred and fifty people. And the fellow says he's got a training school and I ask him: 'Are there any blacks in it?' I ask him questions like: 'What's the population of blacks in the area? What's the population of blacks unemployed?' And he gets defensive and says: 'Gee, you have to be black and poor to get anywhere in this company today.'

"I do have, I think, an ethical thing where, if I'm receiving a salary and benefits from my company, I am obligated to have my goals and objectives similar to theirs, so they can benefit from my work. And that means that I will be saying things, I'll be making recommendations to clients, which are not in what I perceive to be the public interest. And which may not even be in what I perceive to the the client's interest. Because, offhand, rarely will what's best for the client be what the executives—the men who hire you—want to hear. So I tell them what they want to hear. I'll do everything to continue the relationship and have a good rapport. And when they have another problem, they'll call me back.

"I'm exaggerating, I'm pushing this point a little bit, but in all truth, I'm not sure how I'm going to fall. I think, eventually, the conflict is going to be resolved in the sense that I'm going to do what all my clients are doing. Just like the fellow said: 'I'll price differently for different markets, because that's best for *my company*.'"

December 8, New York City:

(Ben Davidson *talking*)

"Over the last three months I have finally done what I should have done all along. I have thought and discovered that I, Ben Davidson, really haven't been following Ben Davidson's wishes. That all along I have been following the wishes of other people.

"I used to figure that if I wasn't happy with the milieu I was in, that was the price one pays; that you have to make some kind of sacrifice in terms of the people and the places, as it were. But I have found, over the last couple of months, that it takes a whole kind of psychology to exist in this world. Everyone is telling you a different story, based on *his* needs, *his* perspective, *his* own particular frame of reference. Everyone is protecting his own interests. It's a very hard world and, you know, why should I have to deal with this kind of people? Why should I have to become an overbearing manager? Because my father would like me to? Because that's the image of me he's got?

"Sure, I could spend my life trying to change that world. But why should I? Why should I spend my life trying to change something which . . . doesn't *want* to be changed?

"A lot of business people would say that if you do a good job, if you are efficient, if you are providing goods at the most efficient price—you're satisfying business' debt to society. But that's not being realistic. Business—big business—is part of the Establishment, and I don't care what people say, if you are established you are way ahead of the game. You are more prone to hear of opportunity, to partake of opportunity; it increases your odds of moving ahead. So if there is an Establishment—which I'm positive there is—then I feel this Establishment owes something to the people who aren't part of it: the working people, the . . . the underprivileged people. They are owed something. A shot at, a better shot, at equality.

"Certainly, the American system is a good system. You can make a million bucks in America today, even if you haven't had a college education. But there is a tremendous amount of inequality. And I believe that if the country is to exist, it must stand by what it says: equal rights. And business and everybody personally have to give up something to ensure equal rights.

"So, two weeks ago last Friday, I sat down with my dad in his office. We had a long talk and I told him what we both knew was coming—that he should count me out. He has never tried to talk me into taking over the business, and he didn't try it then. He smoked a great deal and he wasn't concentrating too well, but he didn't say much. He can't understand what I'm doing, but he made a great effort to let me know that he is wishing me well. I have to give him a lot of credit for that.

"Now we have a new president. He is twenty-seven years old, not much older than I am, and he has been in the textile business for four or five years. Time has come for me to move out. As they stand, my plans are to go into teaching and consulting in the human behavior area.

I'm going back to school—not necessarily to Harvard—to get a Ph.D. in industrial psychology.

"Now that I look back on it all, I wish it hadn't ever happened in the first place. You know, I wish we had been of more humble means, with less . . . less wealth and less . . . less . . . less opportunities. It has taken me a good part of my life to realize that really I've given up a lot of freedom for an opportunity which I now see wasn't for me. Better you should do what you want to do. Better you should be the kind of person you want to be than to make all this sacrifice for something that seems like an opportunity just because it lies in front of your nose.

"Some people will say I'm copping out. A lot of Jewish people who see the son stepping into the father's shoes as a logical progression, and see a father working all his life to have a business to hand over to his son—they think I'm nuts, that I'm betraying my father. But some things can be changed, some can't, and my father will always treat me as his son and not his partner.

"I haven't faced the ice water yet. But when it comes to jump, when it comes to sacrificing money for . . . for being what I want to be, I'll sacrifice the money—you can check me on that at our tenth reunion."

December 15, evening, Cambridge, Massachusetts: Terner and Terner's wife, who had been staying in Cambridge through summer and fall and into yet another winter, were sitting on one of those beat-up benches on the left bank of the Charles. He held her close to keep warm, their bodies —with the heavy coats and scarves—forming a kind of cozy, tangled heap; their breaths curling into one another in white ribbons.

The woosh of the rush-hour traffic from the big highways on both sides of the river blurred their words, and behind the Business School, the yellow sun, like a burning log, cracked on the sharp edge of the horizon, sending up a flight of brilliant sparks to light the shapeless, seamless pit of coming night.

Only high up, on the gables of Aldrich, did some of the light linger—a kind of dark-red vapor, rising from the cool silver of the tiles—making the dark that wrapped up the building seem darker, hiding its massive walls, reducing their brutal proportions to a very far and light and almost pleasing shape.

As usual, the snow has turned gray early, from the traffic, and over at the School, all the lights are going, as if we had forgot to turn them off. The withered pretense, the false airs lie out there, along the two years, like the glittery debris of a costume party. The ticky-tacky fronts we had put up are razed; a lot of myths have been exploded like balloons.

If the Business School is great and daring, it is in its ambition to help people make sense of the million little problems which make up the big one—life. To acquire those basic habits, that undefinable mix of thought, intuition, and faith in one's basic abilities that people, for lack of a better word, call "common sense." That even the longest voyage must start with the first step, and that once you understand a problem, you have half its solution.

This is the ambition. And then you remember Stahl, who went into the Army. And Rosen. And Leroi, the SA rep. And the Saturday WACs. And what went on in class. You know that something went wrong. Yeah, you did pick up some of that common sense, a surprising lot of it. It helps, and you are sincerely grateful. But no matter how you look at it, the price seems unreasonably high.

As in college and in high school, throughout your education really, they started out by saying how education is to make you a better man or woman. How you have to question everything and not accept anything at face value. How they have faith in man and his goodness. And then they turn on the pressure. They expect 200 per cent out of you. And you realize they haven't got faith in anything except pressure, fear, and terror.

And that is what the real game was at the Harvard Business School. Only this time the promises were even grander and the reality even further away. Students, professors, even the secretaries—it was as if everybody were fighting to get out of some corner, and they were not worried too much about habits of thinking and questioning anything, but content to accept *that the maximization of long-range profit is why God hath created the earth.* They were living the shortest of all possible short-range strategies, the only object of which was to survive.

It is surprising how long the Business School has been able to continue on in this way, miraculously untouched (or only lightly touched) by dissent and demonstrations; amid mounting proof that its way, the American way, was leading the nation into a heap of trouble. The American way, that outworn, hilariously twisted and disfigured ethic which urges people to compete for the sake of competing, achieve for the sake of achieving, win for the sake of winning, and which honors him who does all this without pause or letup—the fastest, the richest, the smartest, the nicest, the sportiest, the artiest; because things wouldn't be the way they are unless God meant them to be.

The school doesn't want to hear the tumult outside. That the American way of death is about to poison, shoot, and burn America. That something is going on out there—a second reformation which is preaching *love* and *togetherness;* which doesn't want anything to do with the idea that man is the enemy of man, and which is repudiating the ultimate American belief, *that in all things the individual is supreme.* A reformation whose long-haired apostles proclaim that to put the individual above society is to be asocial. *That America is an asocial society.*

All this the Harvard Business School can't hear because it is up against the worst obstacle to progress—success. It is producing too many millionaires, too many presidents and chairmen, too much fame for itself to need to change substantially. True, it accepts more blacks and women; it keeps putting in cases on pollution and social responsibility. But it isn't really doing anything to change the mood, the attitude, of the place. The professors continue to be more interested in sharing than in harnessing business' power; the school remains more concerned about placing its graduates and getting business' financial support than about whether business is using the nation's productive resources for the good of the nation.

The really disquieting thing is that other business schools, the nation's law and medical schools, the whole so-called professional establishment seems to be doing much the same thing. How else could you explain that those most in need of medical attention have such trouble getting it? That those most in need of justice can't seem to get it? That the majority of those who produce a factory's profits have no say in the disposition of them; those whose entire lives are tied up with a business have no influence over its objectives? How can you explain all this other than by concluding that the first concern of medical schools is with the health of doctors; the foremost concern of law schools with the rights of lawyers; that what business schools are after is promotions, not production.

For too long, the professional establishment has shielded itself from those it is supposed to serve by incomprehensible jargon and mysterious procedures. For too long it has seemed indecent for even its own members to ask the most obviously necessary questions. People would have said that you were stark raving mad if you had told them that students were going to strike at the Harvard Business School. And all of a sudden, the professional establishment, the professional schools, are under attack by the people they assumed had too much to lose to make trouble—their own students!

But as true children of the affluent society, this generation of graduate students takes a decent standard of living for granted. If they are worried about growth, it is about growth's cost and its consequences. Because that is what they see and smell; that is the reality they are growing up in; that is what they need to talk about, and that is what they are going to talk about, whether their schools like it or not.

Yet the real problem they, along with everybody else, are up against is not that people want to achieve, but that they no longer know why. Not achievement, not competition, not individualism are the enemy of society. But individualism gone mad, having lost sight of its goal. Unless, along with everybody else, they understand that they will, one of these days, abuse the individual as the individual now abuses the community; they will exchange senseless competition by senseless co-operation; only to put in place of an inequality exaggerated all out of proportion a totally unnatural equality. Not until they remember the goal will individualism and communism, will co-operation and competition, equality and inequality, lose their threat and become what they are—*means to an end.* Each with its specific advantages, depending on the task at hand, the ability of the people involved.

Unless America's students make an effort to ask themselves *why*, what it is they along with everybody else are struggling and suffering for, they may end up solving the wrong problem. They will, some of them, insist that the real alternative to mindless achievement is dropping out; that the good of all is best looked after by each looking the other way. But no matter how you feel about it, you have to make an effort. Not because it's right or good or holy, but because you are unfinished, incomplete, always in need of something.

In need of food, love, of rest, air, water. And that isn't just the reason for making an effort. It's the reason for anything anybody ever does, really. That is the why, that so infinitely simple yet infinitely hard to remember why. Why people learn, why they love, why they want to own, why they need to share. Because they have needs. Because they are wanting.

True, effort isn't enough. You also have to be lucky. That you don't get the measles at the wrong time. That your teeth hold up. That there is no death in the family. But as Karl Hoffmann would say, you have to be ready for your luck, you have to seize it.

And that is why it won't do to try to replace the old "winner psychology" with a new "loser psychology." Because, in spite of its obvious excesses, the Business School has reminded us that growing comes at the price of struggle. On Sundays. When you have a headache. When you have a thousand good excuses to do something else. That there is no such thing as a "human computer," or learning without effort—you know, the sorts of fantasies people have about what it means to be brilliant.

Now maybe there just aren't tests fine enough to detect anything but geniuses. Or, if there are, we were educated enough to beat the testers at their own game. More than likely, however, there aren't enough true geniuses in the world to fill a front row, let alone an entire business school. But if you are willing to make the effort, even at Harvard, a false genius will do.